RECOVERING DOROTHY

THE HIDDEN LIFE OF DOROTHY WORDSWORTH

POLLY ATKIN

Saraband

Published by Saraband
Digital World Centre
1 Lowry Plaza, The Quays
Salford M50 3UB
www.saraband.net

ISBN: 9781913393175

Printed and bound in Great Britain by Clays Ltd, Elcograf S.p.A.

CONTENTS

LIST OF ABBREVIATIONS

DW – Dorothy Wordsworth

WW – William Wordsworth

MW – Mary Wordsworth

JP/JM – Jane Marshall (*née* Pollard)

HCR – Henry Crabb Robinson

CC – Catherine Clarkson

De Q – Thomas De Quincey

EQ – Edward Quillinan

Dora – Dora Wordsworth

IF – Isabella Fenwick

GJ – Dorothy Wordsworth's *Grasmere Journals*
(from Woof edition)

RJ – Dorothy Wordsworth's *Rydal Journals*
(from manuscript)

INTRODUCTION

Around tea-time on December 20, 1799, just as the light was failing, aspiring poet William Wordsworth and his sister Dorothy arrived at a small white-washed cottage in the hamlet of Town End, in the Vale of Grasmere, in the English Lake District. This was to be their home for the following eight and a half years: a home recorded and eulogised in both their writings. A creative home, in which the days were filled with reading, writing, walking, and gardening. It will be the first real home they have had together since their mother died when William was only seven and Dorothy six, and Dorothy was sent to live with relatives. Dorothy recorded their daily life in Grasmere in a journal, which fed into William's poems: poems that would at first be ridiculed by critics, and later make him famous around the world. 208 years and six months later, give or take a day, I moved into an attic room three doors up the road. This is where my relationship with Dorothy Wordsworth begins.

I moved to Grasmere to do field research for a doctoral degree. My focus was not just on literature, it was on Grasmere itself; on how a place becomes a particular place, and what William Wordsworth and his poetry had to do with creating, intentionally or unintentionally, the Grasmere I came to live in. My research was based at the Wordsworth Trust, a museum and archive centred around the home the Wordsworth siblings had moved to in 1799. Under the name of Dove Cottage, Wordsworth's home at Grasmere has been a museum and literary shrine since 1890. Today, the Wordsworth Trust presents the cottage as 'the inspirational home of William Wordsworth', inviting visitors to 'Discover Wordsworth Country'. The Trust has grown to encompass a museum, a research centre and archive, a shop, a tea-room, and numerous offices and houses, ever evolving and changing. In 1997 it was granted designated collection status and named as The Centre for British Romanticism. In 2020, to celebrate William's 250th birthday, it was rebranded *Wordsworth Grasmere*. The Wordsworth Trust has been proud to claim it is the only writer's house museum which also houses the primary scholarly resource for that author. It means William, of course, not Dorothy, or any of the other writers who have inhabited the cottage since.

Under the terms of my funding, I would work for the Wordsworth Trust, learning about the place and how it worked by doing what everyone else did: working in the shop and the cottage and the museum. Sitting behind the desk in the entrance to the museum, greeting visitors, reading novels under the counter throughout the quiet winter months. Pacing the dim corridor-like gallery when exhibitions were showing, spending days staring at Blake paintings and Doré etchings until they were all I could think about. Folding T-shirts with Wordsworth's death mask on them in the shop. Shivering in the temperature and humidity-controlled workroom. Giving tours of the cottage, which I learnt by following other tours around until I synthesised the telephoned wisdoms into My Own Tour; until I could do my tour in my sleep, whilst very drunk, or in any other space that reminded me in some way of the cottage. Even now, if I enter a room with a Victorian stove, it starts playing in my head. I was embedded in the organisation like a spy, scribbling notes to myself under the shop desk when no one was looking. The term I used in my thesis was 'participant observer'. This was a way to explain or brush over how involved I became in the life of the place I was meant to be studying, how I became an active agent in the homemaking I was meant to be documenting. I came to the Wordsworth Trust in the last days of an informal volunteering system that began to morph into a professionalised year-long traineeship only a year later. Back then, anyone with an interest in working there could come, work, and stay for three months or longer. The volunteer staff were an ever-evolving revolving company of arty, thoughtful, and slightly aimless people with hardly any spending money, not much to do, and creative energy to spare. The eighteen months I lived amongst them were some of the most intense and most playful of my life. Anyone who had been there for longer than three months became old guard. We spoke in Wordsworth quotes. If in doubt, we asked ourselves *what would Dorothy Wordsworth do?* The answers would come from the parts of her journals that seemed funny to us as we repeated them over and over again to visitors. *Wash My Head! Make A Shoe! Lie in a ditch and stare at the sky*. It was like a form of divination.

I still think this, all the time. If in doubt, what would Dorothy do? Lie in a ditch and stare at the sky.

We walked to Ambleside not for the post, as Dorothy had, but for the chip shop and the club in the basement of a pub. Time contracted and expanded. We spoke of Town End Time. I moved into my attic room in June, and by the autumn I felt I had had no other home, nor ever could. Because people were always leaving and arriving there was always a celebration to plan. Any celebration – a birthday or a farewell – demanded a themed party. We held parody exhibitions, where the exhibits we made referred to our lives in the museum. One of my favourites was a fire, burning in the kitchen hearth of the communal house the exhibition was being held in. Scraps of paper tumbled out of the grate. The sign named the piece as 'The Hand of Gordon Graham Wordsworth.' Gordon Graham Wordsworth was William's grandson, and infamous for destroying and redacting the letters and journal entries written by his relatives that he felt presented dubious moralities. To us, children of the archive, he represented the questionable ethics of preservation.

Before I moved to Grasmere, I knew almost nothing about Dorothy Wordsworth. I knew she was the sister of the more famous poet, William. I knew she kept a journal. I knew her journals were important to her brother's poems. That's probably it. I knew nothing about her life, nothing about her writing. My mum gave me *The Illustrated Journals of Dorothy Wordsworth* as a present to celebrate getting accepted onto the doctoral programme. I did not know that what was included or not included in those journals – how the sentences were written, what punctuation was used, and what word choices – was an editorial decision and not Dorothy's own. I didn't know that there were different versions of her journals that said different things, included and excluded different details. I did not know there were parts of her journals that had been blacked out, that had been cut out. I did not know that these were not the only journals.

I certainly didn't know then how important Dorothy would become to me. That I would still be discovering new things about Dorothy fifteen years later. That I would come to understand Dorothy not as a silent support to the genius poet, but as an essential equal partner in a creative project that included the making of a life, as well as the making of poems. That that would help me make my own life, as best as I could. That in my darkest moments, I would find in her pain a way to help me understand, and articulate, my own.

By the time I finished my studies I thought I knew Dorothy, or knew my Dorothy. I thought I understood who I thought she was. But there were parts of Dorothy's life I knew nothing about, just as there were parts of the history of Dove Cottage I knew nothing about.

I would move away, move back, graduate, and fail to move away again before I would first hear about Dorothy's other journals, written from 1824 to 1835, but never published.

Dorothy Wordsworth is praised as a nature writer, and as a woman who walked and climbed. She is admired for her physical vitality as well as for her writing: for walking long distances, for stamina, strength, and a certain wildness. Her worth as a writer has become tied to her physical capacity by book after book which repeats these connections. Fewer people know that Dorothy became increasingly unwell later in life and was largely housebound from 1835. She lived another twenty years after that, dying on January 25, 1855, at the age of 84, outliving her brother by five years. This later Dorothy is completely unknown to most of her readers.

*

Dorothy Wordsworth's biographers have had a peculiar predilection for killing her long before her death. Ernest De Sélincourt, in his 1933 biography, separates off the last twenty years of her life from 1835–1855 as 'posthumous life' – life after death.[1] He explains 'the twenty years of posthumous life that followed only belong to the biography of Dorothy Wordsworth in so far as they reveal in fitful gleams something of what she once had been.' No one, he implies, should want or need to know about what he calls 'her days of insensibility or mental vagary.' In a weighty biography that is otherwise thoughtful and thorough in its presentation of the records of her life, this elision is particularly striking. These twenty years of posthumous life are a tragedy it is better not to speak of, or, if one absolutely must, give it eight pages at most.

Helen Darbishire follows this line in her 1958 edition of Dorothy's journals, pointing to a 'prolonged period of life-in-death' before Dorothy's actual death in 1855.[2] In using the phrase 'life-in-death', Darbishire summons the ghastly spectre from Coleridge's 'Rime of the Ancient Mariner', with her red lips, free looks, gold hair, and skin 'as white as leprosy ... who thicks man's blood with cold.' This presents Dorothy as like the mariner – cursed, trapped in an in-between state – neither really living nor free to die. This reflects how many people think about disability, and it begins to explain the desire of biographers and scholars to choose a different ending for Dorothy, one they think is more fitting, more poetic.

Francis Wilson, in her 2008 biography *The Ballad of Dorothy Wordsworth*, reissued in 2021 to mark 250 years since Dorothy's birth, takes it furthest, calling William's marriage to Mary in October 1803 'Dorothy's funeral'.[3] She places what she calls the 'peak' of Dorothy's life as the time between Christmas 1799 and October 1802, and describes her as 'fossilised for us in her *Grasmere Journal* [...] as though nothing happened to her either before or since.'[4] For a woman who lived to be 84, that seems a deliberate denial of much of life. For Wilson, Dorothy becomes some kind of nightmare crone, literally the madwoman in the attic, with her 'long lost [...] reason [...] haunting the top of their house like the discarded first wife in Charlotte Brontë's *Jane Eyre*'.[5] It seems convenient to Wilson to condense Dorothy's later years into 'madness' and a psychosomatic disorder, since to her, she died 50 years previously anyway. Carl Ketchum, in 1978, is slightly more ambiguous, placing Dorothy not in death, but in darkness: 'mental darkness'.[6] This echoes Millicent Fawcett's description of Dorothy in her 1889 group biography *Some Eminent Woman of Our Time*: 'her memory was darkened, and her spirits, once so blithe and gay, became clouded and dull'.[7] For Ketchum, Dorothy's illness in 1829 marks not the end of her life, but the 'end of Dorothy's active life as a wanderer and sightseer'.[8] With her final journal entry in November 1835, 'darkness closes in'. In her 1927 biography *Dorothy and William Wordsworth,* Catherine Macdonald Maclean presents the final decades of Dorothy's life as too terrible to behold, writing 'we turn away from contemplation of these sad inexplicable years'.[9] This is certainly the advice most biographers have taken.

This book arises from two entangled impulses, one more or less righteous or plausible than the other. Firstly, to shine a light into the darkness and restore the rest of Dorothy's narrative. William's marriage to Mary in 1803 was not Dorothy's funeral, literally or figuratively: she lived for another 52 years. But these are years we hear little about. This book hopes, if nothing else, to remind readers that Dorothy was still Dorothy all that time. She did not die, emotionally or otherwise, until 1855. She did not vanish. She was not undone. She may have changed, as we all do, in sickness and in health, but she was still Dorothy.

The second is perhaps more dubious: a desire to understand her illness. We always read through the prism of our own biases. When some people look at the skeletal hand of Victorian poet Elizabeth Barret Browning they see a woman with an eating disorder. I see a woman with a physiological illness that was dismissed in her own lifetime and continues to be dismissed by generation after generation of scholars. I see hundreds of years of medical gaslighting. I see hints of a connective tissue disorder that could explain all the symptoms she records, including her dietary experiments, and her miscarriages.

This is my bias. At 34 I was diagnosed with a hereditary connective tissue disorder, and then, a year later, a hereditary iron-loading disorder, after decades of seeking diagnosis and being rebuffed. The myriad ways I have been told my symptoms were imaginary, stress-related, psychogenic, emotional – stemming from my over-sensitivity – could fill many books.

So, when I see readers, scholars and biographers look at the lives of dead writers – writers they claim to admire – and disavow their testimony of their own bodies, I see what I have experienced myself. I cannot be certain that I am right and they are wrong. This is why I say the second driving force behind this book comes from a slightly dubious place. I believe it is both ethically and medically dubious to diagnose dead people from the partial record left from their writings and descriptions of them in other people's writings. Biographies of writers' lives are full of posthumous diagnoses of conditions we cannot be certain of. I know this. But I also know that the compulsion to know what is wrong is strong.

Since the first time I saw a lock of William Wordsworth's hair in Dove Cottage looking more like his badger-brush shaving brush than human hair, I have joked about wanting to conduct a forensic pathology on the Wordsworth siblings. I have pitched my dream series – a mix of *Time Team* and *Embarrassing Bodies*, in which writers and artists are exhumed to prove or disprove diagnoses – to friends so many times it has stopped being wholly a joke.

I know that we can't know. All we have, in the words of Dorothy, from her poem 'Thoughts on my sick-bed', are 'known and *un*known things'.

Part of the problem with diagnosing Dorothy at her worst comes from assumptions about what she was like at her best. Iris Gibson's article 'Illness of Dorothy Wordsworth' begins with an assertion of Dorothy's spectacular vitality: 'Dorothy Wordsworth was a very striking woman whose intelligence, character, and sensibility impressed people at first view as vital and unique.'[10] Gibson is only echoing many other reports, which focus on Dorothy's stamina and vitality. Some of these ideas stem from first-hand accounts of her, particularly those by Samuel Taylor Coleridge, and by Thomas De Quincey. Coleridge writes of Dorothy in 1797 as the 'exquisite sister' of William. Coleridge is not evoking the most obvious meaning of exquisite as lovely or beautiful, but exquisite as highly discriminating, as sensitive and intense. Quoting his own poem on Joan of Arc, 'Destiny of Nations', he writes:

> She is a woman indeed!—in mind, I mean, & heart—
> […] But her manners are simple, ardent, impressive—.

> In every motion her most innocent soul
> Outbeams so brightly, that who saw would say,
> Guilt was a thing impossible in her—.

> Her information various—her eye watchful in minutest observation of nature—and her taste a perfect electrometer—it bends, protrudes, and draws in, at subtlest beauties & most recondite faults.

(STC to Joseph Cottle, July 3, 1797).

This is a Dorothy with almost preternatural powers of perception and intuition. She is receptive and sensitive. The perfect electrometer. An electrometer is a device used to measure electric charge, made of two fine leaves of gold hung over an electrode. When charge is detected, the leaves of gold foil repel each other, so they seem to shift, like tree leaves in a breeze. Coleridge paints a picture of a woman who sees and understands the world in a way other people cannot, echoing her brother's reports of her. Coleridge also shows us a woman who is somehow completely herself: there is no artifice or lie to her. Her soul outbeams brightly from her. She cannot hide. She is as open in her presentation of herself to others as she is in her reading of the world around her.

De Quincey recalled his first meeting with Dorothy in 1807 in an essay published in 1839. De Quincey's Dorothy has 'wild and startling' eyes, 'hurried in their motion'.[11] She is short, slight, tanned. He described her as having a 'warm' and 'even ardent' manner, with a 'constitutionally deep' sensibility. He saw that 'some subtle fire of impassioned intellect apparently burned within her'. She was quick-witted, sensitive, full of restless energy. Like Coleridge, De Quincey turned to scientific comparison to try and pin down his impressions of Dorothy, comparing her to light itself: 'The pulses of light are not more quick or more inevitable in their flow and undulation, than were the answering and echoing movements of her sympathizing attention.'

But De Quincey also said that Dorothy 'walked with a stoop'. Could the problem be that it does not occur to later readers of these accounts that Dorothy could be at the same time sharply intelligent, wildly vivacious, and also sick, or disabled?

When I read Dorothy's journals as a new post-graduate student, I found in them records of a young woman, a little older than myself, who struggled with continual ill health. Headaches, stomach aches, toothaches. Days spent in bed, unwell. Days which she had to give up on, unwell. I recognised these days. I recognised the bafflement with which she sometimes met the overwhelmingly vivid world on days when she was wavering more towards ill than well. Yes, she walked at length, and often. Yes, she spoke and wrote with passion. But it did not occur to me that these things would be seen as contradictory, as impossible cotenants in the one body of Dorothy. It had not occurred to me how casually even the most well-informed readers would assume that a person cannot be both active, and sick. Creative, and sick. Mobile, and sick. It also had not occurred to me how much I took it for granted that a person could be all of these things, until my own health deteriorated. In the summer of 2014, at the painful peak of a quest for help for my own mysterious illness, I found myself sitting through yet another conference paper that repeated the same old ideas about Dorothy's illness. Poor Dorothy, it said, as so many have said since and before. Poor Dorothy, to have been so wild and free and mobile and articulate, and be reduced to this! I sat in that room, and felt my face get hot and my hands go numb and my eyes fill with water. I wept for Dorothy, and for myself. For everyone whose personhood has been discounted because of disability, whose experiences have been invalidated, whose life has been deemed less than, worthless, empty, silent.

JUST AS SHE IS NOW

Frances Wilson's biography of Dorothy Wordsworth introduces her with a discussion of the two well-known portraits of Dorothy made within her lifetime – a paper silhouette cut in 1806 when Dorothy was 34, which has hung since 1890 in Dove Cottage – and a painting by 'a Cumberland artist' Samuel Crossthwaite, made when Dorothy was 62 in 1833.

Since Wilson wrote *The Ballad of Dorothy Wordsworth*, a third possible portrait of Dorothy has come to light – a miniature painted on ivory around the same time as the silhouette was cut. The miniature shows a young woman in a white dress and red drop earrings, with dark hair, a long fringe, and large brown eyes which seem to hold the viewer in a steady gaze. The miniature is believed to have been one given by Dorothy to her niece Dora, William and Mary's daughter. Dora gave the miniature to her friend, the poet Maria Jane Jewsbury, as a remembrance of her aunt. Richard Walker of the National Portrait gallery judged it as 'showing a striking likeness to [William] Wordsworth himself at this age'. It now hangs in Rydal Mount, alongside the painting of Dorothy in her later years. In 1832,

Maria Jane Jewsbury asks Dora if her father could supply a memorable quote about Dorothy to keep with the portrait, then, when she learns of Dorothy's serious ill health, offers to return the portrait to Dora via their friend, Edward Quillinan:

> Your account of dear Miss Wordsworth, disturbs me – In London, I shall give or send, to Mr Quillinan, my portrait of her […] you are not satisfied with it – but the time may come, where it will be precious – & much as I value it – you have the first claim. (MJ Jewsbury to Dora W, August 2, 1832).

Feeling the gravity of Dorothy's illness, Jewsbury worries the small portrait may soon become a precious memento, whether or not Dora thinks it a good likeness (which she clearly didn't). As it evolves, Dorothy recovers from that particular worrying illness, and the following year the new, up-to-date painting is made of her. Dora, no longer fearing she might need the miniature to remember her aunt, gives it away again, this time to Sara Coleridge, daughter of Samuel Taylor Coleridge, and another close family friend.

Dora describes the making of this painting in September 1833 in a letter to Edward Quillinan's daughter Rotha, who would later become her step-daughter. Dorothy has been very ill in the months beforehand, but at the time the portrait is painted, she is well enough to come downstairs and spend time with the family and friends. She is able to walk a little, unsupported and unaided, for the first time in months. Crossthwaite – 'a self-taught artist – a native of Cockermouth & a weaver by trade until he was twenty years of age' – comes to Rydal Mount to paint William, the famous poet. That he also paints Dorothy is an accident of circumstance, but Dora finds he 'has done wonders & has delighted us all by making an admirable likeness of my Aunt – & such a pretty picture!' She writes of their 'gratitude to the little man for putting us into possession of a thing so valuable'. This portrait, with its genuine likeness of Dorothy, becomes the valuable memorial the miniature could not be. In the painting, Dorothy is 'taken just as she is now is', Dora writes, 'sitting in her large chair with paper case on her knee & pen & ink on the table on one side'. On the other side is Dorothy's dog, 'little "Miss Belle" […] looking so pert & funny'. Dorothy was apparently delighted not only that her dog was in her portrait with her, but that Nep, Dora's dog, had managed to get his head included in William's portrait – again a 'striking likeness' of the pet. Dorothy's large red chair is at a slight angle, and she looks out and up from it to the viewer, or the artist, unsmiling, but with what seems to me a slightly amused look in her eyes. She wears a dark dress, a beige blanket or shawl draped around her shoulders, and a frilled white bonnet on her head. In her right hand, she loosely holds a pair of spectacles, which are resting on the papers on her knee. Although Dora says it is a paper case on Dorothy's knee, it looks like her commonplace book, in which she drafted so many of her poems during this time. There are bound pages covered in writing, loose pages tumbling out, fragments and notes. To her left, the garden is seen through the window, with creepers growing round the frame, and tall colourful hollyhocks, in front of distant fells and a glimmer of lake. The sky is clouded, with flashes of blue. In front of the window, there is the table, draped in a cloth the same red as her chair. On it there is a tray, with ink wells and a pen. The ink pots glimmer in the light. Dorothy looks studious, busy, industrious in her writing. She looks thoughtful. Pamela Woof suggests that Dorothy 'looks elderly and an invalid' in the portrait, but there is no sign of sickness in the image, unless you were to consider her shawl a medical aid, or her age itself invalidity.[12]

What is unmistakable is that she is presented as a writer, in the act of writing.

'It is telling', Wilson writes, that Dorothy is 'depicted with pen and paper' in the portrait.[13] Pamela Woof has made the same observation: Dorothy in this painting is memorialised as a writer, and it is through her writing that we know her. But there are parts of her writing and her life that we don't know, parts that we haven't been given to access to, and parts that have been erased from the record. Dorothy's *Rydal Journals* reveal that there was another portrait made of her, in February 1826, by a Mr. Dawson when she was visiting friends in Manchester. What happened to this portrait is not clear.

ROMANTIC MEDICINE

The medical treatments and interventions that the Wordsworths had available to them here in what was then Westmorland might seem in turns quaint and barbaric to modern readers.

In 1806, when Mary's sister Sara Hutchinson is ill, she is bled by leeches, given foxglove (*Digitalis*) and nitre, and medical blistering under the treatment of the Grasmere medical man, Mr. Scambler. John Wordsworth, William and Mary's son, was ill at the same time, and was also treated with bleeding to the jugular, and blistering to the neck. Blistering was achieved by spreading a powder on the surface of the skin. As Dorothy explains in a letter to William, blisters were an 'external stimulant' believed 'to divert any evil action that there may be in the Body to another part, as in the case of inflammation in the side, in the lungs etc.' (DW to WW, June 22, 1812). Like many available treatments, even at the time they were known to be damaging if the patient, or the affected area, were too weak.

Medical advice beyond specific treatments was often centered around diet or activity. When Thomas Hutchinson has an accident in 1806, William is in London, and asks for advice from Mr. Carlisle – 'one of the ablest Surgeons in London'. The advice is mainly to eat only vegetables and bathe in Epsom Salts to reduce inflammation. Many treatments, like this, focused on trying to limit the effect of symptoms as best they could. Advice could be bafflingly contradictory. In 1811 Thomas Beddoes recommends warm salt baths to the family as therapeutic, but in 1815 Mr. Scambler advises William and Mary's children Dora and William should be washed all over with cold water every morning to try and improve their constitutions. Dora, Dorothy reports, put up a struggle the first time.

When William and Mary's daughter Catherine had seizures as a toddler, her gums were lanced, she was fed the purgative calomel, julep (presumably a medicinal syrup), and given an enema – a 'clyster' – to empty her bowels and was then put in a warm bath. When her condition relapsed in 1812, she was also given blisters to stimulate her. Dorothy explains that they also considered using an 'electrical machine' they had in the house as a stimulant to help Catherine. Mr. Scambler advised this might have made things worse, not better. Electricity had been used in medical contexts since the 1740s, and medical electric machines designed to give people a small shock had been available for home use since the late 1780s, when Edward Nairne patented a compact electrical machine. John Birch – surgeon, medical electricity advocate and fervent anti-vaxxer – established an Electric Department at St. Thomas Hospital in the 1780s. Medical electrical machines were recommended for any number of complaints, including headaches, paralysis, toothaches, eye problems, gynaecological problems, melancholy, and much more besides.

The Wordsworths had friends – like Humphrey Davy and Thomas Wedgewood – who were at the very forefront of scientific and medical progress. They seek medical advice from the experts of the day and try innovative treatments as well as relying on traditional and accepted medicine. In 1804, Dorothy asks her friend Catherine Clarkson to pass on a query to the famous doctor Thomas Beddoes about her digestive problems and headaches, and Beddoes replies with recommendations for treatment. Through Dora's illness in adulthood, she was treated with mustard blisters, bleeding and rest, but also an experimental medicine, 'a preparation of steel recommended as a trial.' (WW to HCR, May 1835). An innovative 'shower-bath' is bought in 1835 in the hope that it will help her when her spine is thought to be inflamed. Catherine is treated with an experimental massage therapy after her seizures leave her partially paralysed. The family friend who recommends the treatment after it helps her recover from a broken hip describes a regime similar to contemporary physiotherapy and rehabilitation. Despite the brutality of the side effects of many treatments, it is clear that Dorothy trusted her physicians. She dedicated a poem to Mr. Carr, her doctor in her own later illness, and assured William of the excellent care given to Catherine by Mr. Scambler:

> If you had seen Mr Scambler—if you had seen the humility, the tenderness, the watchfulness with which he administered the medicines—if you had heard him speak with the calm confidence and satisfaction that we did you would have been satisfied. You could not have wished for any thing to have been different. (DW to WW, June 22 1812).

Although leeches and blisters might sound terrifying and alien to us, they were accepted treatments at the time, and the latest medical advances even reached Westmorland. How much help or hinderance they were is another matter.

The Covid-19 pandemic has reminded us all – whether we needed it or not – how much of the body and the body's workings remain mysterious. Experts have written of Covid's 'known unknowns'.[14] The pandemic has generated extraordinary scientific and medical advances precisely because it has spotlighted these unknowns'. It has also been a stark reminder of how devalued disabled lives are in a society that connects value to productivity and activity. At the same time, the response to Long Covid has shown how quick some people are to assume that any illness without a simple identifiable cause and mechanism must be psychological in origin. The desire to discount Long Covid as rooted in psychology not physiology has been frustratingly and horrifyingly familiar to many people with chronic illnesses which have been mischaracterised as psychogenic. It is easier for some medical professionals to claim that a condition does not have a physiological cause if they cannot determine that cause, in much the same way that it is easier for some people to believe Covid-19 itself must be a fantasy if they haven't experienced it themselves.

It is no surprise to me whatsoever that so many people have wanted to believe that Dorothy's illness was psychological, or even emotional. It is the assumption too many people have to push against to gain adequate care and treatment still, 250 years after Dorothy's birth. When cold-water swimming is presented as a cure-all in twenty-first century media, can we really sneer at Mr. Scambler for ordering little Dora and Willy to be bathed in cold water every day back in 1815?

My own experiences have taught me that the best doctor is one who can admit what they don't know, or don't understand. This last year has shown there is much about the world that is still unexplained, undisclosed. I am not a medical expert. I am not even a medical historian. This book is full of things I don't know. It is not an attempt to diagnose Dorothy, but to recognise her. It is an attempt to re-centre her in her own life, through turning to her own words, and those of the people who knew her. What I do know is that Dorothy deserves better than the stories that have been told of her. She deserves what anyone does when they try to articulate their pain: to be listened to, and to be believed. This is what this book hopes to do.

To try and give as full and as useful a depiction of Dorothy's illness as I can in this book, I have approached it in two different ways: narratively, as in the chapters 'Five years of sickness' and 'Lost fragments shall remain', which follow Dorothy chronologically through the years from the onset of her serious illness in 1829 to her death in 1855; and by symptom group. The symptoms I highlight in 'Undiagnosing Dorothy' are, like this entire project, informed by my own experiences and my own biases. Like all those who have gone before me in assessing Dorothy's illness, I see in her symptoms what is familiar to me and understand them through the frame of my own knowledge and interests. A different writer would categorise her symptoms differently, as others before me have done. I have tried at all times to be led by her own descriptions of her condition, and accounts from the people who knew her best, but I am still party to the confirmation bias that leads a migraineur to read Dorothy's headaches as migraines. There are many theories that easily present themselves from her pathography. I hope to lay out enough information that readers can bring their own knowledge and draw their own conclusions.

This book is not in any way intended to be the final word on Dorothy's illness: it hopes to be the beginning of a bigger, more nuanced conversation. A conversation about retrospective diagnosis, about ableism in academia, about women and illness, about disability representation, and about disabled lives. When I hear scholars describe Dorothy's later years as non-time, as darkness or nothingness, I cannot help wondering how they would describe portions of my own life. This book is underpinned by the assertion that the lives of disabled people are as rich and as worthwhile as the lives of non-disabled people. Even if you do not see us or hear us, we are still here. Her worth is not in her youthful vigour, nor is it lost in her illness, nor is she herself lost. This book hopes to let Dorothy's words live, as well as her silences, and the silences imposed upon her by others: the cut pages of her journals removed by her great nephew. This book is my attempt to recover Dorothy.

ONE

MANY
DOROTHIES

Dorothy Wordsworth was born in Cockermouth, a small town on the fringes of the North-Western Lake District, on Christmas Day, 1771. She is the only daughter of John Wordsworth, law-agent to Sir James Lowther, and Ann Cookson. She already has two older brothers, Richard, born in 1768, and William, born in April 1770. Two more – John and Christopher – would follow, in 1772 and 1774. When her mother Ann dies in March 1778, aged only thirty, Dorothy is sent away. There is no place for an only girl in a motherless household. So, at six years old, Dorothy is sent to live 150 miles away in Halifax with her mother's cousin Elizabeth Threlkeld. Her life in Halifax seems busy and mostly happy, full of books and other children, including her best friend Jane Pollard and Jane's many sisters. She is brought up alongside the five daughters of Elizabeth's sister, who too had died and left them motherless.Aged fifteen, Dorothy is sent away again, this time to her grandparents in Penrith – her mother's parents – where she spends an unhappy, lonely year, punctuated by meeting her brothers for the first time in nine years. They are all orphans now. Their father had died at the very end of December 1783, five days after Dorothy's twelfth birthday. Dorothy was unable to travel back to Cockermouth for the funeral. Later, she will say that after her father's death, she and her siblings were 'squandered abroad'. Lost to each other, and their home. This meeting with them in the summer of 1787 will change Dorothy's hopes and plans for her life. They begin to plot a home together. That autumn she befriends two orphaned sisters, Peggy and Mary Hutchinson. They are drawn together by, amongst other things, their shared losses. That December 1787, Dorothy's grandfather dies, and her life in Penrith is further destabilised. The following autumn her uncle, William Cookson, marries and moves to Norfolk. Sixteen-year-old Dorothy moves with them. In the Cookson's active household she regains some freedom. She reads. She writes many letters, to the Hutchinsons, to Jane Pollard, to her brothers, especially William. By 1789 she is running a Sunday school for younger girls, passing on her education. She later describes herself at this time as 'mad with joy'. William is by now in his third year of studies at Cambridge. During his long winter holiday, he stays at the Cooksons with Dorothy, and their bond deepens. A vision of a shared home glows brightly in their minds. In 1791 William graduates from Cambridge, and travels to France to see the revolution unfolding first hand. He falls in love. He has begun to be certain that he could not make a career in the church, as had been hoped for him. For Dorothy, this threatens the dream she had formed of a little rectory they could live in together. In 1793 she writes to Jane, imagining the three of them in a fantasy home:

> I could almost fancy that I see you both near me. I hear you point out a spot, where, if we could erect a little cottage and call it our own, we should be the happiest of human beings. I see my brother fired with the idea of leading his sister to such a retreat. Our parlour is in a moment furnished; our garden is adorned by magic; the roses and honeysuckles spring at our command; the wood behind the house lifts its head, and furnishes us with a winter's shelter and a summer's noonday shade. (DW to JP, July 10, 1793).

Dorothy does not imagine a future for herself of marriage and children: she wants a stable home in a beautiful place, with her two best friends by her.

Whilst Dorothy was writing this letter, William was on a walking holiday with a university friend, Raisley Calvert, who would through twist of fate become the benefactor of that home. Raisley had always supported William in his ambitions to become a writer. He himself was a sculptor, one of a family of artists, and he understood the need William had to 'make work that might live'. Unlike William though, Raisley was a young man of means. By the time he was twenty-one, Raisley was also a young man with Tuberculosis. William, directionless, and increasingly depressed about his hopeless future, nurses Raisley through his last sickness. When Raisley dies in January 1795 he leaves a £900 legacy to William, so that William might be free to live and work as he chooses. He specifies that some of the legacy must be made of use and benefit to Dorothy. For the Wordsworth siblings, this money was life-changing. Their own inheritance had been tangled up in a legal battle with Lord Lowther since their father's death in 1783. There was no telling if and when it would ever be resolved, and what money might be left by the time it was. Raisley's legacy allowed them to set up an independent home together, and enabled everything that followed. In the autumn of 1795 Dorothy and William move together to Racedown Lodge in Dorset. Two years later they move a few miles to Alfoxden House, a vast, echoing manor in the centre of a deer park that they occupied only a few rooms of. It is here that Dorothy begins her famous journal, writing regularly from January to May 1798, which she would continue once they settle in Grasmere at the close of 1799.

The next few years of Dorothy's life – until she ends her *Grasmere Journal* in January 1803 – must be some of the most read, most written about and most over-written in history. Poetry enthusiasts, scholars, walkers and nature-lovers have pored over her words since they were first extracted by her nephew in his memoir of William in 1851, and when they were published alone, edited heavily by William Knight in 1897. In his book about how William's Victorian readers received and bent his words to fit their own purposes, Stephen Gill writes that there are 'many Wordsworths'. He looks into some of the many different people 'involved in constructing and diffusing "Wordsworth"', where 'Wordsworth' is not simply the man or the poet, or a combination of both, but a kind of collaborative Frankenstein's Monster of different cultural requirements.[15] He means William, as most people do when they say Wordsworth. But so, too, are there many Dorothies.

Dorothy the orphan.
Dorothy the devoted sister.
Dorothy the oppressed sister.
Dorothy the wild-eyed.
Dorothy the sensitive.
Dorothy the walker.
Dorothy the diarist.
Dorothy only more than half a poet.
Dorothy the devoted aunt.
Dorothy the spinster.
Dorothy the put-upon.
Dorothy the stifled.
Dorothy the creative partner.

These versions of Dorothy spin out from readings of her famous journals, and from letters and biographical speculations. They mean different things to different people. Dorothy the walker is a vital facet of a hidden history of women walking. Dorothy only more than half a poet, the oppressed sister, is an emblem of female creativity squashed by male needs and domestic tyranny. The one this book is about is the one you won't hear about – the one I didn't hear about for years.

Dorothy the invalid. Dorothy housebound, bedbound.
Dorothy unable to walk. Dorothy in pain.

Dorothy unable to write, to pick up a pen.

Dorothy limited not by her family but by her own body.

But to try to understand this other Dorothy, and why she has been forgotten, erased, written over, written out, we might have to go back to the beginning. The beginning of her own story, and of stories about her.

A LITTLE BOOK

The first biography of Dorothy Wordsworth was written by a man called Edmund Lee. *Dorothy Wordsworth: The Story of a Sister's Love* was published in 1886, forty-one years after Dorothy's death. In the foreword to the first edition, Lee explains why he has written what he calls his 'little book': because there is no book about Dorothy, and she deserves one. Lee laments that at that time 'to the best of knowledge, she does not even occupy any place in the numerous sketches of famous women which have from time to time appeared. At the same time, the references to her in the biographies of her brother and in the reviews of his works are many.'[16] In other words, she gets mentioned all the time when people are writing about William, but is never given space of her own. Not that much has changed since then.

Lee eulogises Dorothy as 'the most perfect sister the world hath known'.[17] To Lee, Dorothy is more than just a support to her brother. She plays a vital role in 'influencing the revival of English poetry'.[18] Lee credits Dorothy with 'uplifting' William from the 'gloom which had gathered around him' in the early 1790s.[19] It is partly her 'clear insight' that allows her to see 'deeper into the sources of real satisfaction' and bring her 'helpful and healing sympathy' to guide William on his poetic path:

It remained for Dorothy, if not to awaken, to draw out and stimulate her brother's better nature, to dead what was unworthy, and to encourage, by tender care and patient endeavour, that higher life towards which his mind and soul were turned.[20]

Her influence on him became 'a moulding and an educating power'.[21] Dorothy here becomes Merlin to William's Arthur: his guide, his spiritual advisor, and his support. He wields the sword, but it is she who has the magic. Lee cannot overstate the importance of the role Dorothy played in William's life and artistic development. He describes her as 'the loadstar of his existence', his guiding star, leading him on and keeping him on the right path, not just of his poetry, but of his life.[22]

This has a knock-on effect. Because of Dorothy's role as 'the close companion and stimulator of this great poet during the years of preparation and discipline … we owe it indirectly to Dorothy Wordsworth that Nature has become to us so much more than she was'. Dorothy, through William, has inspired new generations to love Nature, to see it in a 'clearer and brighter light', and to be uplifted to a 'higher soul-inbreathing and restoring atmosphere of repose'.[23] Dorothy, it seems, could be responsible for saving humankind. Lee prepares readers to seek echoes of Dorothy in the landscape of the Lake District. He imagines Dorothy's continuous presence in the places she wrote about and loved, which are 'immortalised' in William's poems because of her:

> If the spirits of the departed ever return and hover over the scenes of the earth which were loved and hallowed in the old-world life, it needs no force of the imagination to fancy that of this most spiritual of women, lingering by sunny noon or shady evening near the haunts where, with her kindred companion, she walked in happy converse.[24]

Lee also cemented ideas of Dorothy and William's life together as a collaborative exercise, one of 'community of thought' in which 'they were all in all to each other'.[25] He describes their first year living together in Alfoxden as 'one of glowing enjoyment and fruitful industry'.[26] Once they settle in Grasmere, this becomes a 'devoted ministry'.[27] Dorothy is described as the best of women, the best of sisters. She is both a 'refined, sensitive young woman' as well as an uncomplaining housekeeper.[28] This comes at her own expense though. His life becomes her life; her own life is absorbed into his:

> with a devotion as rare as it is noble, she simply dedicated to him her life and service, living in and for him. She read for him, saw for him, and head for him; found subjects for his reflection, and was always at hand – his willing scribe.[29]

This is a great and noble sacrifice, he believes; a choice, not an accidental by-product of their shared life:

> With a mental capacity and literary skill which would have enabled her to carve out for herself an independent reputation and position of no mean order, she preferred to sink herself, and her future, in that of her brother, with whom she has thus become, for all time, so indelibly associated. And he was grateful, and returned her devotedness with a love, tender, and almost reverential.[30]

It is a kind of bargain, in Lee's phrasing, which leads to immortality for them both. Importantly, Lee does recognise Dorothy as a poet in her own right, including a selection of her poems at the end of the biography. In his opinion, they show that 'had she devoted herself' to her own poetry, 'she might have attained distinction'.[31] In including poetry, and extracts from her letters, Lee lets Dorothy speak for herself as much as he can.

Lee's depiction of Dorothy's illness is mixed. On the one hand, he is the one of the only commentators on her life to realise that she did not just stop or vanish after 1835: she was not 'a complete and permanent wreck' but 'sometimes relieved by brightness'.[32] On the other hand, he thought the cause of her illness was her doing too much whilst being a woman. Despite presenting her as entirely fulfilled and happy in her choice, Lee still thinks she would have been happier if she had married, and fostered 'cares and interests which would have contributed to the keeping of her mind in a condition of more continuous mental vigour and equipoise'.[33] Instead, she walked too much, she worked too much, and she 'drew an over-draft on the fountains of her life'.[34] 'Nature's powers are limited', Lee argues, 'and Nature in Miss Wordsworth eventually gave way.'[35]

What Lee had to say about Dorothy is interesting to me not just because he was the first person to give her a story of her own, but because his own story is tangled up in the history that would bring me to Grasmere.

In the official histories of the Wordsworth Trust, Lee is repeatedly referred to in simple terms as a Bradford Businessman, and is misrepresented online as a 'London businessman' and a 'wealthy businessman'. But the reason he appears in those histories at all suggests there is more to him than those summaries. The drive to turn Dove Cottage into a museum was fronted by Stopford Augustus Brooke, Queen Victoria's chaplain, dedicated Wordsworthian, critic and amateur poet. Brooke visited Grasmere with his brother in 1889 and was displeased with what he found, lamenting that 'there is no place, indeed, intimately associated with Wordsworth, which is open, except the Churchyard where he is buried.'[36] Brooke supposes other tourists like himself 'would readily pay their sixpences to see the home and garden of Wordsworth' were such an opportunity available, and the dream of turning the cottage into a museum is born.[37] Brooke writes a pamphlet to crowdsource funds to buy the cottage and secure it as a Wordsworth Museum, backed by the Wordsworth Society.

Lee comes into the story here because at the time that Brooke visits the cottage in the summer of 1889, Edmund Lee owns it.

Stopford Brooke slightly patronisingly describes Lee in his pamphlet as 'Mr. Edmund Lee of Bradford who had written a pleasant and graceful book on Dorothy Wordsworth.'[38]

Lee's life reveals not only a long connection with Grasmere, where he lived part-time from the 1880s, but more than a passing interest in preserving both William and Dorothy Wordsworth's legacies. His obituary, on his death in June 1931, calls him 'A Wordsworth Lover'. His house in Bradford was called Rydal Bank, whether by accident or design a close cousin to the Wordsworths' Rydal Mount. In 1909 he buys Ryelands, a handsome neogothic house near the centre of Grasmere, and settles there with his family.

A biographical sketch from 1902 suggests Lee, who trained as a solicitor, only became interested in literature in the early 1880s, through his interest in Wordsworth. Literature becomes the driving force of his life, and that interest in Wordsworth changes not only the course of his life, but its centres.

In the Dorothy Wordsworth section of *Some Noble Sisters* Lee writes:

> Dove Cottage is now National property. For some
> years it was among the most treasured possessions of

the present writer, who, at the solicitation of the Rev. Stopford Brooke and others, recently conveyed it for the purpose of a Wordsworth Memorial. It is now vested in Trustees on behalf of the public in a similar way to Shakespeare's birthplace at Stratford-on-Avon.[39]

Lee wrote not only the first biography of Dorothy, but also a follow-up that attempted to foreground the brilliant sisters of various famous men: Sidney's Sister; Wilhelmina, Margravine of Baireuth; Susanne Kossuth Meszlenyi; Caroline Lucretia Herschel; Dorothy Wordsworth; Mary Lamb; Elizabeth H. Whittier, and Eugénie de Guérin. He also wrote poetry, publishing a collection, *Hinemoa and Other Poems*, in 1898. He was a life member of the Brontë Society, and he supported its foundation in 1894, with the aim of developing a museum to the sisters. It's hard not to imagine that his support of that venture of literary tourism was influenced by his experience with the nascent Dove Cottage Trust. In 1894 Lee revises his book because other publications have made information available to him, which was not in 1886; in particular, the extracts from Dorothy's famous *Alfoxden Journals* and *Grasmere Journals* published in William Knight's *Life of Wordsworth* in 1891. He has also been able to see some of Dorothy's letters. He thanks Jemima Quillinan, Willliam's daughter Dora's step-daughter (Dorothy's step-great niece), who died in 1891, calling her 'a strong link between the past and present generations of the family of which Dorothy Wordsworth was such a distinguished ornament'.[40] He had spoken to people who knew Dorothy, and he is able to do this because by the 1890s he has a relationship not just with the Wordsworths' words, but with Grasmere.

When Lee dies, despite the fact he was the longest-living founding member of the Dove Cottage Trust, he is given no memorial, no particular mention. Lee is buried in Grasmere, not in the churchyard alongside the Wordsworth family, but in the new cemetery on Pye Lane, alongside many of the eminent Victorian and Edwardian Wordsworthians who seem to have treated his continued presence at meetings as an inconvenient consequence of acquiring Dove Cottage, judging by records in the minute books. Lee's elder son, another Edmund Lee, born in 1882 and raised in Grasmere, also becomes an author. His novels include *Helga Lloyd: A Romance of Grasmere*, which combines the attention to rural detail of Hardy with a gothic romance more akin to *Crimson Peak*. He is the secretary of The Poetry Society whilst living in Grasmere, and follows in his father's footsteps to sit on the board of the Wordsworth Trust. Edmund Junior marries Una Heaton Cooper, of the famous Lakes artist family, and eventually the two of them move away. Both Edmund Lee Senior and Junior are pictured in photographs of Grasmere Cricket Club.

Depending on how you look at it, it is either ironic or apt that Lee was a champion of those the literary canon misses out. Although a poet, children's author, independent scholar and founding member of the Wordsworth Trust, Lee is neither lauded nor remembered. Lee ends his introduction to *Noble Sisters* musing on what it means to be forgotten:

> let it be remembered that lives are no less noble for being less known. Happily in many walks of life—lowlier in the fact that their events are unrecorded—beat hearts as warm, and in more limited spheres live deeds as noble and shine influences as pure and strong as those which, through the brighter light of exalted position or conspicuous circumstance, have added to the world's best wealth.[41]

Lee was definitely no less noble for being less known.

Lee's 'little book' about Dorothy sets the tone and a formula for accounts that would follow, including Brooke's pamphlet, which repeats the image of Dorothy haunting Grasmere, but with an important difference. Brooke calls Dove Cottage 'the haunted place', but imagines that in 1889 when he makes his literary pilgrimage, it is 'now uncared for; no sentiment presides over it; it is hard to see the ghosts that as evening falls must inhabit it'.[42] What a blow this must have been to Edmund Lee, who treasured the cottage precisely for its ghosts! Like Lee, Brooke claims to have felt and heard Dorothy as she might have been at the time she wrote her journals. Brooke recounts how when he and his brother 'stood by the wooden gate which opens on to the low-roofed porch' of Dove Cottage:

> It seemed that he and his sister Dorothy were standing with us and that we heard him say to her, "Come in: I will dictate to you the verses I made to-day in Easedale." And in our mind's eye we saw the place as it was in his time.[43]

For Brooke 'the tales of Dorothy ... people the house with love and joy' and allow the initiated visitor to 'see with her eyes the view from the windows'.[44] Dorothy becomes crucial in the haunting of the house, not just because of her importance to William, but because of her close observation of their life there. For Brooke, Dorothy 'is the figure which, as much as Wordsworth, haunts this cottage'. This haunting is so powerful that it is tantamount to a reanimation: 'In this cottage, every room of which her presence fills, in this orchard garden, every flower of which breathes of her, she is alive and delightful, and beloved for evermore.'[45]

This is a complicated possession. The Dorothy-figure filling the cottage is not just Dorothy Wordsworth, the woman and writer, but the version of Dorothy that Brooke finds in William's poems of that era. The cottage 'breathes of her' because she was both written into it, and wrote it herself, building herself into it as a permanent fixture. Most importantly, she will, through her writings 'endear the house to those who visit it hereafter; it will be peopled with memories' through the process of reading. Brooke echoes Lee in claiming 'all lovers of English poetry owe her a deep debt of gratitude.'[46]

Both Brooke and Lee want to honour the spirit of Dorothy Wordsworth, but Lee's dream of quiet reflection turns into an opportunity for public spectacle for Brooke. In both men's vision Dorothy becomes a kind of spirit guide, drawing them into past just as, in their eyes, she drew William to nature.

So Dorothy becomes a mediating figure: mediating between the living visitor and the landscape of her lifetime; between the living reader, the poems, and the poet. This would set a standard for the way her journal would be read and used, and for how her life would be weighed in the balance.

RECOLLECTIONS AND REMINISCENCES

Before Lee's biography, snippets about Dorothy, her life, and her creative role, had already entered the public consciousness.

Lee drew on descriptions of Dorothy made by those who knew her personally, as well as both her own letters, journals and poems, and those of her family. He drew particularly on her appearances in William's poems. 'The Sparrows Nest' gives us one of the most quoted depictions of Dorothy during their childhood together, before they were separated:

> She gave me eyes, she gave me ears;
> And humble cares, and delicate fears;
> A heart, the fountain of sweet tears;
> And love, and thought, and joy.

Dorothy taught William how to look and listen to the world around him, and how to feel with and for it. In 'The Sparrows Nest' he calls Dorothy 'the blessing of my later years', showing the central effect on him of both her presence in his adult life, and the lessons she taught him in childhood. In his long poem *The Prelude* he describes her as softening his 'oversternness', planting his craggy soul with flowers, and 'teach[ing] the little birds to build their nests/and warble in its chambers'. She takes the bare rock of him, and builds a living, self-sustaining world from it. He figures her as the guide others would later understand her to have been:

> thy breath,
> Dear Sister! was a kind of gentler spring,
> That went before my steps.

She is a kind of nature goddess in these lines. She is the bubbling stream, and the hand that arranges. Flowers spring up where she touches. It is no wonder she appears in Lee's book as magical.

Thomas De Quincey was the first person to describe Dorothy in any detail, in name, in print. Dorothy appears as an important secondary character in his 'Lake Reminiscences', published in *Tait's* magazine in 1839, and collected as a book in 1851. He recalls the first time he saw Dorothy – those 'wild and startling' eyes – but also what he learnt of her over the many years he knew her. De Quincey lays out clearly what

William had proposed in his poetry – that there would be no poet Wordsworth without Dorothy – so 'the admirers and the worshippers of this great poet, are become equally her debtors'. It was her mission not only to 'wait upon him as the tenderest and most faithful of domestics', but also 'to counsel him as one gifted with a power of judging that stretched as far as his own'. She 'humanised him'. De Quincey describes a peculiar way Dorothy had of making everything observed expand through her feelings:

> the exceeding sympathy, always ready and always pro-
> found, by which she made all that one could tell her, all
> that one could describe, all that one could quote from a
> foreign author, reverberate […] to one's own feelings, by
> the manifest impression it made upon hers.

Though he says she had 'remarkable endowments intellec-tually', he thought she suffered from lack of a systematic educa-tion. He described her poetry as 'not […] of much merit', and a bit sentimental. In her journals though, he found 'extraor-dinary merit'. He summarises her as 'the very wildest (in the sense of the most natural) person I have ever known; and also the truest, most inevitable'.

De Quincey was also the first person to suggest in print that Dorothy's health problems arose out of a nervousness of dispo-sition and 'self-conflict' – a kind of pre-Freudian psychoana-lytical explanation, that set the tone for all others that would follow. The sensitivity credited by others – her 'most fervid heart' – becomes in De Quincey's telling an 'excessive organic sensibility' that leads to agitation and 'self-counteraction and self-baffling of her feelings'. He describes her as completely beholden to her emotions: 'too ardent and fiery a creature to maintain the reserve essential to dignity [...] so artless, so fervent in her feelings, and so embarrassed in their utterance'. At the same time, he describes her as 'under the continual restraint of severe good sense', so that her quick and ready emotions and her practical nature were in constant battle with each other. She was a 'creature of impulse' but lead by 'her own excellent heart'. In her own writing, this impulsive quickness translates into 'originality and native freshness of intellect' which has a 'bewitching' effect on her descriptions.

He suggests she suffered from a 'self-consuming style of thought', which lent her 'a premature old age, and [...] a premature expression of old age'. The cause of her illness he thought was 'an excess of pleasurable excitement and luxurious sensibility, sustained in youth by a constitutional glow from animal causes, but drooping as soon as that was withdrawn.' In other words, *she felt too much*. He concludes that she might have been happier, and healthier, if she had been able to pour her energies into her own literary career. He is certain if she had been able to make her own career out of literature 'she would have passed a more cheerful middle-age, and would not, at any period, have yielded to that nervous depression which, I grieve to hear, has clouded her latter days.' De Quincey's diagnosis is that Dorothy becomes ill because she is too sensitive and has nowhere to direct her feelings. She becomes ill through lack of publishing.

In his 1851 memoirs of William, Christopher Wordsworth, Dorothy's nephew, included some short extracts of her journal, again making the case for her influence on William. He describes her similarly as:

> endowed with tender sensibility, with an exquisite perception of beauty, with a retentive recollection of what

she saw, with a felicitous tact in discerning and admirable skill in delineating natural objects with graphic accuracy and vivid gracefulness.[47]

In her memoirs, written in 1850 but published posthumously in 1873, Sara Coleridge called Dorothy a person 'of most poetic eye and temper'.[48] One of the last accounts published of Dorothy by someone who knew her as a friend and neighbour is in Harriet Martineau's essay 'Light of the Lake District', published in *The Atlantic Monthly* in 1861. Like De Quincey's Reminiscences, Martineau's essay sought to capture the literary environment of the Lake District for readers. Martineau's Dorothy 'had the true poet's, combined with the true woman's nature', and had been 'a rich household blessing to all connected with her'.[49] Until her illness, that is.

To Martineau, Dorothy's illness was both a moral fable about the dangers of sacrificing yourself for someone else's happiness, and a medical warning 'against overwalking'. Martineau put in print many of the myths that would sustain, all centred on the idea that Dorothy was worn down by her duties to William: 'Dorothy had, not occasionally only, but often, walked forty miles in a day to give her brother her presence. To repair the ravages thus caused she took opium; and the effect on her exhausted frame was to overthrow her mind.'[50] This moralising depiction is all the more perplexing coming from Martineau, who had experienced chronic illness and disability herself. Now we have a term for this: lateral ableism. Martineau only knew Dorothy in her later years, in her illness, and the picture she paints of her is that of a pathetic creature, not only haunting Rydal Mount but horrifying tourists with her ghastly presence:

> Travellers, American and others, must remember hav-
> ing found the garden-gate locked at Rydal Mount, and
> perceiving the reason why, in seeing a little garden-chair,
> with an emaciated old lady in it, drawn by a nurse round
> and round the gravelled space before the house. That
> was Miss Wordsworth, taking her daily exercise.[51]

An early version of this essay was published anonymously as an obituary to Mary Wordsworth in 1859, and friends of the family were distressed at the portrayal of Dorothy as a shame to be hidden away. Crabb Robinson writes to a friend critiquing the obituary, in which, amongst other errors, '– She exagger-ates the infirmities of Miss Wordsworth – and (I believe unin-tentionally) overstates the precautions when to exclude her from the gaze of strangers'. (HCR to Angelina Burdett-Cootts, February 11, 1859). It was not how they had felt. Martineau muddles stories, authoritatively but wrongly recalling that William hoped to build a separate cottage for Dorothy on the field by Rydal Church, so that she could be 'placed in some safe privacy'. This field, now property of the National Trust, was given to Dora, and is known as Dora's Field. Dorothy was never intended to be shut away, but in Martineau's account she becomes an unwanted burden, restricting the poet's capac-ity: 'thenceforth [he] rubbed his sister's feet, and coaxed and humoured her at home, trusting his guests to put up with the inconveniences of her state, as he could not remove them from sight and hearing.'[52]

These ideas are echoed by Edith Morley in 1929, when she describes Dorothy as William's 'chosen companion and friend', even during the 'long years of her invalidism', in her introduc-tion to the *Correspondence of Henry Crabb Robinson*. Disabled, Dorothy became a 'subject of [William's] unremitting care – a care no less affectionate than had been shown for her in the days of strength and comradeship'.[53] In the introduction to her 1958 edition of Mary Wordsworth's letters, Mary Burton repeats this idea of Dorothy as 'a beloved responsibility' to the family 'through all the years of her pitiful invalidism'.[54] Dorothy, in this version, only has light left to give because of Mary's love for her: 'she draws from that twilight of Dorothy's mind all the light she can – consults her, quotes her in her moments of lucidity, reports on her health, describes her happier moments'. In some ways this is true – many of the records that exist of this part of Dorothy's life are in the letters of her friends and family, including Mary, and though these letters give us some insight into Dorothy's day-to-day life, they are also very partial. We only see what Mary lets us see. There is a lot she prefers to avoid mentioning or talks of only euphemistically – Dorothy's bad habits or manners, for example – and there is so much of Dorothy's thinking that Mary has no patience or time to relate. Through Mary, Burton argues 'we hear only a steady, patient devotion, the perfect echo of William's love for his sister. There is no better evidence of the beautiful harmony of these three lives than Mary's attitude after Dorothy is no longer herself but a constant care.'[55] This idea that in her illness Dorothy is 'no longer herself', and instead just a responsibility, a chore essentially, runs through so much commentary on her later life, and circles around this notion that her life essentially stopped when she became ill. It also reflects a common attitude to disabled people, especially those with intellectual or cognitive impairments. Dorothy is presented as a burden on her family, and their continued care as almost saintly. Though I do see love in Mary's letters, I also see a great deal of frustration and confusion, which will be familiar to carers, and to disabled people alike. What comes through from Mary's letters is how hard the situation is for everyone. What comes through from Burton's commentary is that Dorothy was essentially absent from her own life, so her opinion on it no longer counts. Is it any wonder that this attitude is repeated over and over again?

The Scottish novelist Margaret Oliphant finds a much more positive model of literary companionship in her critical biography of William, published in *Blackwood's* magazine in 1871. Oliphant describes Dorothy as a 'peculiar' character: 'impetuous, impulsive, and irregular', a woman who was 'not pretty […] brilliant, hasty, sensitive, and sympathetic'.[56] Oliphant puts the case forward that William Wordsworth the poet cannot be thought of without thinking of Dorothy, too: that he became 'the spokesman to the world of two souls'.[57] Oliphant sees William and Dorothy as one soul occupying two bodies, a real and permanent 'communion of spirits':

> It was not that she visibly or consciously aided and stimulated him, but that she was him – a second pair of eyes to see, a second and more delicate intuition to discern, a second heart to enter into all that came before their mutual observation.[58]

She argues it becomes essentially impossible to tell them apart, or to unravel who wrote or thought what: 'she as part not only of his life, but of his imagination. He saw by her, felt through her'. She recognizes them both as poets – 'though one was voiceless'. Throughout her long essay on William's poetry, she is also always writing about Dorothy. Importantly, she recognised the influence between the siblings went both ways: 'her journals are Wordsworth in prose, just as his poems are Dorothy in verse. The one soul kindled at the other.'[59] This bidirectional influence is particularly noticeable in Dorothy's poetry: her poems are in conversation with his poems, just as his poems are in conversation with her prose. This vision of a complete communion of spirits would influence later readings of Dorothy's role in William's poetry, and any discussion of her life beyond the poems, which Oliphant largely avoids.

In 1874, John Campbell Shairp publishes the first edition of Dorothy's *Recollections of a Tour in Scotland*. His introduction echoes some of the reminiscences in depicting Dorothy as expending her own literary power on furthering her brother's: 'with original powers which, had she chosen to set up on her own account, might have won for her high literary fame, she was content to forget herself, to merge all her gifts and all her interests in those of her brother.' Together, 'they had the observant eye and the feeling heart which money cannot buy.'[60] Forgetting herself came with consequences, though. Shairp too diagnoses Dorothy as suffering from over-work, but also from the ending of that work: 'The unceasing strain of years had at last worn out that buoyant frame and fervid spirit. She had given herself to one work, and that work was done.'[61] She had been the 'prompter and inspirer of his highest songs' making him 'other and higher than he could have been had he stood alone'. In all these accounts Dorothy appears like a magical entity that has used up her powers by transmitting them through William.

Millicent Garrett Fawcett includes Dorothy as a case study in her 1889 essay collection *Some Eminent Women Of Our Times*, originally published as monthly biographical sketches in *The Mother's Companion* magazine between 1887 and 1888. Fawcett focuses on the positive aspects of the literary companionship the siblings had. Dorothy is dedicated to William in this version, but they both benefit. She is a 'comrade' in the work and the walking, and has her own 'extraordinary physical strength', 'mental gifts', and 'sweet and generous nature' that makes it 'cheerful': 'Dorothy continued to devote herself to him by the cheerful performance of the double duties of domestic drudge and literary companion and critic.'[62] Fawcett recognises Dorothy could have been a literary power herself, too, presenting her as 'a prose poet, who might have become a true poet, if she had not felt that she had another vocation'. She also presents her decision to give her 'whole life' to 'enrich and solace that of her brother' as a willing choice, not as a bad bargain: 'She did not sacrifice herself in vain'. Dorothy brings her 'sunny radiance of […] sympathy' and 'unshaken faith' to William's life at his darkest point. 'She chose to give up all independent cultivation of her own considerable poetic gifts', Fawcett repeats, 'to help him to give utterance to those great thoughts and words.'[63]

Fawcett overthrows the diagnosis of overwalking that Martineau gave, arguing that it is wrong to say she was 'the victim of a very premature decline of physical powers' at all. Rather, since both her parents died young, we should look on a 'failure of health at the age of sixty' as quite good odds. She draws on recollections of friends of the Wordsworths to give a diagnosis of 'brain fever' instead: 'from which she recovered, but with mental and physical powers permanently enfeebled.' Rather than an embarrassment, Dorothy in this account is 'tended with unceasing devotion'. The terrible metaphorical darkness comes in here though, as Fawcett concludes: 'her memory was darkened, and her spirits, once so blithe and gay, became clouded and dull.'[64]

These are the versions of Dorothy that come to dominate. Dorothy as visionary, prophetic, gifted, as she appears in Maurice Hewlett's 1924 essay: 'She tells us much but implies more. We may see deeply into ourselves, but she sees deeply into a deeper self than most of us can discern.'[65] Dorothy as the enabler not just of William's poetry of *all* future poetry, as she appears in Arthur Quiller-Couch's 1933 essay: 'She touched his lips, and through him she has left her benign influence upon all later Romantic poets, to this day. *She* gave them eyes, she gave them ears.'[66] Dorothy as part-William, part-Nature, as she appears in Virginia Woolf's essay in 1935: 'William and Nature and Dorothy herself, were they not one being? Did they not compose a trinity, self-contained and self-sufficient and independent whether indoors or out?'[67] William as unable to think without Dorothy, as in Woolf again: 'Dorothy stored the mood in prose, and later William came and bathed in it and made it into poetry. But one could not act without the other. They must feel, they must think, they must be together.' And then Old Dorothy as nothing but a tragic warning.

DOROTHY'S DOROTHY

Dorothy of course left her own records of her life, in her journals, her letters, and her poems. Pamela Woof estimates that she wrote over 700 letters in her lifetime. Her earliest surviving letters are to her childhood friend Jane Pollard, who becomes Jane Marshall. Her other closest correspondents, outside the extended family, are Catherine Clarkson, wife of the anti-slavery campaigner Thomas Clarkson, and Catherine's childhood friend, Henry Crabb Robinson, both of whom remain close confidantes throughout Dorothy's life. It is her letters to these three that often reveal most of her feelings, and later, her illness. The journals Dorothy kept from 1798-1803 must be some of the most read and best known of literary journals. These journals were kept during the first years she lived with her brother William, after they were finally united in adulthood, first in several rented homes in the Quantocks, and then in Grasmere in the Lake District.

Dorothy's *Alfoxden Journals* and *Grasmere Journals* have their own peculiar publication history, of abridgment, excerption and erasure. Heavily edited excerpts were published by William and Dorothy's nephew Christopher in 1851, in his memoirs of William. This placed the journals in the minds of readers as fundamental to the development of William as a poet.

In 1887 William Knight, a Professor of Literature who was a foundational member of the Wordsworth Society, published his own edition of Dorothy's Journals, including the few entries made when she travelled with William in Germany in 1798. In the introduction he lays out the previous publication history of some of her journals:

> A few fragments from her *Grasmere Journal* were included by the late Bishop of Lincoln in the Memoirs of his uncle, published in 1850 [sic]. The *Recollections of a Tour made in Scotland in 1803* were edited in full by the late Principal Shairp in the year 1874 (third edition 1894). In 1889, I included in my *Life of William Wordsworth* most of the Journal written at Alfoxden, much of that referring to Hamburg, and the greater part of the longer *Grasmere Journal*. Some extracts from the *Journal of a Tour on the Continent* made in 1820 (and of a similar one written by Mrs. Wordsworth), as well as short records of subsequent visits to Scotland and to the Isle of Man, were printed in the same volume.[68]

Knight also explains his decision-making process in editing the journals. Though to him the 'numerous trivial details' of the journals do 'bear ample witness' to the life of the Wordsworth household' he draws the line at details which seem to him to be of domestic work not related to the poetry.

The examples he gives – 'Today I mended William's shirts', or 'William gathered sticks' seemed 'trivial' to Knight, but to other readers, have formed the basis for a full, rich understanding of the everydayness of the Wordsworths' lives. Knight claims 'nothing is omitted of any literary or biographical value' in his edits, but also knows 'posterity must judge', and it did.[69] In his introduction to his 1907 edition of the Wordsworth family letters, he felt the need to comment on criticism of his edits:

> Some critics of the Eversley edition of The Journals of Dorothy Wordsworth have written to me objecting that any passages were omitted from them. They little knew what they had the temerity to wish in claiming to read every word of these Diaries, which were not written for publication [...] Their charm to us now lies in the spontaneity and naturalness, that would never have existed had the eye of others been anticipated. But for that very reason their publication as a whole is undesirable.[70]

In 1958 Helen Darbishire edited a fuller version of the *Alfoxden Journal* and *Grasmere Journal,* keeping truer to Dorothy's own notation, though, like Knight, mis-transcribing some words and phrases. Pamela Woof's 1993 Oxford World Classic edition of these early journals offered an accurate, unabridged version to the public for the first time. This affordable paperback has been continually in print and remains the best way for readers to access Dorothy's early journals. Woof includes helpful maps, timelines and notes which give context to readers, which also show the breadth and depth of her extensive knowledge of the Wordsworths' lives, friends, and work. The last entry of the *Grasmere Journal* is for January 16, 1803.

After the *Grasmere Journal* Dorothy did not keep a journal regularly, and it would be easy to think, as I once did, that she did not keep a journal at all. One of the questions I was asked a lot when I worked in the museum was whether Dorothy wrote anything other than her famous journals.

From my early teens to my early twenties, I kept a journal. I journaled most intensely in my late teens, recording things I would not otherwise remember now, for better or worse. Then I stopped. Not all at once, but in a trickle. My journal entries became less frequent. My notebooks filled with other matter: lists, poems, notes. It did not at all surprise me that the same thing had happened to Dorothy. It is hard to keep up life-writing as a practice when life takes over.

Pamela Woof suggests that domestic duties overtook Dorothy. William and Mary's son John is born on June 18, 1803, followed by Dora in 1804, Thomas in 1806, Catherine in 1808, and William (Willy) in 1810. Dorothy becomes ever more essential not only as an intellectual partner but as a carer.

She kept detailed journals of travels in Scotland with William and Coleridge in the late summer and early autumn of 1803 (which she writes up between autumn 1803 and 1805); a short journal of a tour around Ullswater in 1805. Her 1818 account of climbing Scafell Pike with a friend, Mary Barker, and a guide, is published anonymously in William's 1822 *Guide to the Lakes*. She also keeps a journal of the 1820 tour of the continent made with William, Mary, Mary's cousin Thomas Monkhouse and his new wife, joined by Henry Crabb Robinson. This journal deliberately skips the time spent with William's illegitimate French daughter Caroline, and her two young daughters, in Paris in September 1820. In 1821 Dorothy edits the journal to share with friends and family, writing that she 'amplified and arranged' it.

Dorothy also keeps a journal of an 1822 trip to Scotland, which took place after a difficult few months nursing the wife of their new neighbour Edward Quillinan, Jemima, after she was caught in a dressing-gown fire in their home, now the Rothay Hotel and Badger Bar in Rydal. The rest of the Wordsworth family were away, and Dorothy nurses Jemima herself, and arranges the funeral when she dies. Only the previous winter, Dorothy and Mary together had nursed Jemima after the birth of the Quillinan's second daughter, Rotha, William's godchild, who would later become Dora's step-daughter.

Instead of circulating the journal of this 1822 Scottish tour, Dorothy revises the text of her 1803 Scottish Tour, with the initial hope of making money for herself from its publication to fund more travel.

Her last travel journal is of a trip to the Isle of Man in June and July 1828 with Joanna Hutchinson, Mary's sister, and their eldest brother Henry.

In December 1824, not long before her 53rd birthday, Dorothy had begun again to keep a journal of daily life at home. This she continues, though with pauses, until 1835. These later journals are sometimes called the *Rydal Journals*, because they were written during the years she lived at Rydal Mount, in the hamlet of Rydal, four miles south of Grasmere.

The *Rydal Journals* have been forgotten for exactly the same reasons the *Grasmere Journals* were praised. They have been deemed as having little literary merit. Unlike the *Grasmere Journals*, in which you can read Dorothy's vivid accounts of moments, events and encounters which became some of her brother's most well-loved poems, the *Rydal Journals* have been seen as more personal, and more domestic. Dorothy writes of visits with neighbours and friends, the weather, and her body. They are largely the kind of matter that Knight edited out of his publications. William's grandson, and Dorothy great-nephew, Gordon Graham Wordsworth, felt similarly to Knight. He inherited the family papers, including letters, manuscripts of poems, and all of Dorothy's notebooks. He bequeathed the papers to the Wordsworth Trust, but before he did so, he made his own edits, cutting out pages he felt were too personal to be shared. In November 1907 he wrote that 'the entries … are so full of the minute and distressing details of [Dorothy's] malady that I have had no hesitation in excising and destroying them after making a copy of every record that seemed to me of permanent interest.'[71] He slices eighteen pages out of the journals, covering the time period from mid-December 1831 to April 1833. There is similarly a page sliced out of her commonplace book, in which she copied bits of writing she was interested in from other sources and drafted her own poetry.

It is hard to know what Dorothy would have thought of these edits. As William's fame had grown, Dorothy herself had become wary of private writing being made public. In 1829 she wrote to Coleridge begging him to destroy their private letters rather than let them be used as gossip:

> Now at this day such abominable use is made of every scrap of private anecdote, or transient or permanent sentiment, of every one whose name has ever been at all known by the publick that we are very desirous these letters should be destroyed; and therefore, my dear Coleridge, I must beg of you either to send the letters to us immediately, or that you will yourself destroy them, and give us an assurance, by writing, that this has been done. (DW to STC, November 14, 1829).

A few years later, in 1833, Catherine Clarkson considered similar problems when she wrote to Henry Crabb Robinson:

> Before I left home I had been reading over heaps of old Letters – Dear Dorothy Wordsworth's contain the History of the family & of her exertions – I felt compelled to destroy some of them but many of them are too good to be hastily disposed of –What a heart & what a head they discover! What puffs we hear of women & even of men who have made books & done charities & all that whose doings & thinkings & feelings are not to be compared with hers. (CC to HCR, October 23, 1833).

Although Catherine Clarkson is worried about the letters being used against Dorothy in some way, that they are too revealing, too exposing, she cannot bring herself to destroy such important records of such a remarkable woman's life and thinking. Regardless, I'm not convinced Dorothy would have taken kindly to someone else cutting pages out of her journals, and deciding what got to stay, or had to go.

In 1978 Carl Ketchum published a highly abridged transcript of the *Rydal Journals* in the academic journal *The Wordsworth Circle*. To date, this is still the only transcription of Dorothy's late journals that has been made public, albeit in a reduced fashion, though work is under way to produce an edition of some kind. There is no complete transcription of the late journals available to the public or to scholars. Archived at the Wordsworth Trust, in Grasmere, Cumbria, until very recently, these journals have been treated as literary ephemera. They have been seen as unworthy of publication or further study precisely because they focus more on her physical life, her chronic and acute pain, and the wreck of the body than on the poetic landscape her earlier writing is praised for capturing. They are seen as having no literary merit because these journals were not directly used to help create William's poetry, as the earlier journals were. Yet they are full of rich description and interest, of beauty, of shocking and surprising imagery, of joy in small things: the joy that keeps us going through pain. A bad night is followed by 'a warm, misty muzzling bird chaunting morning'. Even when she is unable to leave her room she writes, 'I have the inexpressible comfort of fresh air in my little cell', where the 'glorious red of anemones' becomes her 'treasure all winter'. In spring, although she records her 'strength much beaten' she also sees 'green things burst marvellously into light'. This is the record she leaves us of her illness. Not of a long twilight, or of darkness encroaching, but of the continual, shocking persistence of growth.

TWO

LITERARY
CO-PARTNERY:
DOROTHY AND THE
CREATIVE HOUSEHOLD

In May 1800, William and John Wordsworth leave Grasmere to walk to Yorkshire, to visit Mary Hutchinson, who will become William's wife. John has been staying with his brother and sister. It is hoped that eventually he will come and join them permanently and their long-held dream of a safe harbour for all of them will be realised. Their family will be re-formed in this place that has already come to epitomise 'home' for them. But in May 1800, Dorothy is left alone. She 'resolve[s] to write a journal of the time till W & J return'. She has two purposes in writing: to occupy herself, resolving 'I will not quarrel with myself'; and to 'give Wm pleasure by it when he comes home again'. (*GJ*, May 14 1800). It is written both for herself and to be shared – to record the details of her life, and her home, with and without William – and to be read back to him. It is not a private diary or notes-to-self in the way that we often think of journals now. It was more like a blog, or social media posts shared with trusted readers. As Susan Levin notes, she did not just share her journals with William and other family members, but 'copied and recopied her journals and poems and sent them to family and friends all over England […] In her hands the journal becomes a powerful narrative of emotional, domestic, and artistic life sustained among a group of extraordinary people'.

The *Grasmere Journal* is entirely wrapped up with the project of making a creative home in which both she and William could flourish. This has, in some ways, limited how it has been read. In the same way that Dorothy's biography is often cut off early, her role in the creative household is often understood only in relation to the journal's timeframe, and the specific influence of the journal on William's poems. But her creative life did not stop in 1803, any more than her actual life did.

In 1904 William Knight uses the phrase 'literary co-partnery' to describe William and Dorothy's collaborative working practices.[72] Edmund Lee described Dorothy as 'a moulding and educating power' on William, and recognised the literary importance of how 'they read and thought and talked together'.[73] This strong influential relationship was so accepted that by 1927 Catherine MacDonald Maclean was able to call Dorothy 'the most poetical woman of her generation' even though few of her own poems were known or published at the time.[74] Her poetical status came from her journal, and her influence on her brother.

Coleridge famously wrote in a letter in 1833 that Dorothy was 'a Woman of Genius, as well as manifold acquirements, and but for the absorption of her whole Soul in her Brother's fame and writings would, perhaps, in a different style have been as great a Poet as Himself.' (STC to Anne R. Scott, 26 August, 1833). This statement sets the ground for assuming we know more of Dorothy's wishes and talents than she did herself, and that she sold herself short because of William. 'The absorption of her whole soul' into his fame leaves nothing left for her at all. This sense of 'absorption of her whole soul' in William is echoed by her editors and biographers after her death.

The prevailing notion that Dorothy's creativity was suppressed by her closeness to William – that, as Harriet Martineau suggested in 1861, 'she had sacrificed herself to aid and indulge her brother' – underpins much of her appearance in scholarship and in the public consciousness even today.[75] Even where her creativity is acknowledged, it is most often, as Tilar Mazzeo puts it, as a "hidden' role in the collective authorship from which William Wordsworth's public work emerged.'[76] This is reflected in popular work about Dorothy, such as Kathryn Aalto's essay, which appears in her collection *Writing Wild* and opens the groundbreaking 2021 anthology *Women on Nature*, and which presents William as 'plagiaris[ing], borrowing, lifting' from his sister's life and writing.[77] When we insist on seeing Dorothy as oppressed and self-oppressing, her agency as a writer and as a person is written over.

Nicola Healey has written compellingly on the reception of Dorothy's writing in her 2012 book *Dorothy Wordsworth and Hartley Coleridge: The Poetics of Relationship*, noting that in portraying her as 'fully invest[ing] her life and identity in her brother' critics throughout the nineteenth, twentieth and twenty-first centuries tend to follow De Quincey in 'emphasiz[ing] the *negative* element of this sacrifice'.[78] In her 1995 study *Becoming Wordsworthian*, Elizabeth Fay echoes Victorian critics in calling for an understanding of 'Wordsworth' the poet as 'a consensual being composed of William and Dorothy': the result of 'the collaborative artistic endeavour on which the Wordsworths embark when they decide to live together'.[79] Whilst this idea of Dorothy and William as one poetic being re-centres Dorothy in the literary production that she has often been erased from, this presentation of her as half of the poet 'Wordsworth' has the unfortunate side-effect of further marginalising her individual personhood, and her individual creative work. It is no surprise then that the later journals, both with their insistence on the physical body of the individual woman and their lack of direct connection to important poems of Williams, have been deemed to be uninteresting, even embarrassing: detritus to be ignored or cleared away.

(MORE THAN) HALF A POET
Dorothy Wordsworth had conflicted feelings about authorship, which she discusses in her letters, her journals, and her own poems. To her, there seems to be a chasm of difference between writing for personal enjoyment, or to share with friends, and

writing to publish, and share with the world. Being a published writer was part of a business enterprise, interlinked but distinct from the creative process. There is writing poetry, and there is Being A Poet.

There is one entry in her *Grasmere Journals* which is often used to support the argument that she wanted to be a Poet, and was quashed in her ambitions. On March 18th, 1802, Dorothy walks home from Ambleside at twilight. By the time she reaches White Moss 'night was come on'. It had been overcast, but as she climbs the hill she describes how 'the moon came out from behind a Mountain Mass of Black Clouds—O the unutterable darkness of the sky & the Earth below the Moon! & the glorious brightness of the moon itself!' At the top of the moss, she can see down to Rydal Water, and the mixture of absolute dark and sparkling light, with the fells 'white & bright as if they were covered with hoar frost' moves her to 'many many exquisite feelings'. The view, the light, the 'sense of something in the air that compelled [her] to serious thought' and her feelings combine, and make her, she writes, 'more than half a poet'. When she gets home she tries to write verses, but gives up 'expecting William'. Pamela Woof suggests the ambiguity in that phrase 'I gave up expecting William' might mean she gave up expecting to write like William; gave up expecting to find herself 'performing' William, or the William-half of their shared being. She is not expecting William to arrive home – as he does the next day – but expecting to summon him through her somehow, in the act of writing, as though calling forth a spirit. If they are halves of one shared being, maybe, Woof implies, she was trying to shift halves. There is a similar ambiguity in the oft-quoted phrase 'it made me more than half a poet', which seems to me the centre of this entry. This phrase is sometimes read as self-deprecating, as saying she is less than a poet, or not quite a poet. But the wording is intriguing. She doesn't just feel 'more than half a poet', she is made so. It is as though she goes through an alchemical transformation in the moonlight on the moss. She is more than half, not just one side of a coin, or one part of a pair. Not sunk into or merged with or squashed under William's other half. Back at home in domestic mundanity, the writing, however, still will not come. This episode reflects her complicated relationship with writing, and particularly with poetry.

The extent of her conflicted feelings about poetry and her own ability to write it become clear in a poem she writes in 1827 for Julia, Jane Marshall's daughter, who was Dorothy's goddaughter. The poem begins querying why Julia would 'ask a Christmas Rhyme' of Dorothy, knowing that in her own youth she 'ne'er strove to decorate the truth' in poetry, but 'told in simple prose/each girlish vision' to Jane, Julia's mother, in her letters. She describes the fantasy home they imagined together – 'a cottage in a verdant dell' where they would live together – and how life took them down different paths.

Why, she questions, didn't she write all these 'pleasant guileless dreams' into poetry at the time? The answer is complicated and intriguing. Firstly, she says she had too much respect for the skill needed to write good poetry – she 'reverenced the Poet's skill' – and feared she didn't have what it took to put a poem together properly. She might, she admits, have had a growing interest in trying, but it was a mixture of 'bashfulness, a struggling shame' that she would get it wrong, and 'something worse – a lurking pride' that stopped her. She was too worried about failing to write to the standard she expected of herself, and thought others would expect, to attempt it. Most of all she feared 'the sting of ridicule' if her work fell short, from adults and from her peers. The exacting standards that would make her such an excellent editor of William's poetry also stopped her from writing her own. Even at the end of this poem, which she titles 'Irregular Verses' in a nod to her failure to keep to a set rhythm, she describes her work as 'laboured rhyme'. She is never satisfied with what she has written. It is this same fear of getting it wrong that seems to stop her that night in 1802. She can't get the words right, in the way she wants them, so she gives up. She would rather not write at all, than write something she cannot be completely proud of. This self-critical inner-voice and fear of external ridicule is a thread that runs through Dorothy's earliest conversations about writing, and if anything, becomes more ingrained as William makes poetry his livelihood.

In 1810, Dorothy wrote to Catherine Clarkson 'I should detest the idea of setting myself up as an Author'. Again, this is often quoted as evidence to back up De Quincey's theory – that Dorothy was too self-critical, too crushed by doubt to claim authorship. But as Nicola Healey points out, this was written in the context of not wanting to publish her narrative of the deaths of George and Sarah Green, a local couple who died in a winter storm, leaving their children orphaned. Dorothy had written the narrative to help raise funds and support to care for the children, but publishing it more widely seemed to her to go against this responsibility of care. Dorothy's concern was protecting the privacy of the children. If it were not for the possible negative effect on the Green children, she would have no objection to seeing it printed, *if*, she adds, it were 'without a name, and nobody would have thought of me.' (DW to CC December 9, 1810). This same worry about authorship and loss of privacy crops up in the 1820s when Samuel Rogers suggests she edit and publish her journal of her 1803 tour of Scotland. She weighs up the happy possibility of earning money to fund more travel with any 'unpleasantness of coming before the public', deciding ultimately that it would be 'impossible to make up my mind to sacrifice my privacy for a certainty less than two hundred pounds'. (DW to Samuel Rogers, January 3, 1823). It is not that she does not value her own writing, but rather than she values her privacy more. As Healey notes, this letter 'reverses the popular assumption that Dorothy was consistently and morbidly self-deprecating throughout her life.'[80]

THE WORDSWORTHIAN LIFE

For Fay, when William and Dorothy set up home together in Grasmere in 1799 it marks the beginning of 'a poetic project which, for the Wordsworths, is the making both of poetic texts *and* of the poetic life.'[81] Fay calls this poetic project – creative, created and 'self-composing' – the 'Wordsworthian Life'. It is not an accident, but a deliberate attempt to live in a particular way, a kind of life-long poetic experiment, writing their world into existence as they live it. Fay thinks of it as 'both autobiographical and mythic', as though their lives in themselves are performance art.[82]

In *Dorothy Wordsworth: Treasures of the Everyday*, Pamela Woof describes this sharing household as 'a rare literary fellowship'. For Dorothy, this literary fellowship, this literary co-partnery, was the realisation of a long-held dream, a fantasy of a creative, collaborative home she had been harbouring since her teens. In 1793, when she is twenty-two, she shares a version of this dream-home with Jane Pollard, who she imagines will join her there:

> I have laid the particular scheme of happiness for each Season. When I think of Winter I hasten to furnish our little Parlour, I close the Shutters, set out the Tea-table,

> brighten the Fire. When our Refreshment is ended I pro-
> duce our Work, and William brings his book to our Table
> and contributes at once to our Instruction and amuse-
> ment, and at Intervals we lay aside the Book and each
> hazard our observations upon what has been read with-
> out the fear of Ridicule or Censure.

The sharing of ideas and work 'without the fear of Ridicule of Censure' is fundamental to both the dream, and the reality. In creating her vision, she quotes from William's poem 'Descriptive Sketches': 'We talk over past days, we do not sigh for any Pleasures beyond our humble Habitation "The central point of all our joys"'. She could be describing an evening ten years later, or twenty. In this same letter she gives a critical reading of William's poems that she has copied out for Jane in previous letters. She sees errors in them that 'a friend would easily have made him see and at once correct.' She sets herself up as that friend, describing how she and their brother Kit (Christopher) amused themselves 'analysing every Line and preparing a very bulky Criticism.' She has already convinced him he needs her analytical eye: 'I regret exceedingly that he did not submit the works to the Inspection of some Friend before their Publication, and he also joins with me in this Regret.' Long before they achieve the reality of the creative household, Dorothy has already started making herself essential to the work that will be carried out in it. (DW to Jane Pollard, February 16 1793). For Fay the creation of poetry in the Wordsworth household becomes 'domestic routine', combining the work of the housewife/gardener with the work of the poet in one performative, collaborative role.[83] She offers a way to see the relationship between the domestic life of the Wordsworth household and their creative output, which is truly collaborative, and does not distinguish between different kinds of activities or who performs them. Literature and domestic work are part of the same creative process. This allows a way of thinking about the work of brother and sister as part of the same process, continuous through acts of housework, gardening, walking, and the straightforwardly literary acts of composing and editing poetry and writing journals. As Anne Wallace writes:

> In Dorothy Wordsworth's journals, and in the poetry of her commonplace book, public ways may become lost in the domestic, the walker's tracks disappearing as they enter the private space of the home. But groves are also figured as households; women's domestic work reappears as public business, cognate with the work of the male poet; and women themselves may speak and compose as they walk.[84]

Everything both Dorothy and William, and then Mary, do is part of The Wordsworthian Life. That includes being ill, which too often is also a shared activity, just as care is.

Nicola Healey builds on this to make an extensive case for Dorothy's involvement in the 'joint labour' of the poetry, and for her own awareness of her role as part of an 'entire collaborative literary process', arguing that Dorothy 'understood herself as half of the Wordsworthian enterprise.'[85] Healey argues that even from the early 1790s, Dorothy saw herself as thriving intellectually in the presence of her brothers: they, particularly William, offer her a vision of 'complete equality and independent growth'.

Dorothy's own perception of her collaborative role in the making of William's poetry can be traced in her journal as she shifts between the use of the single person pronoun 'I' and 'we', in both directions.[86] Although she often talks of shared work done in partnership – 'We corrected the last sheet' (*GJ* October 1, 1800); 'Wm & I were employed all the morning in writing an addition to the preface' (*GJ* October 5, 1800) – this shifts into and out of her solo work. She makes a keen distinction when referring to William's work between 'composing' and 'altering' – for example noting that 'Wm could not compose much fatigued himself with altering.' (*GJ*, October 28, 1800) – and in her own work between 'altering' and 'copying', where the creative element diminishes with each grade. William is seen to be 'composing' or 'working at' poems, followed by a process of 'altering' and 'writing', which often involves reading the poem aloud and taking on comments. Dorothy herself is often 'writing', also 'altering' rather than composing. It seems the word 'writing' for Dorothy is used literally: it means putting marks on paper, and does not cover the aspects of composing and drafting as it tends to do now. On October 2nd, 1800 she writes 'I wrote – the last sheet of notes & preface', and it is unclear whether she means she wrote out (as in copied) or whether there is altering and editorial input involved. (*GJ*, 2 October, 1800). Either way it is clear from her journals that the process of composition involves both of them. When Dorothy writes 'William left me at work altering some passage of the Pedlar' (*GJ*, 14 February, 1802), and later, 'we sate by the fire in the evening and read the Pedlar over' (*GJ*, 9 March, 1802), it paints a picture of a creative partnership; two people working towards a shared goal, in conversation.

In Healey's reading of the situation, such entries show that whilst Dorothy may be the 'willing amanuen[sis]' she is so often reduced to, she also 'constructs herself as primary editor of William's compositions in progress'. Healey points to the number of instances in which Dorothy records how her opinion on a poem or its subject altered the finished product.[87] Most importantly, at times 'Dorothy presents herself overtly as co-author of William's work announcing his literary endeavour as a shared industry and vision'.[88]

Healey suggests it is 'critical fascination with the collaboration of William Wordsworth and Coleridge [that] may have caused Dorothy's influence to become [...] sidelined'.[89] Even Lucy Newlyn's 'first literary biography of the Wordsworths' creative collaboration' tends to sideline Dorothy.[90] Newlyn positions Dorothy as one of three equal partners in the creation of the 1798 *Lyrical Ballads*: 'the names of Coleridge, Dorothy and William are missing from the title page – but all three writers were involved in collaboration and there was no competition for ownership.'[91] Despite this 'partnership in writing', she still gives William and Coleridge priority for undertaking 'a collaboration which would transform English poetry.'[92] Only Margaret Oliphant, back in 1871, called William, Coleridge, and Dorothy the '*three* young originators' of *Lyrical Ballads*, 'for it is impossible to deny Dorothy her share in the book'.[93]

SILENT POETS

John Wordsworth, William and Dorothy's brother, is another hidden body in the literary co-partnery of the Dove Cottage years. In 'Home at Grasmere' William writes of the 'happy band' that makes up his home as including himself, Dorothy, and the 'brother of our hearts' [Coleridge], but also 'a never-resting Pilgrim of the Sea' [John Wordsworth] and the 'Sisters of our hearts' [Mary, Joanna, and Sara Hutchinson]. [94] John was intended to join William and Dorothy in Grasmere, completing their home and the 'happy band'. (DW to Jane Pollard, 27 January, 1789). John's stay in Grasmere in 1800 was eulogised by William and Dorothy after his death in 1805 as those 'blessed months', a time of togetherness, and shared creativity. (WW to Sir George Beaumont, February 23, 1805).

Like Dorothy, John is an often hidden companion at key moments in William's poems and in the composition of the poems. John was with William and Coleridge when they first saw the cottage to rent in Grasmere that became William and Dorothy's home, and that ongoing home was to be founded on the proceeds of John's overseas trades.[95] Dorothy's letters show that John not only hoped to contribute to the home financially, but did so in practical ways during his visit, helping with building, gardening, and general homemaking. If the literary work of the Wordsworth household really is indivisible from the domestic work, then in 1800 John was part of that literary co-partnery, and was intended to become even more intrinsic in the future. Dorothy regularly refers to one of the beds in the house as 'John's bed' long after his visit, and even uses it as her sick bed for comfort. (DW to Mary and Sara Hutchinson, June 14, 1802). 'John's Bed' is echoed in 'John's Grove', the name associated with the fifth of William's 'Poems on the Naming of Places', and with the wood that features in the poem. The poem begins during William and Dorothy's first winter in Grasmere, a snowy winter, when the road is blocked with snow. The poet finds a 'commodious harbour' in a nearby wood, but he cannot find a way through the densely packed trees:

> A length of open space where I might walk
> Backwards and forwards long as I had liking
> In easy and mechanic thoughtlessness.[96]

William cannot pace in the wood as he usually does to write. Months later, he returns to the wood, and finds that his visiting brother had found a route through the trees, and by pacing up and down through them, had inscribed one of his 'own deep paths' in the wood. [97] For this act of writing on the landscape, William calls John a 'silent poet'.[98] He is able, William writes, to make this poem-path, because of his 'habitual restlessness of foot', his 'watchful heart' and 'finer eye', phrases which echo William's descriptions of Dorothy.[99] John's pacing allows William to pace. John's walking literally opens up the space for William to walk, and to make poetry. It is only because of the path that Wordsworth is able to love the grove 'with a perfect love': through John's efforts it becomes both harbour and poetic workroom. The path becomes a conduit, through which the poet-brother and sailor-brother are united, although many miles apart. The sailor is pictured pacing the length of his ship, muttering his brother's old verses, as, at the same time, the poet paces the path the sailor wore down, on land, muttering his new verses. The path becomes a kind of time-travel and a kind of portal.

Coleridge had noted these sensitive qualities, writing to Dorothy after he, William and John visited Grasmere together in 1799: 'Your Br. John is one of you: a man who hath solitary usings of his own Intellect, deep in feeling, with a subtle Tact, a swift instinct of Truth and Beauty.' (STC to DW, November 10, 1799). After John's death, Coleridge wrote of him in his notebooks as a 'loss to *the concern*', the Grasmere household to which John had intended to retire with his profits'.[100] 'The concern' is more than just the household, and more than even the sense of the creative household referred to here, but the whole project of the Wordsworthian Life with all it entails and all it promises. After John leaves, the wood becomes a 'haunt' of the household, even more haunted after his death. Anne Wallace sees Dorothy and Mary walking in John's Grove in

1802 as epitomising 'the encompassing of domestic and poetic labo[urs] in a single corporate household effort.'[101] In 1805, Dorothy worries that Grasmere can never be the same to them, now John has died.

I WAS TIRED A POET

Although the happy band of 1800 could never be recaptured, the literary collaboration of the household did not stop, just like the rest of Dorothy's life, after the end of her *Grasmere Journal*. Over the years different partners left and joined the concern. The birth of William and Mary's children shifted the divisions of labour in the household, adding childcare into the mix, which in turn encouraged Dorothy to write verses for the education or entertainment of the children. In a letter to Lady Beaumont in 1806, Dorothy claims that this is the limit of her poetic talents:

> 'Do not think that I was ever bold enough to hope to compose verses for the pleasure of grown persons. Descriptions, Sentiments, or little stories for children was all I could be ambitious of doing'. (DW to Lady Beaumont, April 20, 1806).

William, staying with Lord and Lady Beaumont, has shared some of Dorothy's poetry with them, reading her lines out loud to them. Dorothy assures Lady Beaumont she is wrong to assume Dorothy is thereby 'capable of writing poems that might give pleasure to others besides my own particular friends!!' This idea seems so preposterous to Dorothy that she adds two exclamation marks at the end of the sentence. She explains she wrote the lines William quoted in a hurry, not thinking much at all:

I happened to be writing a letter one evening [...] I laid
down the pen and thinking of little Johnny (then in bed
in the next room) I muttered a few lines of that address to
him about the Wind, and having paper before me, wrote
them down, and went on till I had finished. The other
lines I wrote in the same way. (DW to Lady Beaumont,
April 20, 1806).

With typical self-deprecation, she describes how she only
shared them with William because she shares everything with
him 'as William knows every thing that I do, I shewed them
to him when he came home'. The fact that 'he was very much
pleased' she claims she 'attributed to his partiality' and nothing
to do with any actual quality in what she wrote. He is not, in
effect, an objective critic.

On the surface of things, this letter seems very keen to put
paid to any idea that she, Dorothy, could be a poet. But even
so, she shows that she both does write poetry, from time to
time, and that she has tried to write more, not for her own sake,
of course, but for others. She says that because her lines 'gave
[William] pleasure for the sake of the children I ventured to
hope that I might do something more at some time or other.'
Lady Beaumont has asked her to send more, but under pressure,
she finds that she has been 'obliged to give up in despair', much
like the moonlit night in 1802 when she almost felt more
than half a poet. The voice of her self-critic is so strong that
it continually tells her she has nothing worthwhile to say that
anyone would want to hear, even if she had the skill – 'the gift
of language and numbers' to make it look right. 'Looking into
my mind', she confesses, 'I find nothing there [...] that I could
have the vanity to suppose could be of any use beyond our own
fireside, or to please, as in your case, a few partial friends'. She

has nothing *useful* to say, and no talent to make it palatable even if she did: 'I have no command of language, no power of expressing my ideas, and no one was ever more inapt at molding words into regular metre'. She admits to having tried her brother's methodology, but it still hasn't produced poetry. The thoughts come, but they are all jumbled, and nothing like what she would expect of good verse:

> I have often tried when I have been walking alone (muttering to myself as is my Brother's custom) to express my feelings in verse; feelings, and ideas such as they were, I have never wanted at those times; but prose and rhyme and blank verse were jumbled together and nothing ever came of it.

She finishes the letter, as usual, apologising not only for writing so much about herself, but also for the messy state of the letter – 'blunders and scrawling and this torn paper' – bad writing in every sense.

This letter tells us so much about Dorothy's ongoing internal battle over her own writing. She wants to write – she thinks she has ideas that want to be put down and shared – but when it comes to the actual finished work, she is never satisfied with it. She worries it is not good enough in style, and pointless in content. In the post-script, she also says she has sent on a copy of the journal of her Scottish Tour for Lady Beaumont to read. She seems to feel more comfortable with this. The writing has a purpose – it describes a journey taken, and people and places seen and met. She does not have the same worries that it might be unfit for sharing, like the odd thoughts that slip into her poems. Any writer will recognise these thought processes – the imposter syndrome – the fear that you have neither anything worthwhile to say, nor the skill to say it well enough. You could take her excessive concern she is not a good enough writer, as proof that she is a writer.

She certainly didn't give up entirely, despite her frustrations.

Accounting for multiple versions of poems in drafts in her journals and commonplace books, Susan Levin collected twenty-seven poems Dorothy wrote over the course of her life. Some of these were published in her own lifetime – anonymously – in William's collections. After her death, they were reprinted in periodicals, and included in collections of William's poems, but many were not published until Levin's 1987 collection brought them together and made them available in a reading text.

Dorothy saw through William that poetry was a dangerous act for a body to engage in. It did not spill painlessly from brain to paper. She saw first-hand how he agonised over his poems. He would go to bed ill over poems, he would have sleepless nights over poems, forget to eat. He would make himself ill in trying to make poems. She learnt from watching him and caring for him that making poems is labour that can wear out all parties involved and make them all ill.

William composed in his head as he walked, which meant that composition often brought on 'bodily derangement'. He tells in the *Fenwick Notes* of an instance when the 'skin [was] rubbed off my heal by wearing too tight a shoe [...] though I desisted from walking I found the irritation [...] was kept up by the act of composition.'[102] In 1810 Dorothy writes to Catherine Clarkson that 'William is not quite well. He has been deep in poetry for a long time, and has written most exquisitely, which has weakened him and rendered him nervous and at times low-spirited; for he has a deafness in one ear.' (DW to Catherine Clarkson, May 11, 1810). It was not just the composing part of poetry that made William ill, but writing it down too. William was notoriously bad at writing – the actual physical act of putting quill to paper – which was one reason the creative collaborative household was so important to him. It was much easier and less painful for him to dictate to someone else, than to write his words onto paper himself. In 1804 he explained in a letter to De Quincey 'I have a derangement which makes writing painful to me […] unpleasant feelings which I have connected with the act of holding a pen.' (WW to De Q, March 6, 1804). Edith Morley thought this was down to 'muscular weakness in the hand.'[103] These mechanical problems with the act of scribing only get worse over time for William, as he develops problems with inflammation in his eyes. By the time of Dorothy's illness in the 1830s, he is mostly reliant on others to write for him, and to read to him.

Dorothy notes all this down in her journal, keeping a record of the dangers of poetry and the Wordsworthian Life as well as the pleasures. Healey suggests this is partly to cement her essential position in the household – she is the caretaker who will tend him – but I think it is also a reminder for herself that everything comes at a cost. Composing poetry could not only put her at risk of ridicule or self-rebuke, it might also risk her already variable health. Somebody had to think practically. In every sense of the word, they could not *afford* to keep a household of two poets both making themselves ill. In the manuscript of Dorothy's journal from March 18th, 1802, when she is 'made more than half a poet', her tiredness becomes entangled with her attempts to write verses. She actually writes: 'It made me more than half I was tired a poet. I was tired'. She corrects herself, but the error remains, highlighting the problem: poetry is exhausting work, and she is already exhausted. This reminds me of Sylvia Plath writing in her journal almost 150 years later, weighing up the costs of raising a family and the costs of making art, asking herself 'am I strong enough to do both well?'[104] I think in those early years of co-partnery Dorothy asked herself the same question, and came to her own conclusion. She was more satisfied with her prose. She let William include her account of her 1818 climb of Scafell Pike in William's 1822 version of his *Guide to the Lakes*. Absorbed into the text, there is no sense that Dorothy wrote this account, or made the climb. In the 1823 version of his Guide, he includes the text of her tour of Ullswater, similarly absorbed into his own writing.

The drudge work involved in writing – editing, copying, correcting – that is Dorothy's mainstay in the collaborative work of the household, is off-putting to her in her solo projects. In 1824 Dorothy seeks advice from Henry Crabb Robinson about her journal of their tour of the continent in 1820, worrying whether the editing and re-writing needed to make it readable was so great that she would be better off to 'make another Tour & write the journal on a different plan'. She insists her 'object is not to make a Book' but to give Dora 'a neatly penned Memorial of those few interesting months'. (DC to HCR, May 23, 1824).

The Wordsworths' lives were certainly not short of models of female authorship that Dorothy could have drawn on, and to suggest otherwise is to erase the many prominent female poets, novelists, political writers, and critics of the day, many of whom were close friends and correspondents of the family. Tellingly, on a trip to London to have her teeth extracted in 1820, Dorothy goes to meet playwright and poet Joanna Baillie, who she calls 'one of the nicest of women—very entertaining in conversation', but tellingly adds 'without the least mixture of the literary Lady'. (DW to Mary Hutchinson, May 5, 1820). Dorothy clearly did not want to be a 'literary Lady'. De Quincey may have thought she would have been happier if she lived the life of a bluestocking, but Dorothy has other ideas.

I NOW WRITE ON THE BED ...

Dorothy's troubles with writing can be separated into two categories – difficulties with putting her thoughts into words she was satisfied with, and physical difficulties with writing with quills. Both of these are present from her youth, and both are intensified in different ways by the conditions of her illness. Dorothy, like William, never found the physical act of writing particularly easy. This is obvious in her journals – in which the handwriting varies dramatically – and is something she continually refers to in her letters, from her teenage years onwards. Many of her letters come accompanied with apologies for bad penmanship, long before she begins to apologise for their brevity. As early as 1804, illness prevents her from writing as she hopes, as she apologises to Coleridge 'my head aches, and I am not over well in my stomach, so dearest Coleridge forgive me for sending you a short and meagre letter.' (DW & WW to STC, March 6, 1804).

It is hard enough to type an email or text when you are feeling very ill. To write a paper letter with ink and a quill must have been much more difficult. She struggled enough with quills at the best of times. In 1806, replying to a parcel of gifts which included some pens, Dorothy tells Lady Beaumont they are too good for her – 'I who spoil a pen with every letter I write'. (DW to Lady Beaumont, June 24, 1806). When she is recovering from a winter illness in 1823, she finds letter writing particularly tiring, more so than other activities, apologising to Edward Quillinan: 'Do excuse my scrawling—though my Disorder has been nothing worse than a bad cold—or Influenza—I am strangely weakened, and the writing of a letter tires me more than any thing'. (DW to EQ, May 6, 1823).

As she ages, her apologies for her bad writing become standard. Almost every letter she wrote to Henry Crabb Robinson she apologised for her 'bad penmanship', and it becomes a feature of their friendship, almost a sign of her regard for him. In 1822 she apologises to him: 'This is a sad dull letter in return for yours – & I am ashamed of blots – scrawling with a bad pen &c, &c, &c —'. (DW to HCR, December 21, 1822). In 1824 she explains 'I know you are not tolerant of bad penmanship. […] I have no excuse for giving you so much trouble except the bad habit of scrawling whenever I write to my best Friends'. (DW to HCR, December 18, 1824). Even in her last letter before her illness, sent from Whitwick in November 1828, Dorothy apologises 'Do excuse this long & dull, & ill-penned letter'. (DW to HCR, November 30, 1828). The people she loves best seem to get the worst-written letters.

Despite her problems with handwriting, large portions of her labour in the Wordsworth household involved writing. It is no wonder that sometimes she did not have any energy left to expend trying to write her own verses down, when she was expending so much trying to make legible copies of William's.

In her illness, these physical problems with writing are compounded by her increasing fatigue, and her inability to sit up at a table or desk. Almost everything she writes after 1829 is written sitting in bed, leaning on her knees for support. It is little surprise her handwriting suffers more than ever before.

Her first letter to Catherine Clarkson after her partial recovery in 1829 sets the pattern for the years to come. She begins her letter with a picture of herself writing: 'I take pen in hand and my blotting paper book on my knee to write to you'. This will become her norm, not her exception. She is delighted to be well enough to do this, but the letter is interrupted. She is too ill to continue for nine days. It takes 'three sittings' to regain the 'power of finishing'. At the close of the letter, she laments 'I must be done – What a little matter is too much for me to perform!' (DW to CC, October 18-27 1829).

She moans at herself for moaning, but it is a performance. She claims to be as 'easy and comfortable as possible' writing in bed, but it could not have been easy or comfortable.

Increasingly, others have to write for her, as she has written for others. Dora or Mary become her amanuenses. In April 1832 Dora apologises to Edward Quillinan that he must receive a letter from her and not her Aunt, who 'has not strength' to write. (Dora to EQ, April 12, 1832). Sara Coleridge imagines Dorothy's 'declining state' in 1832 as breaking the creative household, echoing the language of the 'happy band' of 1800: 'I cannot bear to think of the dissolution of that happy family bond which has lasted for so many years.' (Sara Coleridge to Elizabeth Wardell, April 24, 1832).

In January 1834 she presents her improved handwriting to Lady Beaumont as 'proof of increased strength, and better health' admitting 'there have been many days in which, as an invalid, I have not been able to use my pen'. She has to set the letter aside and take it up again, apologising 'I happened to be a little unwell, and therefore I was obliged to put aside my paper'. This is one of the last remaining lengthy single-authored letters written by Dorothy. (DW to Lady Beaumont, January 13, 1834).

Later in the spring, she finds a long letter to Anne Pollard again interrupted by fatigue:

> Strange to say it! this poor scrawl has been the work of four days, and it is five since I began with it. The truth is, that a small matter stops me, and if a visitor, or two or three in succession, come in, my time and strength do not serve to fill up the rest of the day with other labour. (DW to Anne Pollard, April 12–17, 1834).

It frustrates her that what she is able to write is 'not always legible and at best difficult', apologising in her usual way, 'pray excuse bad penmanship, a wretched pen, and this shabby sheet of paper'. It takes Dorothy five days to write this letter – she begins it on the Saturday and finishes it on the Thursday – because she is interrupted by visits from friends to her solitary bedchamber, and the fatigue these visits cause leaves her unable to write. In September she writes to her goddaughter Elizabeth Hutchinson, and details the physical difficulties she faces with writing. She apologises for sending 'a short, unentertaining, and ill-penned letter', explaining how she writes in bed, leaning on her own knees: 'I lie upon my back in bed and with uplifted knees form a desk for my paper.' (DW to Elizabeth Hutchinson, September 14, 1834). She takes pains – pun intended – to explain that she doesn't write in bed because she spends all day in bed, but because she is too fatigued to sit up for more than six hours a day. She explains, 'I rise late and go to bed before sunset, because it tires, and in other respects disagrees with me to sit up more than from 4 to 6 hours in the day.' This letter has been used as evidence of Dorothy's failing memory. She dates it with the day 'Tuesday' and 'about the 14th Sept' – she cannot be sure of the date. But who in the sickroom can be sure of the date?

As the years go on, and writing in bed becomes her norm, her letters get shorter and shorter, and less and less frequent, until they almost stop altogether. At the same time, her illness disconnects her from the literary co-partnery of the household, and there are others who can now fill that role. In January 1830 she writes to Mary Lamb that Dora has taken over much of the literary work she and Mary used to do: Dora 'is very active and a most useful personage at home—her Father's helper at all times; and in domestic concerns she takes all the trouble from her mother and me.' (DW to Mary Lamb, January 9, 1830). Spending most of her time in her room, and much of that in bed, Dorothy is no longer the helpful workmate: it is Dora who is now the 'most competent and willing amanuensis', taking 'all labour' from the 'aged hands' of the older generation of women.

At Christmas 1834 Mary writes for Dorothy to Jane Marshall. It is obvious to them all 'it may be some time before it would be quite right for her to resume her correspondence – as letter-writing always exhausts her.' (MW to Jane Marshall, December 27, 1834). In May 1835, she writes a brief letter to her nephew Christopher, explaining 'though I write lying on my back it wearies me'. (DW to CW Jr, May 18, 1835). The rest of the letter is written by Isabella, John's Wife, who describes Dorothy as 'dreadfully weak and languid, more so than usual'. Dorothy's next letter is written five months later, and contains only a poem, sent to James Greenwood in Grasmere, entitled 'Five years of sickness and of pain'. She has survived a death scare. She has also retired, whether she knows it or not, from the 'concern'.

MY OWN THOUGHTS ARE A WILDERNESS

The cognitive changes that take place during Dorothy's illness in 1835 further distance her from the old concern. For the first extended time since the beginning of her illness, she struggles to read much at all, and can only listen to others read to her in short bursts. She does not just find it nearly impossible to write letters, but to read them, cutting her off from absent friends and the correspondence which has been so vital to her up until this point. In August 1837 Mary takes the family letters to Dorothy to entertain her with news, but she then writes to Dora, 'I have been forced to fetch the letters unread from Aunt – *she is too ill*.' (MW to Dora W, August 1837). The following month, Dorothy does read a packet of letters Dora sends in return, but when Mary asks her what she thinks of all the news, she tells her 'I think I have forgotten most of it'. (MW to Dora, September 4, 1837). She does write some letters during this time, but they are not always deemed appropriate to send. Mary encloses one of her letters within one to William, writing 'I enclose you a letter Sister sent me down stairs a few days ago to forward – you may do so if you think proper; it at any rate will shew *you* what a firm hand she writes'. (MW to WW, August 28, 1837). The handwriting is good: the contents are questionable. The letter becomes both proof she is changed, and proof she remains the same. Spurred on by encouragement, she writes more letters, some of which she has 'talked of writing for the last 12 months.' (MW to Dora, September 4, 1837). Not all of them seem to have been sent. William almost arranges the publication of Dorothy's tour of Scotland, which she had been revising before her illness, in the hope that 'taking it thro' the Press would be a *profitable* stirring of her mind'. But by the end of the year they have decided against it – it seems unlikely to help in the way they had hoped, and on top of that, they 'feel there would be some indelicacy in drawing public attention to her in her present melancholy state'. (WW to HCR, December, 1837).

In spring 1838, Dorothy writes a short letter to her niece Dora. Dorothy calls for Dora to send her news: not current affairs, but gossip and information about the outside world. 'My own thoughts', she writes, 'are a wilderness'. What does Dorothy mean by this? That her thoughts are wild, unapproachable, untameable, unknowable? It is compelling to read it this way. It might sound as though Dorothy is saying she is not knowable to herself.

Dorothy elaborates on her wilderness of thoughts with a quote from Edmund Spenser's epic poem *The Faerie Queen*:

'not pierceable by power of any star'. The line, from Book One, Canto One of the epic poem, describes a literal wilderness, in which the couple find shelter from 'an hideous storm of raine'. What might seem a negative description – a wilderness of thoughts so overgrown no star's light can pierce their depths – becomes more ambiguous when placed beside the poem. The grove in the Faerie Queene is 'fair harbour' in a terrible storm, with lofty trees clad in summer greenery, under which paths and alleys lead inward to further shelter. Her thoughts, Dorothy seems to be saying, may be fair shelter from hideous weather (of the body or the land). Like the paths in *The Faerie Queene*, however, they might be misleading, beguiling, taking the traveller so far into the harbour that they cannot find their way out, and begin to doubt their own minds.

Dorothy gets one word wrong in her quote from Spenser – the poem reads 'not pierceable *with* power of any star' – an error which has been used to build evidence of the failure of her memory.

The letter itself is as rich as the poem, as layered in meanings.

Dorothy's thoughts are a forest so deep and rich with life she might get lost in them, and not return.

So she asks for news from elsewhere instead – news of the outside world, of other lives. 'News then is my resting-place – News! News!' she writes. Anyone who has needed distraction from their own mind or their own body will recognise this plea. I tend to use boxsets and Netflix rather than gossip, but it forms the same function: I can lose myself for a short time in someone else's world which is less painful than my own. Dorothy needs something from outside to offer a safe resting place in contrast to the false safety her own thoughts represent.

She then shares some news from her home: deaths of friends and neighbours. She admits she has anticipated her own death, but still holds on to life – '*I* have fought and fretted and striven – and am here beside the fire.' Others have survived winter alongside her: 'the Doves behind me at the small window – the laburnum with its naked seed-pods shivers before my window and the pine-trees rock from their base.' The storm, it seems, still rages. Dorothy ends her letter here, claiming she cannot write more.

Has she run out of energy, or time? Is it too physically difficult to write, or emotionally? Is she too much in the storm, and unable to write her way through it?

Both Mary and Dora note at various times throughout her illness that Dorothy cannot be 'relied upon' to reply to letters, even when she says she will. It seems not to be through lack of will to, though. In October 1841, a good six years into the supposed 'darkness', Crabb Robinson sends Dorothy a long description of his travels in Somerset, around the area where Dorothy first lived with William in the 1790s. Mary reports that when the letter is read to her 'she was delighted & assured me, as she generally does on such occasion, that she would answer it *tomorrow.*' (MW to HCR, October 14 1841). It is Mary who replied, though, not Dorothy. It is unclear whether she has forgotten her intention by the next day, or whether she is, as usual, too tired.

DW, OLD POETESS

In her illness, Dorothy seems finally to come to terms with the idea of wanting a literary legacy, of wanting to be remembered.

In a poem for Dora's album, which she writes in May 1832, she asks 'why should *I* inscribe my name,/not poet I – no longer young?' She answers herself with the old accusations of pushing herself forward, of speaking when she should not:

'the ambition of a loving heart/makes garrulous the tongue.' It is a long poem – twelves stanzas of four lines each – for someone who claims not to be a poet. Dorothy imagines she will predecease Dora, and that the verses will remain for her after Dorothy has gone. Dora, she writes, will not need verses to remind her of her aunt, and she herself, in the grave, will not need praises. But the poem ends with an acknowledgement that she does, after all, want a hint of literary immortality:

> Yet still a lurking wish prevails
> That, when from Life we all have passed
> The Friends who love thy Parents' name
> On her's a thought may cast.

In the three years prior to writing this poem, Dorothy has had to face the very imminent possibility of her death, and it seems it has changed her thoughts about legacy. After all these decades in which she has valued her privacy over publication – in which she has hidden her identity, erased herself from the public record – she can now admit to this 'lurking wish'. She does want to be seen, to be read, to be remembered. She does think she has something of value to share.

Dorothy's confinement in her sickroom breaks the machine of domestic creative production that has been, until this point, the mainstay of the collaborative creative lives of all the family.

There is a day Dorothy records in her journal in the midst of her first year of serious illness, in December 1830, when the old pattern seems resumed. She writes: 'This day very cold & clear. Mary & D[ora] are gone to the wood – Edith [Southey] writing letters – Wm busy with poems ... I have written many letters'. The day before she notes she had been 'only confined one day this week'. (*RJ*, December, 1830). But this is a brief respite. Over the coming years Dorothy spends more and more time alone in her room. She is alive, and productive – reading, thinking and writing when she is able to – but she is cut off from other activities in the house.

William increasingly struggles to write poetry during these years, whilst Dorothy's creative life seems to thrive, conversely. A great change that has taken place, in her circumstances, and in her thinking. Dorothy is no longer part of the collaborative engine of co-partnery, putting all of her creative energy into William's work. She might have little energy to put into anything, but she has a sickroom of her own. Now released from any obligation to be useful to others, she can concentrate the little energy she has entirely on her solo creations. In her sickroom Dorothy's ability to write is no longer restricted by other works that need to be done – from washing, cooking and mending, to mending William's poems – but by fatigue, pain, and the physical awkwardness of trying to write in bed. She begins to lose some of her old inhibitions about publication. In August 1834 the publisher Samuel Rogers visits Rydal Mount. Dorothy records he 'sate a while with me & determined me not to withhold my consent from Wm to have some vagrant lines of mine published in his new Volume—going to press.' (*RJ* August 13, 1834). Rogers enters the sickroom and comes out with permission to publish, albeit not in Dorothy's name.

The irony is that the sickroom both frees and limits; it liberates its occupant from domestic duties, but the physical conditions that make domestic work impossible also limit creative work. In March 1835 she writes in her journal 'the greatest evil attending my present disordered state is that I can read or work little or none'. In June 1835 she writes a poem for Dora Hutchinson, Mary's niece, which describes precisely the barrier her illness has built to writing:

My tremulous fingers feeble hands
Refuse to labour with the mind
And that full oft is misty dul & blind.
  (Lines to Dora H, June 1835).

In October 1836 she signs herself in Bertha Southey's
album as 'D Wordsworth, Old Poetess', half self-mocking,
half-serious. She has written two stanzas in Bertha's album
in tribute to her: the first, from memory, part of William's
poem 'Beggars'; the second, off the top of her head, her own
response, writing Bertha into the poem. A note on the manuscript suggests she 'threw off' her second stanza with ease,
almost without thinking. The inner critic that for so much of
her life stopped her words between her head and the paper
seems to have been silenced.

In January 1837 she sends a Christmas poem she has written
to a local friend, a poem that reflects on time passing and inter-
generational families, gathered in togetherness 'where faithful
love through trying years has stood all proof'. ('Christmas Day',
DW to unknown, January 5, 1837). Early in September that
year, she copies out her poem 'Five years of sickness' and sends
it to Hannah Hoare, telling her that these are just some of 'many
verses which have slipped from me I know not how'. (DW to
Hannah Hoare, September, 1837). Mary describes this letter as
having 'gone beyond her usual bound.' (DW to Dora, September
4, 1837). She has struggled to find a clear path through the
many thoughts crowding her mind, like trees in the fir grove, a
chaotic wilderness. But poetry finds a way through more easily somehow; it paces the path out. She also starts preparing 'a
book *with all her Poems* for Jane Arnold', after being thanked
for sending a poem in the letter the previous Christmas. She
called the poems 'a book that would be valuable when she was

gone'. It is slow work, but work she sees real purpose in. Work that is concerned with legacy, with preserving her poetry after she is dead (MW to Dora, September 4, 1837). In November she transcribes 'Five year of sickness' again for a young friend, Emily Merewether, and posts it off. Mary supervises, reporting 'it went off very speedily and respectably' (MW to Dora, November 9, 1837).

In her illness, and the limitation it imposes on her, she finds both comfort and pleasure in her own words. She repeats her verses in company, sends them to friends. She is no longer embarrassed of herself, of her skills, or of wanting recognition. She is no longer so concerned with perfection, but sees that she can find solace in what is uneven, messy, incomplete. She is content at last to be known as the poet she is, and not the poet she could not be.

THREE

FIVE YEARS
OF SICKNESS
& OF PAIN

In December 1831, only days from her sixtieth birthday, Dorothy spent 'one fearful night' thinking she was dying.

On December 1, 1831 Dorothy writes a long letter to Henry Crabb Robinson full of political musings and family news. 'You will be glad to hear also that my health is good', she writes, 'and that my Niece is grown strong and healthy.' The weather is 'so warm & sunny' that she composes the letter bathed in light by an open window. By the end of the month, she is gravely ill.

There is no first hand record of this illness as Dorothy lived through it. Gordon Graham Wordsworth, William's grandson, cut the pages that relate to this time out of Dorothy's Journals after he took control of the family papers in 1907.

Several years later, Dorothy writes a poem about this night, dedicated to her doctor, Thomas Carr, who she calls her 'good and faithful friend.'

The poem begins: 'Five years of sickness & of pain/This weary frame has travelled o'er'.

This opening seems to self-consciously echo the opening lines of her brother's famous poem describing their shared trip to the Wye Valley in July 1798: 'Five years have past; five summers, with the length/Of five long winters!'

In calling up William's poem Dorothy's poem also calls up its themes of remembering and unremembering, of vision and visitations and revisiting. In the poem, William tells of how, since his first visit to Tintern, the wood has stayed with him in memory, enacting 'tranquil restoration' through loneliness and weariness. It has been not only restorative, but transportative, enabling him to 'see into the life of things.'

In the present of his poem, William sees Dorothy, in 1798, as like he had been five years earlier when he first visited the area. She becomes both his successor and his better. The poem becomes his prayer for her, a blessing, which asks for the moon to shine on her when she walks alone. He imagines Dorothy in the years to come, her mind 'a mansion for all lovely forms' and her 'memory ... a dwelling-place', so that if she experiences 'solitude, or fear, or pain, or grief' the mansion of memory in her mind will sooth her with 'healing thoughts'.

It is these healing thoughts Dorothy carries forth into her poem.

At the time she writes the poem, the crisis is over. The poem tells us she has been spared through the kindness of God, and rests 'in quietness of mind' and body 'upon a tranquil shore'. That night, the poem informs us, Carr told her he expected her 'earthly cares' to soon end. He told her she would die. But does she remember this herself, or only what her family tell her about it? William later remarks that she seems to remember little of that crisis. 'They tell me' she writes, not 'I remember'. Whatever happened was so acute, so utterly overwhelming, it is a blur in her mind.

In October 1835 she copies the poem out for a Grasmere neighbour, James Greenwood. (DW to James Greenwood, October 1835). This is the earliest version of the poem to survive. It contains three short stanzas, ending with this second-hand memory of being told her time was over.

In September 1837, Dorothy writes to her friend Hannah Hoare about this frightening time: 'On that night Mr Carr left me because he could do no more for me, and my poor Brother went to lie down on his bed thinking he could not bear to see me die'. She copies out the poem, now titled 'To my kind Friend and medical Attendant T. Carr composed a year ago – or more', and reports that though she still cannot walk without support, she now sits on her chair and writes with 'a clear head – and a thankful heart'. She hopes she may recover the use of her legs. She sends the poem again in 1837 to her cousin and childhood companion, Edward Ferguson, copied into a letter which recounts her struggles. This time she adds under the poem 'true it is, and I doubt not Mr Carr was *surprized* the next morning to hear that I was alive.' Mr. Carr is not the only one surprised by Dorothy's continuance. The family seem to expect her demise at any moment, and her survival becomes a matter of amazement and mystery. The clarity of thought and handwriting in this letter come too as a surprise to the family, and suggest further recovery than they had ever expected possible. Dorothy's refusal to die becomes as mysterious to her loved ones as her illness.

In sending this poem to various friends and relatives, it seems like Dorothy is trying to claim and understand her own trauma – an experience that she has little recollection of, and yet is haunted by. She finds herself repeating and repeating her version of that night, but much of it is a mystery to her. 'A Madman', she tells Edward, 'might as well attempt to relate the history of his doings and those of his fellows in confinement as I to tell you one hundredth part of what I have felt, suffered and done.' (DW to Edward Ferguson, October 8, 1837). Her experience of illness is both untellable and impossible to stop telling.

This poem is Dorothy's testimony of her illness, a way to try and understand her own experience, and a way to try and make it understood by others. She is writing herself back into her own narrative.

*

This crisis in 1831 did not happen in a vacuum, nor was it the first time the family would prepare for Dorothy's death. In November 1828, at the age of 56, Dorothy went to stay with her nephew John Wordsworth at his new home in Whitwick,

Leicestershire. John, William and Mary's eldest son, was taking up a position as a curate for Francis Merewether, who was Vicar of Whitwick and Rector of Coleorton. John had been helped into the position by William's patrons, Lord and Lady Beaumont. It was an important moment in John's adult life, but potentially an overwhelming one. He would be responsible for property for the first time, for budgeting and furnishing and all the roles of the head of house. Dorothy planned to help make the house homely for John and help him settle into his new role. William passes details of her journey and arrival onto Henry Crabb Robinson, telling him of a 'delightful letter' in which 'she speaks with high delight of her journey from Buxton down Darley-dale [...] to Derby and Nottingham' then on to Whitwick, between Loughborough and Ashby de la Zouch. (WW to HCR, November 28, 1828). Dorothy follows this two days later with her own letter, telling her old friend of her journey, her arrival, and her plans for the 'coming lonely winter'. (DW to HCR, November 30, 1828, *HCR C*). She plans to spend six months at Whitwick, before taking a slow journey home via various friends and family.

She writes of her hopes to travel more on the continent, to Switzerland and beyond, though also has misgivings about the plausibility of the ageing household even managing to cross the channel again, as she looks towards her 57th birthday the following month.

In these first few weeks she has found she and John 'are very comfortable & happy together', and she imagines 'Time will not hang heavy on our hands'. She is already considering returning to Whitwick the following winter.

Little does she know that the coming lonely winter will change the course of the rest of her life.

In March 1829, Dorothy is taken seriously ill.

Dora later explains to Edward Quillinan what a 'narrow escape' they believe Dorothy had from death: 'the inflammation was not subdued for <u>forty eight</u> hours – & all that time she was in <u>torture</u>'. (Dora to EQ, April 12, 1829).

Once William and Mary are aware of Dorothy's illness, Mary travels to Whitwick to help Dorothy.

The peak of the illness seems to be over before Mary arrives on April 10. By mid-April 1829 Crabb Robinson writes to William that she is 'convalescent'. (HCR to WW, April 22, 1829).

There is little record of Dorothy's 'dangerous illness' whilst it is at its height. There is a gap in her journal during the illness itself. In May she seems to go back and fill in a few sparse details, only to say that she was taken very ill on April 3, Mary came on the 10, and by May 3 she was able to walk into town again.

In *The Passionate Sisterhood* Kathleen Jones suggests that it is typically selfless of Dorothy to not bother the family until she is some degree recovered. In the context of the similar crises and silences that would follow in the decade to come, I can't help thinking Dorothy was simply too ill to write to her family, too wholly absorbed in being ill to tell of being ill.

She is able to write to Henry Crabb Robinson in late April and again in early May, remembering how she had been boasting of her 'extraordinary health & strength' only recently. She clearly takes her sickness as an admonishment – a reminder not to take one's health for granted – writing, 'My dear Friend what a lesson for us! The old Women at my bedside talked of me to each other as if quite sure that I *must* die.' (DW to HCR, May 2, 1829, *HCR C*). Here we see both the gravity of her illness and her attitude towards it – that it should be something to learn from, spiritually, and bodily.

William, at home and struggling with a painful and debilitating eye problem, dictates to Dora a letter to Henry Crabb Robinson, updating him on the situation. Dorothy's sudden illness raises in him the immediacy of morality, fear of 'snappings off', of sudden losses of loved ones, of failing strength. Her illness, he says, was a 'shock [...] to our poor hearts'.

His fear is revealing of the incredible importance he places on Dorothy. 'Were she to depart', he admits, 'the Phasis of my Moon would be robbed of light to a degree that I have not courage to think of.' (WW to HCR, April 1829). Dorothy is the sun, the original source; William only dull rock lit up by her reflected glow. Without her he has no shine. This seems to describe both their personal relationship and their creative collaboration. Without Dorothy, William has no essential spark. These words also echo Dorothy's from 1805, contained in a letter to Lady Beaumont in which she explains that 'fraternal affection [...] has been the building up of my being, the light of my path.' (DW to Lady Beaumont, March 18 & 19, 1805). This is written after John's death, which has shaken their vision of home, and their hopes of joy. In Dorothy's vision, her brothers seem to walk ahead of her with lanterns, lighting the way for her to follow. But for William, Dorothy herself is the light. Just as Dorothy never quite recovers from this illness, William never quite recovers from the fear of her death, and his letters over the following years of sporadic health crises show a man in constant pre-emptive mourning, expecting and dreading Dorothy's departure at any moment.

Although Mary did not arrive to help care for her until after the worst was over, Dorothy admits to Henry Crabb Robinson that Mary's presence has been vital in her recovery: 'for without her I should not have myself perceived how weak I was, & how much care was needed, & I should certainly have had a relapse.' She hopes she has learnt her lesson: 'In case of a similar attack, however I should know better, & could of myself avoid all risques.'

The same day, Dorothy receives a delayed letter from Crabb Robinson with his best wishes for her recovery, which makes her reflect again on this sudden 'dangerous illness'. In response, she makes a statement that inadvertently draws a line separating her life into a time of remembered health before this attack, and the time that will follow, claiming 'it is the first time in my life of fifty-six years in which I have had a serious illness'. (DW to HCR, May 2, 1829).

There is also the first hint here of the debilitating pain in her legs she will feel in the years to come, which she supposes is rheumatism brought on by the cold, damp weather, because many people experienced similar rheumatic pains that winter: 'at the beginning of the cold weather […] and now again during my illness, I felt rheumatic pains of which till this winter I had not in my whole life had the slightest feeling.' (DW to HCR, May 2, 1829).

She assures Crabb Robinson she is 'perfectly restored to health', though adds '& almost to strength', revealing that she is still in recovery, and not entirely better. She has been told 'quiet care' is necessary for a full recovery, and she admits she feels she needs it – 'my own frame admonishes me that it is' – almost despite herself. She promises to 'be neither rash nor negligent', not for her own sake but for the sake of her loved ones, and to take her health seriously. 'Indeed', she admits, 'I never can forget what I suffered myself nor the anxiety of those around me.' (DW to HCR, May 2 1829).

In May, Mary returns home to Rydal, leaving Dorothy 'improving gradually' at Whitwick. (WW to HCR, May 18, 1829).

Her illness, she says, 'has left a home-sickness behind it' and she is glad to return to Rydal Mount in September. (DW to HCR, May 2, 1829). She breaks her journey to visit her dear Aunt Rawson in Halifax and again becomes 'very ill', with weakness, fatigue, and poor sleep keeping her in bed till after noon in the week she had originally been planning to leave for home. (DW to HCR, April 22, 1830). She later describes this to Jane Marshall as an 'attack of cholera morbus'. Cholera morbus was the term used to refer to a severe gastric attack, involving cramps, diarrhoea, and vomiting. In her commonplace book, she pastes in medical advice for treating cholera morbus.

Back home, she seems to everyone to be 'healthy and well', but finds she is getting unusually tired after walking only a mile or two. On September 14th she walks a mile, 'with a long rest at the end of the mile', but at home she is so 'worn' she has to go to bed for an hour to recover. She blames the fatigue on the damp, and her 'not quite settled' bowels. 'I should be very careful', she writes to Jane, promising 'and so I shall be.' (DW to JM, September 15, 1829).

*

That November Dorothy writes to Coleridge, the first letter she has written to him for many years – so many years she jokes he will have forgotten her handwriting, and not know who is writing. This letter shows her hopeful still of a full recovery and a return to an active, travelling life.

> You have, no doubt, heard of my Brother's pleasant tour in Ireland; and of his great activity in climbing mountains etc etc—I hope my day is not quite over, though at present I confine myself to garden-walks; and drives

> in the poney chaise, to guard against returns of serious
> derangements of the Bowels which have troubled me
> since last March. You will, I know, be glad to hear that
> I am now quite well. (DW to STC, November 14 1829)

Her phrasing hints that this bowel disorder has not entirely left her – that they have troubled her since last March implies ongoing problems, although not as severe as the initial crisis. Dorothy is now taking the advice she was given during the worst of her illness: to rest and to limit activity, to avoid relapses.

In the last week of September, she had felt well enough to fill a week with activity. In her journals she records that on Monday she walked to Grasmere, on Tuesday to Brathay Bridge. On Wednesday she attended the local Book Club, and on Thursday rode to Grasmere, then dined (had lunch) at their friend Mrs. Harrison's. The Friday she marks as William and Mary's wedding anniversary, on which they all go for lunch at Mrs. Luff's.

By the next week she is ill in bed, unable to go to Church. Mr. Carr is called to attend to her. She breaks off her journal until October 23, when she begins to realise how unrecovered she is: 'I have been not quite well at the beginning of this interval but am never strong'. Her frustration at her ongoing illness comes through when she adds 'though I walk not further than garden or foot of hill'. She has seen the effects of pushing herself to do too much too soon, and expects the opposite to work as well: if she does little, she should feel better. The next few years are a long lesson in nothing being that simple.

Reaching out to Coleridge can be seen as an instance of Dorothy searching for a community of care, for solidarity in her illness from those she knows have shared experiences of illness. Coleridge had always been open about his own health problems, unafraid to speak honestly about troubles with bowels, sickness, boils, or whatever ailed him. She knows that if she writes to him about her bowels, he will understand in a way other friends might not. Despite her grumblings about him being a difficult house-guest during his opiate addiction, years previously, she now sees the potential for community in shared suffering.

On October 18 she writes to Catherine Clarkson of her 'inexpressible delight' at being well enough to sit up in bed and write a letter. Catherine Clarkson has long been a confidante during Dorothy's episodes of ill health, and knows her history. It is a huge relief to her to be able to write after weeks where she 'could neither read nor listen to reading', let alone sew or anything similar. At her worst, she 'could not stand for a minute together even leaning upon another' but is now able to 'go up and down stairs without help and walk about in the house a quarter of an hour at a time'. It now gives her 'but little pain' to walk, which suggests walking was quite painful before, although she still has 'a sense of weakness with unconquerable stiffness'. This bowel attack – of 'sickness and violent perspirations – hot and cold' and daily, constant pains in her bowels – has also affected her legs, her ability to stand, and move. (DW to CC, October 18–27, 1829). She is regaining mobility, but slowly, and fears the 'autumnal cold dampness' will hinder her progress. But even the hope expressed in this letter is a troubled hope – this is the letter that takes over nine days to finish, finally, sitting up in bed, having been interrupted by episodes of diarrhoea and weakness during which she could not write at all. 'There has been no tendency to inflammation in the Bowels' this time, she writes, 'I have only had bilious sickness—headaches, and sharp pains of the Bowels'. As much as she wants to see herself as recovered, the problem has not gone away.

*

By April 1830, a year after she has begun to recover from the initial illness, she is keen to assure friends she is better. She has 'had no one ailment since the beginning of January' she reports to Henry Crabb Robinson, though she has been 'enacting the Invalid since the month of November.' She has been on strict orders to continue to rest, 'in compliance with the judgement & advice of those who I suppose are much better judges of what is safe than I am myself' – though she has been pushing the boundaries, from the house to the garden and beyond, as the improving weather of spring has made movement easier.

In her letter, she is at pains to point out that 'there is no hardship' in this limitation. She feels it is her 'duty' to obey the restrictions placed on her; payment in kind to those that have worried and cared for her.

Her letter also reveals an undercurrent of uncertainty about her recovery – when she looks forward to the next winter, she adds 'if I live so long'. She is aware of her situation still as potentially mortal, any relapse potentially fatal.

What has been lost in this illness is her sense of her own capacity, or her trust in it. She hopes by the following year she 'may be safely trusted to [her] own feelings as a Guide in ascertaining the measure of [her] strength.' At the current time, however, she cannot be trusted. Her feelings are not, it is judged, in her own best interest.

This first year of Dorothy's illness sets various precedents which will become ingrained in the years to come: winter is a time of danger; any relapse might be fatal; Dorothy cannot be trusted to help herself.

*

In December 1831 Dorothy becomes again, very ill. Sara Hutchinson writes to Edward Quillinan on January 6 that Dorothy 'has had a very bad attack', though by the time of writing 'all present danger is over – & for four days her recovery has been very rapid'. (SH to EQ, January 6, 1832).

The family believe Dorothy's illness to be a relapse of whatever made her so ill in Whitwick, which they categorise as primarily an inflammatory bowel disorder. In January 1832 William writes to John Kenyon that Dorothy 'has been five weeks confined to her room by a return of the inflammatory complaint which shattered her constitution three years ago'. (WW to John Kenyon, January 26, 1832). Over a year later, he repeats this theory to Henry Crabb Robinson: 'the origin of her complaint was an inflammation in the Bowels, caught […] when she lived with her nephew in Leicestershire three years ago.'

The problem is not constant, but recurring, and each successive episode leaves Dorothy weaker and more disabled. In April 1832 William writes to update their brother Christopher on Dorothy's health: 'Our dear sister makes no progress towards recovery of Strength. She is very feeble, never quits her room, and passes most of the day in, or upon, the bed.' The only pain she has is occasional, William writes, 'from wind and stitches.' (WW to CW, April 1, 1832). William reassures Christopher that despite her limitations, she is happy enough with her situation: 'She is very chearful, and nothing troubles her but public affairs and the sense of requiring so much attention.'

William is clearly worrying about mortality when he reports that Dorothy has been a model of Christian piety through her illness: 'Whatever may be the close of this illness, it will be a profound consolation to you, my dear brother, and to us all, that it is borne with perfect resignation; and that her thoughts are such as the good and pious would wish.' (WW to CW, April 1, 1832).

By the middle of April, Dorothy has been able to sit up in an upstairs room that isn't her bedroom during the daytime for three days, before making it to the sofa downstairs to see her nephew Willy, who has returned home for a visit. (Dora to EQ, April 12, 1832).

But this respite is very brief. In May 1832 William again writes to Christopher, to recount that Dorothy has had a 'relapse' after 'going on well for a fortnight'. This relapse 'left her extremely weak', and William finds it most alarming: though 'less violent' than her previous attacks, he can see that with each one, she loses more resilience – 'her recovery from each attack is slower and slower.' (WW to CW, May 1832).

On May 5th Dora writes to Jemima and Rotha Quillinan similarly that Dorothy 'has been very ill again' and 'has not left her bed since this last attack which was Thursday week – that is 10 days ago'. Dora adds a promising note: 'we hope to get her up for a short time this evening.' (Dora to Jemima and Rotha Q, May 5, 1832).

In June, Dora reports to Edward Quillinan that Dorothy 'has had another relapse & tho' apparently very slight yet it kept her to her bed many days'. She seems to recover only to relapse continually. 'Alas', Dora fears, 'this cannot continue long'. (Dora & WW to EQ, June 26, 1832). In the same letter William refers to his sister's 'deplorable weakness & dangerous illness'. In their eyes, she is still in imminent danger, her future entirely uncertain.

*

Almost a year after Dorothy's terrifying night, she writes one of her last letters of any length to her childhood friend Jane Marshall. It has taken a year, but by early November 1832 she really believes that she is over the worst. She writes:

Enough to say that I am very much better—have now no regular or irregular maladies except the flatulence and pains in the Bowels—and I am certainly much stronger, less susceptible of changes in the atmosphere. My horrid cravings have quite left me.—It is true I have *sinkings* now and then; but any thing is better than the gnawing appetite with which I was for many days afflicted.(DW to Jane Marshall, November 20 1832)

Jane's daughter Ellen has clearly been ill, and Dorothy's reflection on Ellen's illness also tells us important things about her own at this point:

'Dear Creature! often have I thought of her when I felt the bliss of lying down upon my bed—worn out—yet free from pain. I have thought of her and of her grievous sufferings compared with mine. That difficulty in breathing is what I grieve for most in thinking of her. The contrast of my own easy breath makes it doubly felt by me when I lie down. Indeed I have often said that till within the last year I never knew what was the Blessing of a good bed to lie upon.' (DW to Jane Marshall, November 20, 1832).

Although Dorothy repeatedly says she is much better, she still 'keeps upstairs', as Dora puts it in her post-script to a letter to her cousin John that they collectively write in December 1832. (WW, DW & Dora to (nephew) John Wordsworth, December 5, 1832).

This communal letter shows a shared relief and joy in Dorothy's recovery. Dorothy edits the letter as Dora writes, so that Dora's report that 'she is much better than she was three months ago' becomes 'very much better', and Dora's cautious 'she looks better' becomes 'looks much better'. Dorothy adds in a postscript, 'I have been growing fatter regularly for many weeks', though Dora also notes 'she still suffers sharp pain occasionally, and is now and then troubled with sickness.' Her recovery is relative, not complete.

*

There is a gap in Dorothy's journal between January 22, 1833 and April 23, which seems to coincide with another crisis. In January Dorothy's ankles swell and blacken – a new symptom that greatly alarms both the family and physicians.

On January 29 William writes to their brother Christopher 'our dear Sister is very poorly and seems to grow weaker every day'. (WW to CW, January 29, 1833). He explains that a month earlier she became unwell – perhaps only with a cold – but has not been able to leave her room since. During this period 'her legs began to swell—and the swelling is accompanied with black spots'. These swollen legs with black spots 'alarm Mr. Carr much'. Mr Carr thinks she might be dying, and so he increases her dosage of brandy and opium to ease her suffering. Dorothy 'is not at all aware of this danger', William thinks. Afterwards, she will remember little of any of it.

In February 1833 William writes to Henry Crabb Robinson: 'I am come to that time of life, when I must be prepared to part with or precede my dearest Friends; and God's will be done.' William by this point has become resigned to Dorothy's continual ill health and living with the constant threat of her death, but it seems imminent. He had written to Christopher the previous month, 'it cannot be long before we must follow in course of Nature all those whom we love, who are gone before us.' They had lost so many of their loved ones in their lives, perhaps it seemed inevitable that they would experience more grief.

Throughout the month of February, Dorothy seems in grave peril. Sara Coleridge, the poet's daughter, passes on news of Dorothy from Dora to another mutual friend, Mary Stanger, convinced Dorothy may die any day: 'her fate is now sealed & O the difference to that household when she is taken away!' (Sara Coleridge to Mary Stanger, February 2, 1833). A few days later, Sara Hutchinson writes to the elder Sara Coleridge, the poet's wife, with news of Dorothy, who she expects, 'will not be long with us'. The verdict on her condition is clear: 'Mr. Carr gives us no hope of her recovery'. She explains to Sara how 'for the last three weeks she has become much worse – tho' gradually – & her weakness & languor are truly deplorable – indeed without the help of stimulants you could scarcely believe her alive'. With stimulants – opium and brandy – 'she is kept at time tolerably easy – & even comfortable & *cheer*ful'. She has been 'entirely confined to bed' all the time, but 'her patience never forsakes her' and she 'never complains of being weary of it'.

William seems in denial, and 'strives to hope against hope', so that the rest of the family 'dare not breathe the fears which oppress us'. It seems inevitable and unavoidable still: 'he knows too well that we must soon lose her – Gods will be done!' (February 9, 1833). None of them seem to be able to imagine how the family – and William in particular – will be able to manage without Dorothy amongst them. Dora writes to Maria Kinnaird of watching her father trying to manage his fear of losing Dorothy: 'Father was mercifully supported that sad sad night when he thought he had taken leave of his sister for the last time—indeed all through this trying winter—but surely such love as he bears to her is of no common nature, and when the separation does take place it will be hard to support'. (Dora to Maria Kinnaird, February 22, 1833). Mary writes to Jane Marshall, Dorothy's best childhood friend, to prepare her for 'impending separation', having been told by Mr. Carr it cannot be 'far distant'. Dorothy is heavily sedated, so suffering less than before, and does not seem to be aware that she is expected to die at any moment. Her legs are both better and worse: 'in consequence perhaps of her total inability to use her legs, the swelling is abated – but little spots, like flea bites appear upon them accompanied by heat, which symptom Mr. Carr considers almost decisive.' (MW to JM, undated).

In mid-February William writes to Thomas Hamilton that Dorothy 'has now been confined seven weeks to her bed'. The crisis might have passed: 'Mr. Carr a few nights ago prepared us for her Dissolution before morning', though she is since 'a good deal better'. (WW to Thomas Hamilton, February 18, 1833). By February 22 she is well enough to add her own note on the bottom of a letter William sends to Edward Quillinan. She explains:

> The worst of my late illness has been spasms in the legs, excessive langour and aversion of noise. Add to these I could neither write, read nor listen to anyone, Thank God I can now do all tho' very little. (WW & DW to EQ, February 22, 1833).

In March she seems to Dora 'very much better'. On the 22nd she 'sat up for full two hours' which seems to mark an upturn, though she still cannot stand. Dora is delighted 'she can again amuse herself with books & we read to her every evening a long time which she much enjoys'. (Dora to Rotha Q, March 23 1833). Dora writes similarly to Mary Kinnaird on the same day, adding 'the blackness about the ancles which alarmed us so very much is all but gone'. (Dora to Mary Kinnaird, March 22 1833). Sara Coleridge, deep in her own illness, has reservations about Dorothy's progress, writing to Elizabeth Wardell,

'I fear her recovery is out of the question. All we can expect is that she may be spared in tolerable comfort some time longer'. At least they no longer expect her death daily, as they had been doing for so long. (Sara Coleridge to Elizabeth Wardell, March 29 1833). William, visiting John and his family in Moresby, writes home, 'One word for dearest Sister— how shall I rejoice to see her; if any mischief come to her I shall never forgive myself for staying so long beyond the intended time'. (WW to family, April 1, 1833).

A fragment of an undated letter by Dora, which must be written around this time, gives a picture of Dorothy as bearing her suffering as she recovers with almost saintly patience:

> You will be as much delighted to hear as I to tell that our sweet patient cheerful Invalid continues to gain ground surely tho <u>very</u> slowly – the blackness about the ancles which alarmed us so much is rapidly dispersing & the swelling nearly abated & there [were] none of those sad spasms wh. were so distressing [...] She has not yet attempted to put her feet to the ground nor do we mean to allow her doing so until the blackness is quite gone. (Dora to Miss Marshall, undated, 1833?).

In her sickness this winter, Dorothy has been unable to read or concentrate much on listening to people read to her. Time blurs. It has been the shortest winter of her life, and perhaps also the longest. She seems disconnected from everything, including her own pain. Dora describes her as the most perfect uncomplaining invalid: 'never a murmur escapes from her – there she lies perfectly still from morning to night & from night till morning & whenever you enter her sick chamber you are greeted with that same bright smile so full of love & tenderness'.

In late April, Dorothy records in her journal: 'I take the pen having hobbled twice round the room after washing and dressing myself, and having legs bandaged by my faithful Nurse, dear Dora.' (*RJ*, April 23, 1833). Her legs still need bandaging, suggesting the blackened spots developed into weeping skin or needed compression. Her own account of her passive winter seems less uncomplaining than the vision Dora gives: 'Till within about a month I could read none—then very little—no work—no writing—and for two or three weeks could hardly listen to other's reading—thank God I can now do all in moderation'. She is keen to get back to mental activity, and to rides in the garden.

In May, after the worst is over, William sends an update to Henry Crabb Robinson: 'the functions of the stomach and bowels are pitiably impaired – her Ancles are still a good deal swoln but the blackness from which the medical attendant apprehended grangrene & mortification has entirely disappeared.' (WW to HCR, May 4, 1833).They 'hope for further improvement', but her life is still 'in the hands of God' – 'we must be prepared' he warns. (WW to HCR, May 4, 1833).

Through the spring her health fluctuates – 'losing ground' in stormy weather, before settling again. (WW to HCR, May 18 or 28, 1833).

By early June, although the thundery weather has been keeping her sick and she can walk no more than 20 or 30 steps, she is able to concentrate enough to request, via William, that Crabb Robinson find and send her a copy of Gilbert White's *Natural History of Selbourne* to read on her sickbed, and to dictate instructions of where Crabb Robinson should visit on a trip to the Isle of Man. (WW to HCR, June 4, 1833; WW to HCR June 5, 1833).

In July Crabb Robinson finally manages his long hoped-for visit to Rydal Mount en route to the Isle of Man. He writes to his brother that he finds Dorothy 'wonderfully recovered from a state of such debility that her death was looked for from day to day.' (HCR to TR, July 4, 1833). She is weak and tired but 'could partake of conversation' though he is only able to see her for 'an hour at a time', to limit her fatigue.

On July 16 Dorothy picks up her journal again, beginning, 'What a pause! During all this time have been convalescent but so slowly I hardly knew it except by looking back & have been very helpless as to reading & working'. (*RJ* July 16, 1833). She is finally progressing, she thinks, but writing this entry itself has tired her. Two days later, she adds how she wants to write more about her illness but 'it is almost a blank'. She has only just been able to begin to 'employ' herself with the things she calls her 'natural activity': 'work – reading – writing – listening all tired me'. 'It was different', she reflects, 'in the first winter of my confinement'. She can walk with 'wonderful ease' now, 'without pain', although her legs are still weak, and her stomach is more settled, with less wind. Crabb Robinson keeps her entertained and distracted from her pain: 'his company always pleasant when I was strong enough to listen—no need of effort on my part—Patiently would he sit by the hour trying to entertain me—then was my prop in walking—and even led me to my Bed when tired'. (*RJ*, July 18, 1833).

At the end of the month William reports that Dorothy is generally 'much improved', although she has another small crisis – 'a seizure of spasm […] which weakened her much.' (WW to HCR, July 29, 1833). 'She is rallying', he writes hopefully, 'though slowly'. In the autumn Sara Coleridge passes on reports from Hartley Coleridge that Dorothy 'looks well in the face but is very decrepit & aged in figure & motion'. (Sara Coleridge to Elizabeth Wardell, October 30, 1833).

In September, at the time she is sitting for Crossthwaite's portrait, she seems remarkably well again. She has gained strength, mobility and concentration since July. Dora writes:

> 'She has never looked so well or been so well since her first attack 20 months ago as at present – she can read, & write, & work, & talk – & walk about her room (without a stick) & dress herself entirely – drives out every day when weather permits sometimes even comes down stairs to see her friends & takes frequent walks along the upstairs passage [...] going down those two or three steps unassisted except by her stick'. (Dora to Rotha Q, September 10, 1833).

In early October, Dora paints a positive picture of Dorothy's health to Jemima and Edward Quillinan: 'We tell my Aunt she is the strongest of the party now! she takes her drives out of doors & her walks in the house – & often in the evening when we are quite alone she brings her work down stairs & sits an hour or two with us'. (Dora to Jemima & Edward Q, October 6, 1833). In the fine weather, Dora writes, she has been her aunt's 'charioteer', enabling her to enjoy the mild autumn.

But the same day, as Crabb Robinson leaves Rydal Mount again on his way home, he reports Dorothy's health as still 'perilous', fearing 'it is very improbable that I shall see her again.' (HCR to TR, October 6, 1833).

*

Dorothy manages to get through the winter of 1833 into 1834 without a serious relapse. In the new year she writes with thanks to Julia Myers for a Christmas present of oysters, which cheered her up in her 'solitary sickroom', and again she claims she is better than she was – 'wonderfully well compared with last year at this time.' (DW to Julia Myers, January 2, 1834).

The mild spring eases her pain, but she 'does not gather strength as might be expected.' William, dictating to Mary, admits to Crabb Robinson that the family 'all think that she deceived herself' in thinking she has gained no strength at all. (WW to HCR, April 3, 1844). She admits this herself, the same month, in a letter to Anne Pollard: 'There has been little change with me since I last wrote, yet as I have had no bilious attack and no violent attack of *pain* (though seldom entirely free from gentle visitations) I *must* be actually much better; but the change is so very slow that I am forced to check myself and think of the past when I (perhaps some-what peevishly) have exclaimed 'I gather no strength." (DW to Anne Pollard, April 12-17, 1834).

Despite these frequent, terrible attacks, she still clings to the hope of a complete recovery. She is still at this time limited mostly to her 'solitary bedchamber'. Hints of boredom are coming through though, despite her attempts to maintain a cheerful invalid persona. She apologises to Anne that her letter is dull: 'a solitary bedchamber does not furnish a variety of incidents', though 'Friends are very kind and sit with me as much and as often as leisure will allow, except when the apprehension of fatiguing me keeps them away.' All through her illness she has maintained her aim to listen to expert advice, to limit her activity, and to not over-exert herself, but she is feeling less philosophical about her confinement as yet another spring approaches.

She continues through June much the same, weak but 'much freer from pain.' (WW to HCR, June 10, 1834). In July, Dora reports to Crabb Robinson that Dorothy is 'stronger on the whole' than during his visit. Dorothy adds her own note to the letter, elaborating on her current condition. To get outside, she is still reliant on someone to 'drag' her in the chair. 'Alas!' she laments, 'my legs are but of little use except in helping me to steer an enfeebled body from one part of the room to the other. The longest walk I have attempted has been once round the Gravel Front of the House.' (Dora and DW to HCR, July 24, 1834). That she has been able to walk outside at all does show an improvement in her mobility, but not as much as they might have expected or hoped for.

*

At the beginning of October Dorothy writes to the publisher Edward Moxon that her 'health and strength improve, though slowly.' (DW to Edward Moxon, October 2, 1834).

However, the change in seasons seems to bring about a relapse. In October she writes to Catherine Clarkson that the 'autumnal cold and dampness' are once again stopping her from being able to walk outside in the garden, adding 'cold is my horror'. (DW to CC, October 18, 1834).

In November William writes to Henry Crabb Robinson that Dorothy had a relapse – a 'backcast' a month previously – so that she 'does not gain strength' and on measure remains about the same, with her appetite, weight, and digestive discomfort fluctuating over the months. (WW, MW & DW to HCR, November 24, 1834).

In December she has another 'severe bilious attack', which leaves her both fatigued and weakened. Mary reports it 'kept her almost a prisoner to her bed for [...] three weeks'. At the end of it, she is able to sit up again 'in her favourite chair', but only for a single hour, before she must return to bed. Each attack leaves her weaker and more incapacitated. In her journal there is a gap between December 6 and Christmas Eve, the eve of her birthday, when she tries to fill in the missing time:

> I take the pen for the first time, having been confined to my Bed entirely since Monday 7th Decr—At the end of a week a Diarrhoea was stopped, & my appetite began slowly to return but for many days my pain was as great as ever, & constant. (*RJ* December 24, 1834).

Her pains are now 'less violent – & less frequent' and she thinks her strength is returning although she cannot stand or walk: 'body weakness will not let me stand on my legs'. She explains that her 'inside aches constantly', though the pain is bearable, except for occasionally when it becomes a 'piping agony'. Despite this, she has appreciated the mild weather, 'often dazzling in brightness'. The shortest day, she notes, was 'light & long & a lovely sunrise'. Even in her worst pain she can still appreciate the beauty of her surroundings, and the extraordinarily dry, bright weather. On December 30 she writes, 'never surely in the 63 years that I have lived can there have been such brilliant new-years & Christmas days.' (*RJ* December 30, 1834)

1835 starts the same, with a 'brilliant sun-rise'. The beauty of it makes Dorothy wish 'Oh! that men's hearts could be <u>softened</u>! – then elevated by the goodness & beauty of all that is done for & spread before us!' (*RJ* January 2, 1835). But the weather, inevitably, changes, and Dorothy worsens. Throughout January she is fitfully ill, with 'recurring fits of uneasiness' which are 'very oppressive'. (*RJ* January 23, 1835)In February she is a little better, able to work at a rug she is making as a gift, and slowly with 'work & Books'. (*RJ* February 4, 1835).

She is well enough to worry about everyone else's health around her. She has 'many fears' for those she loves (*RJ* February

8, 1835). The rest of the month blurs by in weakness and household worries. The weather is very cold, and on February 20 she records a very painful night, 'starved to marble', i.e., frozen to stone. (*RJ* February 20, 1835). Days later she records a 'dreadful storm in the night' that kept her awake and left her very weak. In her weakness, time is lost – '12 o'clock strikes & I have neither read nor worked—hardly thought'. (*RJ* February 24, 1835).

On March 9 she picks up her journal after a break since February 25, lamenting 'I hardly know how the time has gone'. In her sickness, she explains, 'how to lie easiest & quietest has been my chief care'. (*RJ* March 9, 1835). On March 13 she calls her state 'good-for-nothing'. She has had 'sickness every day'. She ate no meat on March 12, which seemed to help, though she says her stomach is 'unsettled & cannot bear solid food'. (*RJ* March 13, 1835). Mr Carr has recommended some new medicines to help, but on March 14 she writes, 'today (the 4th time) my stomach has repelled my dinner'. On the 15th, finally, she manages to eat, despite feeling 'squeamish' still. (*RJ* March 14–15, 1835).

She has a bad night on March 16, 'with fits of sharp pain', followed by several 'days & nights disturbed by sickness & pain'. (*RJ* March 16, 1835). On the 20th she takes medicine she hopes will 'overcome' the bile. Although her pains have been 'very severe', the heat in her legs is gone, the 'left is much stronger' and the 'circulation improved'. The birds have been warbling all day to her in her bed, when she could 'neither read nor work'. (*RJ* March 20, 1835).

On Saturday March 21 the weather is 'dry, clear & chearing', which seems to promise spring and all spring holds for her: better health, better strength, time outdoors in the garden. But 'a sharp wind brushes away all greenness'. The weather is against her yet. (*RJ* March 21, 1835).

On March 30 she is able to write a longer entry. She has been both 'better & worse'. This is the first day she has felt well enough to 'read a letter'. She has been 'often very sick' and is struggling with her appetite. The only thing she has been able to eat is arrowroot bread and biscuits. (*RJ* March 30, 1835)

April 1835 begins 'cold & dark & calm'. The trees are not budding yet. Dorothy records 'sickness all day' in her journal. On April 2 the weather outdoors has become the weather in the body: Dorothy describes herself too as 'very dark melancholy myself', whilst the wind whistles around her. (*RJ* April 2, 1835). The weather continues 'damp, close & dark'; Dorothy continues 'sick all day'. Mr. Carr comes and brings her more medicine. On the 10th she is a little better and can put more onto paper. She has had 'little pain' but writes that 'weakness oppresses me'. 'In truth', she reflects, 'I have been so often sick, & when not sick so helpless that I have had no pleasure in doing any thing'. (*RJ* April 10, 1835).

The next day, the weather is fine at last. Dorothy is finer too, writing, 'I have not been sick today' then correcting herself, 'except—! Then I am always sick'. (*RJ* April 11, 1835)More time is lost – the next entry is on Sunday April 19. Dorothy laments 'another week & nothing set down'. It has been very cold again, and her pain much worse. Now the weather is milder, and her 'sicknesss has been better – almost gone'. The entry closes with a promise of spring: the frost is over, 'snow gone'. This is the penultimate entry she will make. (*RJ* April 19, 1835).

*

In May 1835 Dorothy, Sara Hutchinson, Mary's sister, and Dora are all taken ill with what seems to be the flu, caused, William hypothesises, 'by the changeableness of the weather'. Dorothy at first appears better than she was the previous month; she seems to 'recruit every day', until she is 'somewhat thrown back by another of her bilious attacks'. (MW to IF, May 13, 1835).

Sara was well enough at the end of May to write to her family to update them on Dorothy's condition:

> Poor Miss W. does not rally at all – you never saw any one look more like a picture of exhaustion. & yet there does not appear to be inwardly either in mind or body any great change – her faculties are the same – & I think she complains less of pain – but is greatly affected by a sort of nausea which obliges her to lie perfectly still – & when you go into her room she is lying generally as if she were in a state of insensibility or half asleep... (SH to Mrs. Hutchinson, May 30-31, 1835).

Throughout this illness, Dorothy is 'always craving air', giving them a slim hope that the 'change in the weather' as spring unfolds will help her. Sara is interrupted in her letter and by the time she takes it up again the next day, she is feeling unwell herself, with a 'plaguey pain'. In June William writes to Henry Crabb Robinson of the 'distressing state' of all three women's health. Although Sara 'has been dangerously ill in a severe rheumatic fever' she seems to be recovering. It is Dorothy who appears to be in the most danger. She 'grows weaker and weaker, more & more emaciated.'

In March, Sara Coleridge had written to Mary Stanger that 'Miss W. is confined to her bed– but full of life of mind and kindly interest for the dear friends of this world whom she is well aware that she may probably very soon take a last leave of'. (Sara Coleridge to Mary Stanger, March 25, 1835).

Now, with the added pressure of this virus, William prepares himself yet again for the fact that Dorothy might die at any time, certain 'it is impossible that my beloved sister can put on for any length of time.' (WW to HCR, May 1835). Weeks pass and the situation does not improve. She seems certain to die. To Mrs. Williamson he writes, 'as to my own dear Sister, it is with her a mere question of time; as it seems, humanly speaking, impossible that she should rally in any effectual degree.' (WW to Mrs. Williamson, June 7, 1835).

On June 16 Sara Coleridge writes to Dora with full expectation that Dorothy will not survive this latest crisis. Sara imagines memories of Dorothy in happier times soothing and elevating her in the years to come:

> I feel assured that her last days and hours on earth will be as full of quiet joy and humble yet exalted hopefulness as her blest and blessing life has ever been. Will you give my sincere and grateful love to her: it is nothing to say that I shall never forget her face and voice, and the many happy occasions on which I have seen and heard them; may they be frequently present with me for useful influences – to support, to soothe, & to elevate! (Sara Coleridge to Dora, June 16, 1835).

On the same day, Mary writes to Isabella Fenwick 'Rydal Mount is at present a *Hospital* – Miss. W. has rallied to a certain point, which is almost a miracle, but a week ago we considered her to be dying.' (MW to IF, June 16, 1835).

To the family's great shock, it is Sara who dies, on June 23, after five weeks of illness. Dorothy, to everyone's surprise, comes through her fourth major crisis in five and a half years. William writes to Henry Crabb Robinson with the sad news. 'My poor Sister is very feeble', he reports, 'but we are all in health much better than our friends can think possible.' (WW to HCR, June 24, 1835). In early July, a week after Sara's funeral, William writes again, relating changes to Dorothy's memory and thinking since 'the event', and that her 'health of body seems to have suffered less than her mind'. (WW to HCR, July 6, 1835). She seems not to be able to remember the illness or the time around it, and is aware of the change in her memory and thinking, 'complain[ing] of weakness & foolishness of mind'. Physically, she is slowly improving – 'the bilious sickness and cough & expectoration which harassed her and weakened her so much are gone', but he expects when the weather changes that 'the sickness without catching cold' will return. In her confused state 'she complains of faintness & hollowness & has an incessant craving for some thing to support her.' William is so exhausted from caring for Dorothy his hand shakes as he writes. 'She has a great craving for oatmeal porridge', he relates, 'principally for the sake of the butter that she eats along with it and butter is sure to bring on a fit of bile sooner or later.' His role has become one of 'refusing her things that would be improper for her' – meaning unhealthy.

*

There is an intriguing parallel between Dorothy's acute attacks during these years and the illness which disabled, and later killed, her niece Catherine. Catherine Wordsworth was William and Mary's fourth child, born in September 1808. Dorothy describes her as the 'only funny child in the family' – the only one to make you 'laugh outright'. (DW to Lady Beaumont, February 28, 1810). When she was eighteen months old, Catherine experienced over seven hours of convulsions which left her paralysed down her right-hand side.

Dorothy writes to Catherine Clarkson at the time that 'it was evident that the palsy proceeded from a rupture in some vessel of the brain'. (DW to CC, April 12, 1810). Little Catherine Wordsworth had had a stroke. She lost the speech she had already learnt.

Over the next year Catherine regains some use of her right arm and leg. They employ an experimental therapy that they learn about through Dorothy's Aunt Rawson – the woman who raised Dorothy after her mother died – who had recently lost mobility after breaking a hip. The therapy, developed by surgeon John Grosvenor, was a 'cure of lameness by friction' – massaging the muscles in her weak side for an hour every day, and another hour down her spine. (WW and DW to Lady Beaumont, May 10, 1810). In May Dorothy reports, 'With leaning against a chair she can stand upon both legs, and even move, though very lamely, from one end of the sofa to the other.' (DW to CC, May 11, 1810). It is the fine weather and hot sun, Dorothy thinks, that has helped Catherine the most. But on the evening of June 3, 1812 Catherine has another seizure, and this time she does not recover. She dies a little after 5am. Dorothy was present when Catherine was first taken ill in 1810, and blamed the initial seizures on over-consumption of raw carrot – carrot bullets that her older siblings had made to shoot out of guns carved out of elder wood – carrot-shooters rather than pea-shooters. The doctor had no doubt that it was eating these carrot bullets that caused the seizures. Catherine vomited heavily before the convulsions begin. The doctor suggested castor oil to empty her digestive system, producing a 'copious evacuation' which cleared 'many lumps of carrot'. The convulsions in 1812 had no discernible cause, and, the doctor assures them, could not have been prevented. Grevel Lindop and Muriel Strachan have proposed that Catherine Wordsworth had Down's Syndrome, a diagnosis that did not exist during the Wordsworths' lifetimes. The evidence is compelling, but just as we can't know what the cause of Dorothy's ill health was for certain, we can't know for certain whether Catherine did or did not have what we now know as Down's Syndrome. Regardless of what the actual cause of her convulsions was, Catherine must have been in Dorothy's mind as she herself craved and was denied certain foods, for fear they would bring on a relapse, and as she herself lost the use of her legs after spasms and convulsions. When William rubbed her aching ankles and legs to help them recover from swelling and semi-paralysis over these years, he too must have had Catherine on his mind. I also wonder if Dorothy remembered the words she wrote to De Quincey after Catherine's death: 'The disease lay in the Brain, and if it had been possible for her to recover, it is much to be feared that she would not have retained the Faculties of her Mind.' (DW to De Q, June 5, 1812). Later that month she wrote similarly to Catherine Clarkson: 'we only prayed for her release in death; for it was plain that had she lived she could not have recovered the use of her limbs, nor probably of her senses'. (DW to CC, June 23, 1812). In positioning death as a welcome release from disability, Dorothy was far from alone, in her time or ours. The same belief that it is better to be dead than disabled fuels ableist responses across society, ranging from the cartoon of Steven Hawkins drawn after his death showing him walking out of his wheelchair towards heaven, to the filicide of disabled children. Dorothy was responding to the prevailing conditions of her time, in much the same way as her friends would later respond to her disability.

Early on in her illness, Dorothy seems the perfect invalid: pious, never complaining through her pain. William in May 1832 writes that 'her thoughts are what they should be'. (WW to CW, May 5, 1832). Dora, possibly around the same time, writes to Jane Marshall that 'it is beautiful to observe' Dorothy's forbearance. She is the model of the worthy sick. But as time goes on, Dorothy changes. She is no longer patient, no longer resigned to her suffering. She fights her nurses and family. She is angry when she isn't given what she's offered. She has become a problem to be managed.

As Dorothy recovers from an acute episode in May 1832, William writes to their brother Christopher of the death of Mary's sister Elizabeth – long disabled – and that her death is a 'happy deliverance' because her 'mind was disordered'. (WW to CW, May 5, 1832). Neither Dorothy nor William would know that her dear friend, Henry Crabb Robinson would soon write similarly of her. In 1836, hearing her physical health is good, Crabb Robinson writes to his brother that in her current 'melancholy state I do not consider this as good news.' (HCR to TR, January 7, 1836). His clear implication is that it would be better for her to have died, than to live as she is doing. When Dorothy does finally die in 1855, he calls it a 'merciful bereavement'. (HCR to MW, January 29, 1855). I wonder whether Dorothy would have retained her belief in death as a merciful option if she had known how her own life would also become dismissed and devalued.

*

After this major crisis in spring 1835, Dorothy stabilises, but never regains the health she hoped for.

In October, she sends the poem for Thomas Carr to James Greenwood. It is not clear exactly when she wrote it, though in 1837 she dates it at over a year ago. The poem places itself at least five years after she became ill – which she may be dating from April 1829, or she may be dating from the following winter, when she first really thought of herself as an invalid. Either way, it could not have been written earlier than the spring of 1834.

It seems likely that the last perilous episode in 1835, in which Sara is lost, returns Dorothy to the crisis moment three and a half years earlier when her family prepared for her death, and the poem is written in summer or early autumn 1835.

In the poem, all she sees is the past danger, and the present calm. It may well be that she sent it soon after writing it, when it was fresh in her mind, that it was simply the most recent entry in her commonplace book when she was searching through it looking for something to send in response to a neighbour's request. In the poem, her mind is quiet, and her heart 'never shall forget' the past danger, and how she has been led through it. But in the months to come, her mind would remain unquiet and unsettled, and she would forget so much more. In November 1835, Mary describes Dorothy as, in her own words, 'struggling' with a 'melancholy state'. Though her physical health is good, 'her mind is [...] in a state of childishness.' It is at this point, due to her good physical health, that they decide to withdraw laudanum use, with the hope that this will help her. Withdrawing the drug seems to be entirely 'without bad consequences', but it also effects little change in Dorothy's cognitive function. (MW to HCR, November 1835).

Yet on November 11 she composes and copies out a poem for John Carter, an assistant of William's and general handyman, who was instrumental in landscaping the gardens of Rydal Mount. The eight short lines of the poem begin, 'When shall I tread your garden path?', asking when she will be able to walk freely outdoors again. The second stanza repeats and riffs off the language and tone of her poem for Thomas Carr, mixed with another written in April 1832, figuring herself as captive to her illness these five years: 'A prisoner on my pillowed couch/Five years in feebleness I've lain'. The earlier version rejects the idea that she is a prisoner: 'No prisoner am I on this couch/My mind is free to roam'. But three more years have passed like this, and it is harder to think of her illness as a 'warning mercifully sent' and not as a permanent state. Her poem on the garden path ends questioning a future when she may be able to 'wander, free as air' again, resting half-way between hopefulness and lament: 'Oh! Shall I e'er with vigorous step/Travel the hills again?' A week earlier, on November 4, she had written her last journal entry. It begins, 'I take up the pen once again, After a trying illness'. She is 'without pain at present', but the present is short. She gives three bits of news concerning the others, typical of her journaling throughout the years: 'Wm is at Workington – John has been in Radnorshire – Dora not unwell'. (*RJ* November 4, 1835). Then the entry stops, with no full stop, as though Dorothy was interrupted mid-sentence. The entry is misdated 1815, not 1835, which Carl Ketchum calls 'an indication of her mental state', but if it is, what is it meant to indicate? That she forgot the previous twenty years and thought it was 1815 (unlikely, considering the content), or that she mis-wrote a number? The word 'unwell' is drawn out, larger and longer than the others and thicker in ink, as though she has had to refill her quill or was having a problem with it. At the bottom of the page there is a large blot. 'I have risen to dinner', she wrote in between the news of her body and the news of her loved ones. Perhaps dinner called her away. Perhaps her body intervened. Perhaps she got snagged on the word 'unwell' and could not go on. Whatever the reason, her journal ends there, on the word 'unwell', and she does not pick it up again.

FOUR

SICKBED
CONSOLATIONS

Dorothy's *Rydal Journals* are full of pain, fatigue, and frustration. But they are also full of beauty and joy; moments of sudden gladness in which she is taken out of her pain.

During her illness, there are three main things that bring Dorothy comfort: nature, memory, and poetry. For Dorothy, the three are tangled up in each other. Poetry becomes a way of both reigniting memories, and bringing the natural world into her mind, and her room, even when she cannot leave her bed. Her greatest consolation is to be out in the fresh air amongst other living things. When she cannot be outside, she brings the outside – plants and creatures – in. This happens literally, and in memory and imagination. Her poetry brings all of that together.

In 1832, Dorothy begins to make a collection of poems within her commonplace book, which she calls 'Sickbed Consolations'. Dorothy's sickbed consolations were begun at a time when she had been ill, on and off, for over two years, but did not imagine she would be ill for the rest of her life. She saw her life in the sickroom as a temporary disruption, not as a permanent state. It was something she had to be patient through, and learn from. The poems reflect her hopes for the future, for recovery, but more than anything, they show her attempts to work out how to live with her new reality. It is a struggle shared by anyone with an acquired disability, and by many people with life-long illnesses as their condition changes over time. They are meant as consolations – both in the making of them – and their message. They are poems which speak of finding solace, of light in the dark, but her drafts show her struggling with the notion of consolation, and with coming to terms with her confinement.

In spring 1832 Dora relates the difference Dorothy found in her second winter of sickness, versus her first. In the first winter, she had said that even during 'all her suffering her mind was so active that it was truly "A mansion for all lovely forms'" & her memory was "a dwelling place for all sweet sounds and harmonies'". Dorothy quotes William's 'Tintern Abbey' to explain her state of mind that first year – the mind as a mansion, a dwelling place she can escape into. She is completely absorbed in being completely elsewhere, soothed by the 'healing thoughts' William wished for her in his poem so many years before. Dora explains '& so her days past as pleasantly & <u>more</u> profitably (so she tells us) than they had ever done when she was in the full vigour of health & strength'. In the first year of her sickness, being able to think, uninterrupted, was its own consolation. She was ill, but not too ill as to not be able to write, read, dream, create. The second winter, she tells Dora, 'appears to her the shortest winter she ever past as her mind has lain perfectly fallow (she not having the power to think)'. Each day could be any other day. The winter has been short in one way, but also interminable. In her inability to think 'each day has been so monotonous'. (Dora to Jane Marshall, n.d., 1832).

Dorothy is describing a feeling so familiar to anyone who has been seriously ill. Time in the sickroom both seems to slow down to a point at which it almost stops entirely, so that one day or one hour or one fraction of an hour can stretch to the length of several lifetimes, but also lose all sense of progression. Time in the sickroom piles in all at once or repeats in a glitchy loop. As the years of sickness go on and sick year piles on top of sick year, Dorothy's grip on conventional time becomes looser and looser. She loses days, weeks, months to sickness. Often, she will start her journal again after a break and remark that she doesn't understand where or how the time has gone.

In recent years, these changes in time experienced through the sick body have been named 'crip time'. Ellen Samuels describes crip time as 'broken time', relating how 'it requires us to break in our bodies and minds to new rhythms, new patterns of thinking and feeling and moving through the world.' She also describes crip time as 'time travel': 'disability and illness have the power to extract us from linear, progressive time with its normative life stages and cast us into a wormhole of backward and forward acceleration, jerky stops and starts, tedious intervals and abrupt endings.'[105]

Dorothy after 1829 lives in the alternative time of crip time, travelling not only through time but also through place in her poetry, and in her vivid, visionary memory.

After 1836, William claims she 'never feels time hang upon her' anymore. (WW to Edward Moxon, August 30, nd). She has achieved dislocation from clock-time.

QUITE FEARFUL OF THE AIR

After her first serious illness in 1829, Dorothy willingly, if slightly grudgingly, submits to a regime of dramatically reduced activity, which is recommended to her as part of her recovery.

In October Dorothy writes to Catherine Clarkson that her daily walking has been interrupted by the shift to the 'cold dampness' of autumn. Dorothy hoped to take a kind of health hibernation over that winter, when she could rest and concentrate on 'laying in a stock of strength' for the following summer.

She has been trying to get back some strength and stamina by extending her activity in a slow and measured way. Without the change in weather, she says, 'I think I should now be able to walk far enough to have a Look at the prospect from the old Terrace' – still within the garden, but at least a view. But the season's shift has put paid to it: 'cold is my horror; for it flies instantly to my bowels so I must not execute this large scheme till we have Spring Breezes and sunshine.' She 'hopes that the Spring may find [her] no longer on the invalid list or at the very bottom of it'. (DW to CC, October 18, 1829). No one is allowed to forget that her illness was brought on by walking outside in the wrong weather, or so it was believed. William writes to her from Penrith with genuine fear that she will endanger her life by trying to walk too soon: 'My dearest Sister you must not walk not even in the garden to *fatigue* yourself—everything of the kind is to be avoided like the grave.' (WW to DW, October 1829). He gives examples of two friends who almost died by 'premature exertion' after illness. To rest seems to be innovative medical advice from a London doctor – Dr. Ainslie – against the traditional advice of a local doctor.

Although Dorothy does not dare risk her health by walking beyond the house in the colder October weather, she does still get outside, either in the small open-top carriage the family kept, driven carefully by Dora, or in a second-hand bath-chair, acquired from the Curwen family, which a servant wheels 'round and round the garden and upon the lower new-made green terrace'. Dorothy's garden outings are partly made possible by William's use of pacing as a poetic practice – he built flat terraces in the garden on which he could walk to and fro to compose – but they gain a second, vital purpose in allowing a level surface for Dorothy to move around the garden. Her movements in the bath-chair, which she calls 'that little carriage', and later, self-mockingly, the 'baby rides', are limited to the new terrace by steps. It 'cannot be drawn up the steps leading to the old Terrace', she remarks, 'and I have not been there for several months.' Jane Marshall's sister lends her a muff, tippet, and a fur-trimmed merino wool gown to wear when she is in the carriage or the chair, to keep her comfortably warm.

During the winter of 1829 into 1830 it is 'decreed that [Dorothy] must stay at home' to conserve her strength. She writes to Henry Crabb Robinson of the consolation she finds in her locality – 'surely it is no punishment to be confined to this beautiful spot'. (DW to HCR, April 22, 1830).

But restricted to Rydal in 1830 she becomes increasingly beholden to the weather to allow her out or keep her in, and the weather has been bad. 'Whenever the weather has been tolerable', she writes, 'I have gone out in the poney-chase – or walked; but not farther than the Terrace.' Her walks have been limited to the garden – metres not miles.

It is not just the weather that Dorothy is beholden to, but also the support of others. She records how on one fine-weather day 'by way of special Treat', their servant James Dixon and William together carried her up to the old terrace on a chair, which she described as her 'first mode of taking exercise out of doors' after she arrived home. In her weakness, and with the limited mobility aids available, she has become dependent on others to let her outside. To go further than the terrace, she must be given use of the poney-chase. In the years to come she will be taken outside in a merlin chair bought specially for her, a kind of proto-wheelchair, but not one she can propel by herself. Like many disabled people, she has become reliant on others not just for her essential care – to feed, wash, and clothe her – but also to move around. The notable independence of her younger years, when she would take long walks alone, has turned into interdependence.

The winter of 1830 is not the first winter she has been confined to the house and garden. In the winter of 1823, she is kept at home with what she thinks to be a bad cold, or possibly influenza, and her walking is 'confined to the Garden and Terrace.' That winter her restrictions seemed to make her surroundings even more beautiful, and she told Mary Laing that she enjoyed the winter more than normal because of it. The house and garden became a safe harbour for her in a cold season: 'Whenever the sun shines in a morning we have it glittering upon the

Lake—and are at all times sheltered from Storms.' (DW to Mary Laing, December 28, 1823). By May, she is recovering a little.

In the first winter of her serious illness, she must have thought the same thing was happening again. She would hunker down during the bad weather, and then she would get better. It had happened before; it could happen again.

In March 1830 William sets to work making yet another terrace in the garden. Dorothy writes to Maria Jane Jewsbury that William is 'delighted' with his new terrace, as is she herself, 'who now confine my walks to our own parapet'. This new terrace gives her more variety in her view: with 'the three terraces together we have a very great length of walk with constant variety of slope and level, and prospect.' (DW to MJ Jewsbury, March 22, 1830).

Spring seems to bring a resurgence of energy and hopefulness to her. She tells Crabb Robinson 'since the trees began to bud I have extended my walks a little further; and I do indeed feel myself equal to much more than I venture to attempt.' This pattern of withdrawal in winter and recovery in spring and summer will repeat for Dorothy over the next decade, with the winters increasingly accompanied by pain and health crises.

She adds a postscript to the end of the letter:

> We have a very wet and mostly *cold* spring after an unrelenting winter [...] Our shrubs are budding – larches green but the trees very backward & the soil is so soddened with wet that even the flower look comfortless. (DW to HCR, April 22, 1830, *HCR C*).

It is a cold spring in 1830. The plants are late blooming, and the birds late migrating and nesting. On April 29 she records hearing the cuckoo for the first time, 'his visit to our shores unusually late'. (*RJ* April 29, 1830). This slow spring seems to speak as much to her internal weather. It is spring, and spring does bring some hint of bodily relief, but not the absolution or cure that might be hoped for.

The signs of spring come to hold particular importance to her and begin to dominate her journal. On April 30th she is told that 'the Doves are building a nest of their own with sticks blown into their cage'. Even in her room, she can hear 'all the birds are busy shouting, warbling, or building'. (*RJ* April 30, 1830). May Day hints at a positive change. After a rainy day, the 'sun bursts out before setting'. The scene to Dorothy is 'unearthly & brilliant – calls to mind the change to another world. Every leaf a golden lamp – every twig bedropped with a diamond.' But as with her health, 'the splendour departs as rapidly.' (*RJ* May 1, 1830). It remains cold, even when it is not raining. The weather is a continual worry. Her journals show her frustration on the days the weather keeps her in, and her reliance on good weather to let her out. On May 10th, 1830 she writes in her journal that she has walked out, but 'huddled up in winter Garb' still. She still keeps a fire burning in her room. (*RJ* May 10, 1830).

Increasingly, her journal becomes a record of interlinked weathers: the weather outdoors, and the weather of her body, one dependent on the other.

In the summer of 1830 she is so glad to be outdoors that the journal's mood is pleasant too, all fine mornings, bright gleams, and clear moons. On June 2 she describes 'a bright clear morning – & all day sun – & unusually clear blue sky & soft blue water – the new Terrace – clad in summer greenness'. (*RJ* June 2, 1830). She reads on the terrace, walks a little, and is driven out to see friends. When the rain comes in August it does not seem ominous. On Sunday August 1 she writes 'our eyes (all unexpectedly) open on a rainy morning'. (*RJ* August 1, 1830). The rain can have its own compensations. On September 9 it rains all day, cancelling a hoped-for trip to Patterdale, but instead she sees 'A glorious Burst of light before sunset – silver drops – smoky steam – yellow lights – Rainbow complete'. (*RJ* September 9, 1830). The autumn is wet and stormy, with floods through November, but Dorothy keeps walking on the terrace when the weather allows, even in the first half of December before the cold sets in. But by December 20 it is 'very cold' and she 'durst not face the cold to make calls'. (*RJ* December 20, 1830). Even though it keeps her in, the cold brings beauty. Her birthday, Christmas Day, begins with the 'loveliest of frost' and closes with Aurora Borealis, although Dorothy underlines that they did not see it. She carries on walking between rain storm and frosts, on the terrace, and further when it is fine. (*RJ* December 25, 1830).

February 1831 begins with a week of heavy snow falling, then a thaw, which reveals 'snow drops in warm places – hanging their bead like heads'. (*RJ* February 12, 1831). By the end of the month it is snowy again, and Dorothy laments there is 'no greenness' in the cold: 'our spring flowers ever melancholy'. (*RJ* February 28, 1831). There are storms again in March that keep her in, but her walks are getting more adventurous when she can embark on them – as far as the wishing-gate in one direction, or up to the waterfalls at Rydal. She seems to keep improving through the spring of 1831, as far as her journals give away. There is a brief break between the end of May, and June 11, during which she has 'entirely neglected' her journal. Dorothy continues delighted with the world. Everything that could be lovely is lovely: 'Never was there a more delightful week than this last (of June) has been'. (*RJ* June 30, 1831). As the summer goes on, sometimes all she makes note of is the weather. Her body remains quiet all year, as far as the journal admits, until December, when the crisis comes, and the pages are cut out to save us from knowing of it.

After the crisis of 1833 the garden is again seen as a healing space, but sometimes even the effort of being outside can make her more ill. In July she notes she has been 'mostly out in chair' in the garden, 'but yesterday did too much & aching inside paid me for it—kept me in bed all the evening and disturbed at night'. (*RJ*, July 19, 1833). The weather has been against her again: 'All the latter part of June was cold & wet or with thunder fits & pulled me down'. She is beginning to realise the limits of the therapy the outdoors has to offer her. It can make her feel better, but it can also make her feel worse. Feeling better in itself can also be a double-edged sword. In late July she is delighted with her progress. She is able to get out of bed by herself, and increasingly, to walk unsupported. On July 23 she declares her 'legs never so strong as this morning', when she could walk 'all round the room & about & about without stick'. (*RJ*, July 23, 1833). The next day she goes out in her chair on the terrace to be 'dragged' around but is 'much stronger in limbs'. With excitement she records she has 'walked down stairs several times – & as much as 3 or 4 on long passage & am very much better'. (RJ, July 24, 1833). But on July 26 she has 'sad news' – 'violent pains in right side'. She has done too much; pushed herself too far, fooled by her apparent recovery. (*RJ*, July 26, 1833).

In her 1834 journal the cold and damp appear as dangerous antagonists, imprisoning Dorothy in her room. The cold, she explains, 'affects my inside'. (*RJ*, November 21, 1834). Autumn becomes a threat, a shutting down which presages something worse. Her descriptions of the garden, and of the plants and creatures she loves, seem increasingly metaphorical.

In October, 'damp & comfortless gloom' turns into a storm that floods the valley and damages trees, leaving the 'ash tree torn & mangled', and Dorothy subject to 'sad painful' days when she cannot get up at all. (*RJ*, October 19, 1834).

When the storm passes, it leaves Dorothy with 'frosty air, which suits me not'. (*RJ*, October 25, 1834).

On October 26 she notes it is 'very fine & bright, but too cold for me'. 'With a large fire' the thermometer is at 60°F (15.5°C). She repeats 'the air too cold for me', and the next day she finds herself 'very weak in limbs & body'. (*RJ*, October 26, 1834). On November 1 she remarks 'I feel the cold sadly'. It is a fine day for the time of year, but the creep of autumn cold is punishing. (*RJ*, November 1, 1834). On the 11th she writes 'the cold air wrecks me'. (*RJ*, November 11, 1834). By the 13th – 'cold and clear' – she admits she is 'quite fearful of the air'. (*RJ*, November 13, 1834). It soon becomes a tragic lament: 'This cold! this cold alas! alas!' (*RJ*, November 17, 1834). On the 27th her journal entry is one phrase only: 'I am disordered within'. (*RJ*, November 27, 1834).

At the close of the year, it rains after a month of dry, cold weather. She writes of how William comes to talk to her in her sickroom and 'rejoiced to hear thickly falling rain after so long a pause'. She remembers taking 'many a moist tramp' with him in the past, and 'could not but feel a touch of sympathy' for William's excitement to hear the rain fall. But walking in the rain is a threat to her now, not a balm. She would have preferred 'bright moon & stars'. There is a chasm between the siblings now: the gap of understanding between the generally healthy and generally sick. Although he knows bad weather affects her badly, William seems not to have thought about how Dorothy will feel about this rain. Dorothy, typically thinking of others' suffering in parallel to her own, notes how Dora too 'could not rest for it against her window'. (*RJ*, December 30, 1834).

January 1835 throws up all the bad weathers, like a gang of villains – 'frost, now hail – wind'. 'The weather', she writes on January 22, 'has been very trying'. She has withstood the attack, she thinks: 'my weak body has girded to all changes, & sometimes suffered severely'. The next day's entry begins with relief at a change in atmosphere: 'A mild thaw & the sick may be thankful.' (*RJ*, January 22–23, 1835).

PILFERED OF THIS SUNNY SPRING

Dorothy's 'sickbed consolations' return time and again to questions of confinement and imprisonment, and where freedom may be found. It is a repeating theme, explored in length in her poem 'Thoughts on my sick-bed', written in May 1832. The first of the consolation poems, it becomes a foundational text that the other poems of her consolations sample from, expand on, and argue with.

'Thoughts on my sick-bed' begins by questioning how spring seems not to have worked in her body this year, the way it has worked on the land. It begins with an 'and', as though mid-thought, mid-argument:

> And has the remnant of my life
> Been pilfered of this sunny Spring?

She wonders how her heart, normally so responsive, has sounded 'no echoing string' to spring's sounds this year. Has her relationship with nature been broken by her illness and the long confinement it has brought?

She does not really believe it could have done. Her body may now be only a 'feeble frame', but there is a 'hidden life couchant' within it – sleeping or resting, not dead – that has been so 'enriched' by the 'unsought-for' gifts the natural world brought her in her youth that it cannot die. She describes herself as a young woman 'in quest of known and *un*known things' in the world around her. She and William were 'Companions of Nature', co-habitants with the flowers and birds. Here again Dorothy echoes William's words in 'Tintern Abbey', when he described himself as a young man as 'a worshipper of Nature'. Dorothy describes a different relationship, not one of devotee and god, but of a meeting of equals.

Her illness has given her an even deeper relationship with nature. The poem goes on to explain how friends brought 'the first flowers of the year' to her on her 'couch of rest', and the flowers unlocked something in her. First she has 'sad thoughts' but then joy overtakes. Her '*hidden* life' – that old connection with nature – is suddenly 'no longer hidden'. It has come back to her, to 'consciousness'. She feels a 'Power unfelt before' that overrides her 'weakness, languor, pain'. In her inward eye, she is on the Terrace walk, on the hills, in Tintern – she is free to travel anywhere, in her mind at least. This magic is enacted both by the flowers themselves, a kind of Proustian explosion, and how they bring to mind William's 'prophetic words' in 'Tintern Abbey'. She has 'No need of motion, or of strength,/Or even the breathing air' to travel now. She only has to *think*, and she is there. The same language of imprisonment and release appears in her 'Lines for Dora H.', written in June 1835 in the early stages of her recovery from her third great crisis. She shifts from excusing her inability to draw a pretty picture in the album, to explaining her current condition: 'My failing strength my tottering limbs/Into a prison change this room'. These lines in particular are repeated and repeated in fragmentary drafts in her journals at that time. In this poem too, she attempts to turn the prison of the sickroom, in verse, into a sanctuary:

> Though it is not a cheerless spot
> A cell of sorrow or of gloom
> No damp cold walls enclose it round
> No heavy hinges grating sound
> Disturb the silence & the calm

She knows her room is *not* a prison, although at times it might feel like it. In March 1834 she describes the weather as 'provokingly fine', and herself a 'poor prisoner' who 'cannot stir out beyond the garden.' She wants to find the best in her situation, adding 'It is blessing enough for me to look on it.' (RJ, March 18, 1834). When she is well enough to write, she is well enough to think herself into thinking herself lucky. But she wavers between these two realities: the room is a prison/it is not a prison. She is free in her mind/she is trapped in her mind in her body.

In the drafts of 'Thoughts on my sick-bed' she moves between describing herself as 'a prisoner in this quiet room' to 'a prisoner in this lonely room', to 'imprisoned in this lonely room', ending up with 'no prisoner in this lonely room'.

In her 'Lines for Dora H.' it is the window that turns the prison into a sanctuary. The open window allows 'free entrance' of the 'summer breeze' into the room, and lets her look out onto 'the leafy trees/the sky the clouds the gleaming showers/craggs lakes & odiferous flowers'. She may not be able to reach them, but they are still, in some way, with her, just as her friends and loved ones are in 'faithful recollections'. But the great power in 'Thoughts on my sick-bed' seems to be waning: she does need the breeze, she does need to see the landscape. She still feels nature's gifts, but she needs to experience them with her bodily self, not just in thought. She needs external stimulation: the mansions of the mind and the dwelling-place of memory are not enough. She is trying so hard in these poems to find something good in her situation, to not feel sorry for herself. She is trying to find the moral in the riddle of her own life. In drafts of 'Thoughts on my sick-bed' she writes of 'feelings kept down & repressed by exuberant health & thought', of blessings 'strengthening as the Body decays'. She explores the idea that illness has released something in her, something pushed aside by her busy restlessness in years gone by. This disappears from the neat copy, but lingers in the idea that the bliss she feels when the flowers are brought to her is greater than anything she had felt before. This echoes an idea in her earlier poem 'Irregular Verses', written in 1827: 'the saddest heart feels deepest gladness'. She wants to find not only consolations, but gifts in her sickroom.

In a letter to Edward Quillinan in May 1832 Dora explains how Dorothy wrote 'Thoughts on my sick-bed' after they brought flowers into her room: 'I hope she will sometime let me send you an affecting poem she has written on the pleasure she received from the first spring flowers that were carried up to her when confined to her sickroom'. Dora quotes a little of the poem, adding 'You must excuse limping measure – Aunt cannot write regular metre'. Whilst Dora is writing her letter, Dorothy is outside, making the best of the weather and the 'lovely garden': 'I see her out of my window making her way by help of my Mother's arm towards the Green terrace Father is very anxious that she should see the improvements he has been making in that bit of ground & I think they will accomplish it – for she says "I am quite strong"'. Dorothy makes it to the terrace, leaning on Mary: 'I have been to see her she <u>has</u> walked to the terrace & is now sitting on the grass plot giving directions to Father who is busy with his axe among the trees'. Dora says 'it is beautiful weather for her a perfect poet's May': just the kind of weather they are all certain can heal her. (Dora to EQ, May 25, 1832).

The 'green terrace' Dora mentions is the flat terrace outside the house, which William has been extending. William describes the changes to Edward Quillinan in a letter in June 1832: 'the green terrace has been lengthened towards the church 34 level feet so as to make a charming quarter deck walk & at the termination will be a seat & in time an arbour if the wind will permit.' (WW and Dora to EQ, June 26, 1832). It becomes, in its extension, a step and slope free space that Dorothy can use more freely over the coming years. The draft of 'Thoughts on my sick-bed' in her commonplace book has a note in pencil added in at a later date alongside the title; it reads, 'the first spring time', though it was during the second spring time that she was largely confined to her room. Does she mean something different by first? The first spring time she knew she was disabled? Or the first spring time of her consolations?

MY MIND IS FREE TO ROAM

Through her illness Dorothy sought solace from nature, and increasingly, as the years passed, from her Christian faith. As yet further time passed in the sickroom, it became increasingly obvious that neither could nor would give her the healing she initially hoped for. In 1832, in a lull between health crises, she writes a poem for Edith Southey, the daughter of the poet Robert Southey, and a close family friend. She has known Edith all her life. This is a long-promised poem, written 'in recollection of a request made by her some years ago'. It is only now, as 'the evening sun shines on [her] bed' that Dorothy is able to fulfil it. 'Lines intended for Edith Southey's Album' describes a complicated relationship with Nature, which mirrors a relationship with God, who both 'afflicts' and 'heals the wound'. This poem wants to find in 'sickness, pain or pining grief' a necessary warning not to be thankless and thoughtless.

In 'blithe Health', she writes, we can become 'forgetful of wise Nature's skill/To soothe, or rouze and elevate'. 'Sickness and sorrow, grief and pain' become 'precious' teachers, not unlike Nature itself. Health, meanwhile, is a trickster, who wants us to forget what really matters: 'health brings joy/That dazzles us'. This poem feels like another attempt to comfort herself, to find meaning in 'the fearful rush of pain'. Written in bed, about bed, it really is a sick-bed consolation. Two years after writing 'Thoughts on my sick-bed', Dorothy writes a poem she titles 'Lines written (rather say *begun*) on the morning of Sunday April 6th, the third approach of Spring-Time since my illness began. It was a morning of surpassing beauty'. Her journal on Sunday April 6th, 1834 reads:

> Loveliest of Sabbath morn.g How I long to be free in the open air! The Birds are all singing—Rooks every busy The earth & air & all that I behold seems a preparation for worship & Sabbath rest—the Bird & Beast have this one days security from Snare or slaughter— (RJ, April 6, 1834).

If I were counting years since her illness began, I would place this day during the fourth spring time since her illness began, but maybe she really is counting her years of illness from a different starting point, as the pencil note on 'Thoughts on my sick-bed' suggests. Or maybe she is folding springs into each other, confused by the non-time in which she spent that second, fallow winter. Either way, her journal allows us to date the poem as written in April 1834. That day, she records that she read a bit – 'the Bible – & a few Essays' and that everyone was at church 'except William', and herself, of course, though she does not say so. The journal entry ends there, with everyone at church, except her and William. Did she then look out the window, and see the vision of the poem? The poem describes this Sunday of 'surpassing beauty', rich 'with the full choral hymn of birds'. The day is quiet but active, a kind of strange peace has dropped on all living things, which include the landscape and its inhabitants:

> A robe of quiet overspreads
> The living lake and verdant field
> The very earth seems sanctified,
> Protected by a holy shield.

Surveying the scene, she has a kind of epiphany about the 'heavenly ... spirit of earth', and how to feel it. 'Visible stillness' becomes the means by which 'Nature attunes the pious heart' to 'the cheerful voice/Of living things in budding trees & in the air above.' Out there in the field and by the lake, things are coming into spring liveliness, and she cannot join them any more than she can join the procession of people called to the chapel below. She seeks 'pious hope and fixed content', and she think she finds it in the revelation that her sickness, her stillness, is opening up a new world of understanding. She still wants to reframe illness as a grace or a blessing: a 'gift' amongst other gifts allowed her in her stillness. She chooses to see 'leisure, peace, and loving Friends' not as compensations, but as 'the best treasures of an earthly home'. Why would she want more, this poem asks. Her 'mind is free to roam', even if her body cannot any longer. She is adamant this time: 'No prisoner am I on this couch'. Yet we know from her journal how much she 'long[ed] to be free in the open air'. When she notes the day's respite the birds and beasts have, is she also thinking of herself: could she have just one day of respite from entrapment?

In the poem, Dorothy makes her contemplation of her confinement into a religious meditation. Like all her poems, this one is in conversation with William's, and particularly with his sonnet which begins, 'Nuns fret not at their convent's narrow room'. His sonnet is not about actual confinement of the body in a cell or a citadel, but of the poet's imagination 'within the sonnet's scanty plot of ground'. It is a poem about surprising compensations that arise from restriction, and how creativity can bloom within a limited framework. It hopes others will find 'brief solace' within its bounds. William's poem wants us to believe there is nothing good or bad, but thinking makes it so: 'In truth the prison unto which we doom/Ourselves no prison is'. We doom *ourselves* to prison, by thinking ourselves imprisoned. Dorothy's Sickbed Consolations play and replay this theory, as though running it through a computer and getting a different answer every time. Is she a prisoner, is she not a prisoner? Can she think herself out of imprisonment? If she cannot think herself out, is she failing herself, Nature, and God? Is she learning from the 'warning mercifully sent'? Through the years of her illness, her relationships with both Nature and God shift. By 1837 she is neither seeking nor expecting a cure from either. What she wants and seeks in Nature and in God is compassion, comfort, and meaning. What she finds in them is pleasure, joy, and understanding. They know what they are doing. Their workings may be mysterious to her, but she believes they have their own logic. This is her faith.

I FEEL THE WEATHER

As the years go on, Dorothy is increasingly affected by the whims of the weather. It takes on personality for her, and visceral power. In 1834 she writes, 'thunder calls but I cannot hear her', as though the thunder were a visitor she did not want to see. Later that summer another storm reverberates through her 'body & limbs'. 'I feel the weather', she writes. (*RJ* August 21, 1834).

In spring 1833, after a bad winter that leaves Dorothy unable to walk, they hope the change in weather will affect a change in health. Dora writes to Rotha in March that 'she cannot yet attempt to stand but her progress has been so great the last ten days that we hope in a short time she may be able once again to move about as she did last spring.' (Dora to Rotha Q, March 23, 1833).

Instead, thundery weather seems to bring on a relapse. William writes how 'thunder always used to disorder her, and we had some very hot weather which produced that state of Atmosphere.' (WW to HCR, May 18 or 28, 1833). In June, he notes that whilst Dorothy is 'upon the whole considerably better', she is 'sadly subject to injury from the changes of the Weather.' By this time 'she can walk about 20 or 30 steps, but always with exhaustion', but 'when the weather is favourable she is always wheeled about in a chair, for an hour or two, in the Garden.' (WW to HCR, June 5, 1833).

When Dorothy relapses in December 1834, Mary writes, 'We could not trace the cause of this attack to any other source than the changeableness of the weather'. (MW to JM, December 27, 1834).

As Dorothy's mobility is increasingly limited by each successive crisis, she becomes even more reliant on others for access to green spaces. In the summer of 1834, regained enough strength to walk on the gravel at the front of the house, but she cannot reach the greenery of the garden. She longs for Crabb Robinson to return and 'drag [her] on the green Terrace.' (Dora and DW to HCR, July 24, 1834).

The garden becomes a place she can only access with assistance, a place closed off to her body by her body. In April 1834 she had written to Anne Pollard of her frustration at waiting in her 'solitary bedchamber' for the weather to turn:

> I sometimes of late have chid myself for impatience; for the sun shines so bright and the birds sing so sweetly that I have almost a painful longing to go out of doors, and am half tempted to break my bonds and sally forth into the garden; but I must be contented to wait till the wind changes its quarters; and before that happens rain will surely come, which may still keep me confined, for damp is almost as dangerous a foe as the East wind. (DW to Anne Pollard, April 12–17, 1834).

When she is able to access it, the effect is immense. She describes to Anne the extreme joy she feels to be 'surrounded again by sunshine and fresh air' and all the busy life of spring outdoors: 'Yesterday with a thankful heart I revisited the garden and green-terrace in my little carriage. I cannot express the joy I felt, and though much fatigued I did not suffer in any other way.' The effect is all the greater for her reliance on others, and the amount of time she spends indoors: 'No one but an invalid, after long confinement, can imagine the pleasure of being surrounded again by sunshine and fresh air, budding trees, flowers and birds.' (DW to Anne Pollard, April 12–17, 1834). In the sickroom, Dorothy is shut away from the things she has turned to in the rest of her life to give her comfort – trees, birds, the sky – anything bigger and beyond herself and bustling with life. In this letter, Dorothy explains how she has tried to bring some of that into her sickroom:

> Do not think, however, my dear Friend that my confinement has been irksome to me. Quite the contrary, for

within this little square I have a collection of treasures and on the outside of my window I have had a garden of ever-blooming flowers, and you know what a beautiful prospect. Never have my flower-pots been seen unadorned with flowers in addition to the bright berries of winter, the holly etc. I have plenty of good old Books and most of the news are supplied by Friends or neighbours [...] As to personal comforts I need not say that I never want any thing that I can desire or wish for. (DW to Anne Pollard, April 12 – 17, 1834).

Her journal records these attempts to bring the outdoors in, a kind of green therapy. After the crisis of January and February 1833, the family begin to fill her room with pot plants. William described to Edward Quillinan how they 'have now in the room a beautiful bunch of Primroses, which is full of promise for her, transplanted from our green terrace.' The flowers are not only a beautiful distraction in and of themselves, but a promise – a kind of pact that if she keeps holding on, they can see another spring together. Later in the same letter William adds: 'The Hounds are this moment making a most musical cry, which penetrates the sick room, but the silent looks of our little friend the Primrose are still more agreeable as they announce that the winter music must be near its close.' (WW & DW to EQ, February 22, 1833). Her pots and branches will come to have a powerful significance to her – the 'beauties of my room' as she calls them in June 1834. Decking her flower pots becomes a regular activity for her – refreshing her room, and changing its mood according to what is growing in the garden, like refreshing the décor. The trees and flowers become her dear friends, like the 'forlorn almost horizontal branch' she describes, 'which, when I lie on my Bed I would not part with for £20' (RJ June 14, 1834). In her journal in spring 1833, Dorothy writes of 'two glowing anemones and a snow-white companion [...] in a pot on my window ledge, and two knots of blue primroses of the Alpine purple', which cheer her in her room until she will be strong enough to go for 'rides in the garden – then of a wider Range'. She hopes to soon be reporting of 'gradually returning strength', but for now she has 'all the Birds of sky and earth [...] singing – & all is wrapped up in a happy brightness'. The spring is late – 'the grass with hardly a tinge of greenness –& even larches & lilacs are but just showing green' – but a change is coming outdoors, and she hopes it will come for her too. (*RJ* April 23, 1833).

Bringing greenery indoors has a knock-on effect, and her room becomes a kind of miniature garden, with its own non-human inhabitants: butterflies, birds, and bees who visit her sickroom gardens. From within her room, she hears rooks and owls out in the trees. In December 1834 Mary records how unusually fine weather that Christmas has allowed Dorothy to keep her windows open, and those open windows 'have allowed free entrance to a pet Robin that is almost a constant companion to her – its nightly perch is often upon a nail from which hangs one of the pictures, with which the walls of her room are now almost covered, and its soft warbling is most delicious and soothing to her feelings.' (MW to JM, December 27, 1834). In the notes on the poems he dictates to Isabella Fenwick, William describes Dorothy's robin as choosing to '[take] up its abode with her'. In his description, the robin becomes both entertainer and therapist: 'It used to sing and fan her face with its wings in a manner that was very touching.' A threat is presented in the form of a 'beautiful white cat' sent to the family by Mr. Pearson. As beautiful as the cat is, Dorothy can only see the harsh inevitability of what Nature may take away in it, writing in her journal 'my tears fall for Robin who has just treated me with his best song – & perched on my table whilst I scattered for it its food'. (*RJ* December 2, 1834). Although this pet robin is a new friend this winter, robins have been singing to her in her sickroom throughout her illness. In November 1830 there are 'warbling robins' at her window despite the rain. Dorothy here appears like an aging Cinderella, with songbirds for company in her exclusion from human society. Her solitary sickbed becomes a kind of bird hide. Her quietness and stillness allow the creatures to come to her, that before she would have been restlessly seeking. The threat of the cat is never realised: it is kept out of the room; Robin is kept safe. Mary in her letter adds that 'under such circumstances – knowing the nature of our Sister – I need not add to you that she has been, and is happy'. The sickroom, with such blithe company, can become a place of genuine joy.

In February 1835 a spell of 'unusually mild' weather reminds her of the unerring presence of the birds around her, even when the weather is 'oppressive with dullness & dark': 'here I will record that not a day of last year, or of the beginning of this has passed without the song of Birds – one or more'. (*RJ* February 3, 1835). In her sickroom she bears witness to even the sparse music of winter. Her stillness – her imprisonment – enable her to listen in a way she never would have done before, and enable her to hear that the song is continual. It never stops. Even in the 'days of keen frost' when many of the birds are quietened, 'even then', she marks, 'my own companion Robin cheared my bed-room with its slender subdued piping'. Throughout the next month of sickness and weakness, the 'birds warble all day' regardless. (*RJ* March 20, 1835).

Dorothy's dependence on nature to give her solace and healing is a blessing and a curse. Flowers can transport her and entirely change her state of mind and being, but a lack of flowers can destroy her. The Wordsworths knew as well as any that Nature could be as destructive as it could be restorative. Nature had been their teacher, their companion, but it had also taken loved ones from them. They believed both of their parents' fatal illnesses had been precipitated by cold and damp. In 'Tintern Abbey', that background to Dorothy's thoughts on her sick-bed, William writes that 'Nature never did betray/the heart that loved her', but they knew that it could kill just as surely as heal. As Dorothy writes in her 'Floating Island' poem: 'Nature, though we mark her not,/Will take away – may cease to give.'

In February 1834 Dorothy's flower pots are blown down by a storm, and coincidentally, she is 'very ill after dinner'. The illness comes on suddenly and perplexingly: 'why or wherefore I know not – pain – sickness – head-ache – perspirations – heat & cold'. Trees and flowers are like her own body, and subject to the same storms. The next day starts 'bright & cold' but then 'a hail shower falls from dazzling silver – & dark clouds to remind us of past times & warn us not to expect a calm suddenly'. The weather is a warning and also a punishment. So often she describes rain as 'threatening'; when it is so entangled with her pain and sickness the threat is bodily and can produce real harm. That same evening the weather gives an answer in 'rain by pailfuls driven against my window'. (*RJ* February 19, 1834).

Even in the worst of the storm – both literal and metaphorical – she seeks calm, and the promise of ease. On Monday March 9, 1834 she writes that 'the rain will not depart from its accustomed strong holds', but even so, the rain is beautiful – 'glittering showers' that 'travel over us'. She has been tending the little garden in her room after the storm of the previous month, setting something in motion, she hopes, or creating the environment for positive regrowth:

> I have been sticking leafy bright green twigs of Elder
> among my Spring and winter flowers—my garden of <u>all
> the</u> seasons visited by the Bees who solace me with their
> gentle humming while the bids warble sweetly – & there
> is the industrious chearful bittern taking no rest— (*RJ*
> March 9, 1834).

Spring still brings her 'warbling birds' and 'warm misty muzzling bird-chaunting' mornings, through and with her pain. In
April she writes of 'my flowers everlasting', but she is continually reminded that her body has limits. (*RJ* April 9, 1834) She
enjoys the spring weather too much and 'the air and exercise'
aggravate her bowel condition.

On April 7, William's birthday, she writes, 'still very fine but
too cold for me they say, yet there is something in the air that
oppresses me'. (*RJ* April 7, 1834). The next day, she 'dropped
asleep before an open window' and woke up more exhausted,
as though the air itself wore her down. It is hardest for her when
it is sunny but still cold, as on April 12th, when she complains,
'Sunshine to make me long to go out & feel it—but the blight-
ing East wind still bars me up'. (*RJ* April 12, 1834). The cold
wind is both her prison and her guard here, keeping her shut
indoors. By the 17th she is able to open her window and enjoy
'the inexpressible comfort of fresh air in [her] little cell'. She
reflects on the glorious red of anemones' in her room, which
have been her 'treasure all winter', looking forward to when she
can see the rest of the flowers in the garden. The next day, she is
finally allowed out. (*RJ* April 17, 1834).

The garden does not have the effect she hopes. On April 23rd
she records that 'the air has not strengthened me according to
expectation & yesterday I suffered much'. (*RJ* April 23, 1834). She
has a bad few days of pain and fatigue, forced back to bed, too

sick to be up writing '& there I lay chill, dark & wholly unable to read unfit to talk & unable all'. (*RJ* April 30, 1834). But May Day brings a change – the 'rain continues cold' but 'green things burst marvellously into light'. (*RJ* May 1, 1834). The next day, she writes, 'should have been May-day—The sharp wind is gone the sun shines—birds warble—grass grows so fast & so green you do indeed "almost see it growing". Trees at once bursting into half-leaf'. (*RJ* May 2 1834). Each set back is overly disheartening. 'I am no company', she admits on May 4, but by May 8 things are turning again: 'Spring advances with speed – Lilacs in full bloom – small red roses – Sycamores & Elms quite green – in small leaf'. (*RJ* May 4–8, 1834). The next day is a 'sweet gleamy morning' and she is brought a new supply of 'various flowers' for the miniature garden in her room. She helps 'to place them in the pots til my poor legs will bear me up no longer'. But the work has consequences. The following day she is exhausted, and in 'twisting pain'. The brighter the consolation in these months, it seems, the deeper the sink afterwards. (*RJ* May 9-10, 1834).

When she can go outside, she is convinced it helps. On May 24th she describes 'a delightful airing (1 ½ hour) on green Terrace […] The day charming—a newly-fledged Thrush could not fly to the top of the wall—The little wren very busy—Robin & white moth—' Afterwards she is 'tired but a sound sleep quite set me up again'. She is convinced 'the air now does me much good—I feel it day by day—' (*RJ* May 24, 1834). On May 27 she writes she again, 'had a delightful visit to Green Terrace & was much benefited', though she is terribly ill the next day. (*RJ* May 27, 1834). She is so excited to be outside that, even after all her years of practice, she pushes herself and suffers afterwards.

Dorothy's crisis in June 1835 seems so particularly alarming to the family partly because of the time of year. They are used to her coming back to light and life with the garden each spring.

Sara writes to Dora, 'I was in hopes that the summer would in some degree have restored your dear older sufferer, instead of trying her so deeply – but God's will was otherwise.' (Sara Coleridge to Dora, June 16, 1835). That summer does not heal her this time seems to indicate that nothing ever will.

When the family are struck by the extent of the change in Dorothy's cognitive abilities in the spring of 1836, Mary repeats again and again the hope that 'when she can get into the garden a change may take place.' (MW to Mary Anne Marshall, May 4, 1836). In April, Mary writes to the Staniforths that being in the garden seems to improve Dorothy's focus and state of mind – 'upon her being taken into the garden; she was able to look about and enjoy all she saw'. In comparison, she recalls, 'last summer she was unable to lift her head, the only time she was in the open air'. (WW & MW to Samuel & Mary Staniforth, April 16, 1836). To Jane Marshall she writes, 'we hope when she is able to be taken into the Garden & be again introduced among the flowers, & other natural objects in which she delighted – that all her present illusions may depart.' (MW to JM, probably May, 1836).

When she is able to go out, she is overcome with emotion. William writes to Crabb Robinson, 'my sister was out yesterday & wept abundantly at the sight of the spring flowers.' (WW to HCR, April/May 1836). Mary writes to Jane Marshall:

> On first going out she wept aloud like a baby, being overcome by the beauty around her, and asked to be taken to a certain border, when she has lately been supplied with flowers.
>
> At first she was too overpowered to look upon it; afterwards she became calm, and enjoyed everything she saw, like her old self. Then, being brought homeward, a

new sensation was created when she reached the shady green lawn. On a sudden she began to sing, which she continued to do till James took her into the house...
(MW to JM, May 7, 1836).

Part of what overcomes her is seeing the flowers she has kept in vases in her room, growing at large in the garden. The experience is so overwhelming she has to sleep afterwards. It is a kind of sensory overload, after which she has to reset her mind and body.

It had been hoped that being outside in the garden she loves would affect some kind of miracle cure, but by July they have given up the hope they had 'of her mind strengthening as a consequence of her being able to get out and be amused in the fresh air.' (MW to HCR, July 4, 1836). Though it does not heal her to be outside, or restore her as they hope, it continues to bring her pleasure. Mary details how 'she has now her drives – & daily exercise in a Merlins chair, in the Garden –& for a time enjoys it –& she is very happy – but no permanent change follows.' (MW to HCR, July 4, 1836). There is no Nature Cure available to Dorothy, but there is comfort, enjoyment, and pleasure.

This continues right until the end of her life. In July 1852 Mary reports on Dorothy's good health and calm mental state during a period of fine weather:

Nothing could be conceived so delightful as the change which had taken place & continued, for a few days – with the only change from perfect quietness in bed, or in the Garden Chair – always in good humour humour "quite well," & always had been well– could walk as well as ever – required no hot bottles – or fire – in short not had no wants – & often said she was as "happy as an Angel" – such

was her state, & her smile ever upon her countenance was
that of an innocent Child. (MW to the Hutchinsons, July
18, 1852).

As always, her state changes with the weather: 'But alas! with
the bad [weather] this has passed away – & yesterday & this
morng – she has been in her <u>worst old</u> way.'

At one end of Dorothy's commonplace book, under drafts of
her poem 'Loving and Liking', a neater, earlier note can be read.
A title, declaring the page 'Dorothy Wordsworth / Journal', with
no date, is followed by brief remarks on the weather – 'Bright
sunshine – cold air – bitter wind – high seas' – and the price of
fruit and vegetables. Details – the 'fine cauliflowers in October'
– date the journal entry to the 1820 trip. It ends abruptly with a
list of items on sale: grapes at 'seven sous the pound', compared
to red grapes at '3 sous under Montmartre 4 sous the green –
cheeses of Neufchâtel'.

After leaving Paris in October 1820 the Wordsworths stayed
with their friend, painter and poet Mary Barker, in Boulogne-
Sur-Mer for two days before attempting to sail back to England.
Their ship ran into trouble trying to leave Boulogne harbour,
and they had to stay another week before making their crossing. Mary had moved from Borrowdale to Boulogne just the
previous year in the hope of living well at less cost. The cover of
the commonplace book shows that it was bought from a book-
seller and bookbinder in Boulogne, Griset Fils Ainé (Griset,
the Elder Son). An advert for the shop that September in an
English-language French paper tells us they sold 'an assort-
ment of the best traveller's guides through the different coun-
tries of Europe', as well as maps and books. It is not hard to
imagine Dorothy entering the shop with the excitement of a
traveller in a bookshop in a strange land, and taking away this

large notebook, so different from her home-made ones, as an indulgence and a souvenir of her travels.

It would seem Dorothy is writing there, at Mary Barker's, looking out at the sea and the 'paved roads', comparing what she sees to what she saw in Paris. This brief note on the market prices of grapes may be the only record Dorothy kept of her time in Paris in 1820. After the short fragment of journal, Dorothy has transcribed a recipe for 'Miss Barker's White Salve', presumably taken down from Miss Barker during this stay. Directly below that is another salve recipe, and then she seems to have left off using the book for several years, when she takes it back up again as a commonplace book. Why she breaks off this snippet of journal in October 1820, we cannot know, but it makes a strange echo through the later material that does fill the pages of the book. It also brings a world outside the sickroom into the sickroom: a world of international travel, of mountain climbing (Mary Barker was Dorothy's companion on her famous ascent of Scafell Pike in 1818), of the company of creative women. Later in the book, Dorothy has transcribed a poem by Mary Barker into its pages, bringing her into the room too. She is not a prisoner, she is not alone, so long as she has her consolations.

FIVE

LOST FRAGMENTS
SHALL REMAIN

Like many people in the earlier stages of an ongoing illness, in the early 1830s Dorothy imagines a recovery narrative for herself. She is better, her poems say, or will be. The struggle is over, her letters say, time after time.

In some ways, after 1835, the struggle is over. She does not have another life-threatening crisis. Her health fluctuates, but with fewer extreme ups and downs. Though she does not regain full mobility, and is not able to walk for any distance, by 1837, on her better days she can walk a little around the house. But the final crisis of June 1835 does something to Dorothy that changes the rest of her life. It is impossible for us to know exactly what happened, but it seems likely that during that terrible crisis, she sustained a non-traumatic brain injury of some kind.

Over the next 19 years, the almost-twenty years considered her years of 'darkness', or her 'long twilight' she continues much the same: not unwell in her body, but different in her mind. She becomes 'Poor Sister', or 'Old Aunty'. She is dependent on the care of the family and servants. She has a maid dedicated entirely to her care, both because she may need attention at any time, and to manage her daily laundry. Her head is shaved for convenience, and she is kept in 'beautiful neatness and cleanliness'. (MW to Dora, August 1837). Dorothy's life is not without fun and joy in these later years. She is aware and responsive to changes around her, both positive and negative. On her good days, she sings in happiness and makes jokes, and delights in other's company. On her bad days, she weeps or rages. She writes poetry, she recites poetry.

Although Dorothy did not keep a journal after 1835, she did write occasionally in her commonplace book, making notes, copying interesting stories and bits of writing, and drafting poems. There are entries dated 1848 and 1849. She wrote some letters we know of, and more which may not have survived. In some ways, this is beside the point. She did not need to write her life down for us to believe in it.

Since I first heard that term 'darkness' applied to Dorothy's later life I have wondered time and again what is actually meant by it. She was not in literal darkness, mental nor physical.

Increasingly, I came to think that what troubles people about this period of Dorothy's life is her inarticulacy. It is not twenty years of darkness, but it is twenty years of leaving little or no account, no record of herself in her own words.

I began to think the people who repeat this coupling of darkness with Dorothy's illness were confusing writing with life, with light. It's easy to see how, as academics and literary critics and writers themselves, they would conflate the two. When writing is the centre of your life, it can seem like life itself. I have at times myself felt that if I cannot write my life down as I go, I cannot be sure I am living it, but this fear, like any assumption that equates articulacy and intellectual output with quality and worthiness of life, is rooted in ableism. To assume that only people who are able to turn their days into words and write them down are in the light of their lives does a terrible disservice to non-speaking and non-writing people.

I also wonder if what they mean is that these later years are the Dark Ages of Dorothy – not years in which Dorothy lived in darkness, but years which are an obscure darkness to us, as later readers – years about which we can know nothing, because we have no record to draw on. This is untrue now of the historical period once known as The Dark Ages. I hope one day it might also be untrue of Dorothy's later life.

RISEN FROM THE BED OF DEATH

In December 1835, shortly before Dorothy's sixty-fourth birthday, William writes to Basil Montagu, who he and Dorothy cared for when he was a child, that 'there is no prospect of her being other than a prisoner in her bed or room for the remainder of her days.' (WW to Basil Montagu, December 10, 1835).

That Christmas, Mary once more takes on the task of thanking Jane Marshall for her presents to Dorothy. Mary shows a degree of doubt about Dorothy's own testimony about her symptoms, one which is repeated and reflected in so many accounts of her illness. 'She has complained a good deal', Mary writes, 'of pain in her bowel', but it is only 'to a certain extent' that they think they have 'proof'. There is a mistrust of Dorothy as patient here that many chronically ill and disabled people will recognise from their own experiences. When Mary takes the present up to Dorothy, she is 'in her disturbed way', but the presents calm her. Mary writes that 'every sensation of irritation or discomfort vanished, and she stroked and hugged the Turkey upon her knee like an overjoyed and happy child'. If the discomfort can be removed by a Turkey, it is inferred, it is discomfort of the mind, not the body. On a simple level, Jane's gift works as a tool of distraction for Dorothy. It doesn't mean her discomfort was not real, but that the joy of receiving the turkey temporarily takes her away from her pain. Nowadays, patients with chronic conditions are taught distraction techniques to help manage intractable symptoms. We are taught to list items we can see out a window, or to count. Sometimes I use Netflix to distract me from bad, disturbed days, sometimes cat photos, but an unexpected gift from a dearly beloved friend would work well.

But Mary does not know this. All she sees is a complaining patient, who becomes inexplicably calm and happy when given a gift. Dorothy, Mary is clear, cannot be trusted. She behaves badly, is selfish, forgetful, greedy. Unless there is evidence that confirms her account of herself, her account cannot be taken for granted. She has become an invalid in every sense of the word.

Dorothy writes her own short addition to this letter, thanking Jane. The postscript is in two parts, both signed, as though written, perhaps, at different times. The first recalls the seriousness of her recent illness: 'My dearest friend, risen from the bed of death I write to you with a thousand thousand blessings on y^r dear head and on all your family.—May we meet again in this world.' She signs off, then begins again, reminded maybe of the purpose of the letter as a thank you note, remembering to thank and send wishes to the rest of the family. (MW and DW to JM, December 1835). I can't help but wonder if Dorothy read Mary's part of the letter before she wrote her own, or between the two additions. How did she feel to read about her feelings in the third person? Did she recognise herself in Mary's account? 'Too lazy to rise from her pillow' in the words of her niece; childish and ungovernable in Mary's? Did she recognise herself as the untrustworthy, ungrateful invalid she is presented as in the letter? And what did she think of her 'dear, dearest friend' reading this account? Mary's letter, although loving, reveals a distaste for excess that carries through into the reception of Dorothy's journals from this period. Dorothy's insistence on her bodily reality is just too much for everyone around her, and for her later readers. Even Laura Shapiro in *What She Ate*, more sympathetic than most towards Dorothy's great appetite and cravings, writes that in '1835 she had discovered self-pity […] she was whining now, feeling sorry for herself as assiduously as if she had decided to make up for lost time.' No one wants to know about how painful her bowels are, how the cold hurts her. They do not want to know about her hunger. She is no longer the good, grateful invalid, thanking God for the health she does have, and for the glimpses of the outside world that sustain her. She has to be cared for and the house must revolve around her needs. She will not thank anyone for the trouble they take over her, and instead, attacks them for it.

In Mary's account we can also see the exhaustion of the carer, the frustration of the carer with the cared-for, and the strain of expectation. We also see the strain of trying to care for someone who is angry about their care. In a letter to Henry Crabb Robinson the following February, Mary passes along a message from Dorothy: 'Miss W. sends her love and bids me say that "she has had many a *sad tug* since you went and that she has been very ill used, and has wanted you to protect her."' This suspicion of the people close to you can be common to brain injury and dementias, but it also shows the vulnerability of the sick person at the complete mercy of those around them.

Before this illness, Dorothy was responsible for so much of the caring in the Wordsworth household – she was the good aunt, who carried so much of the weight of emotional and domestic labour. She was always busy, making and doing for the family. In her illness, the situation is dramatically reversed. William notes at one point in a letter to Edward Moxon how striking it is that she doesn't busy herself with sewing or reading anymore, 'as she was one of the industrious of the earth'. (WW to Edward Moxon, August 30, undated).

It has been argued that Dorothy's central role in family life itself causes her illness. Some critics follow a psychoanalytical reading in which Dorothy's illness has an emotional or psychological root. She has been the carer for so long: illness allows her to be the cared for instead. In effect, in this theory she becomes ill in order to perform the kinds of selfishness Mary's letter records with no guilt or accountability. Others follow a mechanical reading in which Dorothy is so physically and emotionally worn out from caring so much that her body and mind break down. Neither of these seem satisfactory reasons for me, and both seem to ignore the physical and cognitive reality of Dorothy's daily existence.

In January 1836 William reports to friends that Dorothy's mental capacity has become a worry, and there is no improvement in her overall health. Yet the stabilisation of her physical condition means that, for the first time in seven years, she is no longer considered at death's door. Crabb Robinson visits in the new year and writes to his brother of Dorothy's changed prognosis: 'she is likely to live years as I am told by the medical man here'. (HCR to TR, January 7, 1836).

At the end of the month, Mary writes to her sister-in-law that Dorothy 'still continues in the same state, only her memory is improved – and she *can* talk continually for a short time together, but otherwise her habits, etc. are the same'. (MW to Mary Hutchinson, January 30, 1836). This is the first record that up until this point Dorothy has *not* always been able to talk continually, to piece sentences together, since her acute illness.

By February, she seems to be recovering physically, but is still struggling cognitively. William writes to Christopher, his nephew: 'Your poor Aunt is in general bodily health much better—she is grown quite fat; but she cannot stand unsupported; and her mind, owing *we think* to some inflammatory action in the brain, is sadly weakened and disturbed.' (WW to CW Jr, February 8, 1836). Mary reports to Isabella Fenwick that Dorothy does have some 'revived memory', but otherwise her 'mind [is] continuing in the same shattered state'. She has had some 'temporary relief' from this perceived inflammation of the brain – or at least 'disease confined to the brain' – from medical blisters. Still, there is 'no progress towards *permanent amendment*.' (MW to IF, February 10, 1836). Her bowel condition seems to have calmed down, or settled to a new baseline, but the cognitive disturbance the last attack brought on has not settled at all. In mid-March, William writes to Henry Crabb Robinson that Dorothy is 'greatly improved in bodily health' and is able to walk a little with support. 'Her mind however', he notes, 'is still feeble in all that relates to her illness, of which she has a strangely confused recollection.' (WW and MW to HCR, March 17, 1836). By late March something seems to have shifted – she has recovered enough to send a letter to her nephew requesting his urgent help in making a speech for his father. After the main point, she adds a summary of her health. She has 'got through a mighty struggle'. She claims to be 'as well as ever I was in my life', with one key exception – 'I have not recovered the use of my legs.' She adds, 'my Arms have been active enough as the torn caps of my nurses and the heavy blows I have given their heads and faces will testify'. If taken literally, it seems Dorothy is bragging about abusing her carers, and this is how some people have read it. But I think she has gained enough distance from her 'ungovernable passions' and her physical weakness to joke about them. This kind of grave humour is a familiar coping strategy for people who have been through great physical suffering, but it can seem inappropriate to people seeing the experience from outside. (DW, MW, and WW to CW Jr, Late March 1836). William adds some more details about Dorothy's condition to the letter, though. Her mind is not 'disturbed by fits of violence as it used to be' but is 'still very weak on some points'. He confirms again that Dorothy is 'indeed upon the whole in very much better bodily health', though still in a good deal of pain 'not unfrequently', and often 'uneasiness and discomfort.'

Her recovery from such serious illness is clearly baffling to them all, as is the partial nature of the recovery.

In July, Mary writes that 'her bodily health continues good' but they have given up hope that her memory would return. (MW to HCR, July 4, 1836). By Christmas 1836 Dorothy is well enough in mind and body to write to Jane Marshall herself to offer condolences on the death of Jane's son, John, as well as to thank her for sending turkey for Christmas dinner. The letter, dated Christmas Eve 1836, is short, but lucid. After she signs her name, she adds: 'How my heart yet beats at the sound of Christmas day—'. She still feels hope and life, after all they have all been through, at the anniversary of her own birth, as well as Christ's. She has survived, against all odds, another year. The 'tremendous struggle', Dorothy hopes, is over.

TOO BUSY WITH HER OWN FEELINGS

In January 1837 William reports Dorothy to be not better, but 'no worse'. At best 'rather more comfortable'. (WW to HCR, January 28, 1837, *HCR C*).

In February, William and Mary consider leaving Dorothy at Rydal without them for the first length of time since her illness. Mary writes to Isabella Fenwick that she is 'as to bodily health, perfectly well – and as she does not suffer from the absence of anyone, and having an exemplary attendant constantly with her, and each member of the house always ready to please her, I feel perfectly at ease in the prospect of leaving her'. (MW to IF, February 16, 1837).

Dorothy is delighted when they return home in June. Mary gives a good picture of her to Catherine Clarkson: 'her bodily health good – tho' unable to move off her Chair – and her mind still more (as I thought at first) enfeebled'. Although she is largely immobile, she is generally comfortable and contented: 'it is a comfort to see that she is *happy*: that is she has no distress or sorrow that oppresses her more than the transient sorrow of a spoilt child: to such a one only can be liken her.' If she is distressed, it seems, it is momentary. She also has moments of clarity and sharpness: 'if you can *fix her attentions* – her intellect is as bright and she will express an opinion, when asked, with as much judgement as in her best days: but alas these gleams are short lived.' This is the only place Mary records that Dorothy seems to be suffering an ongoing discomfort in her head – 'which she rubs perpetually' – a sign of 'something amiss going on in the head' to which they attribute her 'restless feelings'. This restlessness 'prevent[s] her finding quiet from reading – nor will she often *listen* to it.' When asked if she wants to read, or listen to others reading to her, 'she says "she is too busy with her own feelings".' (MW to CC, June 1837).

What did Dorothy mean by 'too busy with her own feelings?' Was it that she couldn't bring her mind to focus, that her body and mind in their discomfort were too noisy, or that they were infinitely more interesting than anything anyone else had to offer?

In her letter to Hannah Hoare that September she calls it 'a hard task to write at all among the many thoughts which press upon me'. Her head is so occupied with chaotic thoughts, they seem to press upon her – a physical weight or pressure. Is this what she is rubbing at when she rubs her head? Not a pain, as such, but the migrainous pressure of teeming thoughts and feelings?

OLD AUNTY

In the summer of 1837 Henry Curwen Wordsworth, Dorothy's grandnephew, comes to visit. He is just three years old. At first, he is disbarred from seeing Dorothy, as another child was frightened by her noises. Mary promises he will only be taken to see Dorothy 'when she is *nice* and quiet'. (MW to Dora, August

1837). Dorothy's mobility has been improving surprisingly. Her dedicated maid, confusingly also called Dorothy, reports to Mary, 'she one day walked to her bedroom window with a stick and with leaning upon her very slightly: and another day the length of the passage, and she has many turns in her sitting room'. This is a great improvement from a few months previously, when she could only walk supported by two people, moving her feet, but not bearing her own weight. She seems to be returning to the level of mobility she had regained before her last acute attack. They 'hope she will walk soon, as she seems very desirous of doing so.' Dorothy seems to be walking through force of will. She is so eager to be able to move around herself, even around her room, to not be at the mercy of others to move her. By early September Dorothy '*really* can walk without hold […] she walked across the back room – and again the length of her bed one day *supported*, and she only wants courage'. As it was in 1833, her muscles are affected, and her legs are weak, even when they are not painful. (MW to Dora, September 4, 1837). Henry and Dorothy develop a sweet relationship, essentially playmates outdoors, neither of them expecting anything of each other but what they find. 'When *she is nice*', Mary writes to Dora, 'she is much delighted' with him: 'I often taken him to say his prayers, which he does sweetly, in her room – and she always observes "how delighted his Grandfather will be to hear him"'. They spend time together in the garden, Henry riding with Dorothy in her chair, 'sitting at her feet', and imagining he is driving a carriage with horses.

In mid-September Dorothy shows how much her movement has improved by '*walking* alone from her chair to the top of the back stairs, and then making her way ½ way down on her bottom before she was helped'. She achieves this great feat with a single purpose: 'to get herself roasted by the kitchen fire'. The fire in her own room has gone out (Mary blames 'her impatience' for poking it out) and she cannot wait for another to be lit. Once she was by the kitchen fire 'she was the gayest of the gay', and her happy noise soon brings little Henry to join the party. The scene is one of great and unexpected joy – Henry and his aged Great Aunt making a party of the kitchen – but it also shows the lengths Dorothy would go to to get near a fire. Only great discomfort from the cold could make her risk the greater discomfort of falling on her way down the corridor or stairs, or the pain and fatigue of attempting the short journey.

Mary cannot see Dorothy's insistence on a fire as anything other than a sign of the confusion of her mind, so she sees Dorothy's determination in seeking out fire on this morning as just more proof of her baffling contrariness and stubborn resistance to good sense. She knows that without a fire Dorothy will be agitated; that if she is allowed a fire it calms her. It does not occur to her that the fire could be giving Dorothy the exact physical comfort that she needs.

Pamela Woof reads this need for a fire as psychological, that to Dorothy 'hearth meant home'. My broken inner thermostat and I understand what it is like to want a fire in the summer months, even on a hot day. How it feels to be unable to get warm without an external heat source, no matter how many clothes and blankets you layer yourself up with. How it is to feel like your bones are made of compacted ice when everyone around you is sweating. It is not unreasonable or implausible to me that Dorothy needed a fire to make her feel comfortably warm; to me, it seems a sign of physical confusion, not mental confusion.

The following summer Mary complains again about Dorothy, when indoors, insisting on 'relaxing herself over a large fire', often with 'a basin of hot water' on her knee, in which she washes her hands and shaven head'. (MW to Mary

Hutchinson, June 18, 1838). This seems to be about both the physical comfort of the warmth, and a kind of self-soothing technique. Mary describes Dorothy as playing with the water in a childlike way, 'amusing herself with her nail brush – and *soap lather* reaching to her chin'.

Henry himself is a bit like the fire: a simple comfort. In the letter she writes to Edward Ferguson that November, which surprises her family so much with its clarity of content and appearance, Dorothy mentions her enjoyment in Henry's visit, telling Edward, 'My Nephew John is here with his eldest Son, a charming little Boy, whose prattle amuses me (old Aunty, as he calls me) very much.' (DW to Edward Ferguson, October 8, 1837). Henry's presence seems to allow her to relax into her inevitable new role of 'Old Aunty': he has never known her as anything different. He has no expectations, and no pity. They can just enjoy being around each other.

In the letter, as well as hinting at the indescribability of what she has 'suffered and done' during her illness, she gives news of others, and responds to news. It is 'Through God's Mercy I am now calm and easy' she writes, and contemplating the illness of Mrs. Rawson, adds 'but God is Merciful', echoing the lines in the poem she includes. She also mentions their friend Charles Lamb, who had died in 1834, and his surviving sister Mary, describing her as 'a solitary twig – patiently enduring the storm of life'. She must have seen the potential parallel in her and William's situation, when she adds 'in losing her brother she lost her all'. Mary is left only with 'the remembrance of him, which cheers her the day through'.

In the note Mary sends along with the letter, she describes the unusual effort Dorothy seems to have put into the letter: 'since her confinement she has never before fixed her mind for so long a time I think to one effort, as must have been called for to accomplish this very nice letter'. (MW to Edward Ferguson, November 9, 1837). But she also describes how confusing it is to them to watch Dorothy work, as it does not look like an effort in process: 'to *see* her write, the act seems neither to require *time* nor *thought*, she is so rapid; and when tired or done she flings her paper aside and in a moment appears the same uncomfortable – and I may indeed say – *irrational Being* she too commonly is.' Mary is baffled by what seems to her a disconnection between the great effort Dorothy says it takes her to write, and how it appears when she is doing it. But so much of the effort is unseen. It is not necessarily the actual writing of the letter itself that is so particularly hard, but getting both the mind and body to a state of clarity and activity at the same time, at an appropriate time, and ensuring there is enough energy to finish it. As Mary reveals here, sometimes Dorothy flings her paper aside when she is too tired, rather than when she is 'done'. She has to control both her 'tottering' will, and her 'feeble' body to bring them both to the paper. It might look effortless, but it clearly isn't. And no wonder she collapses back into herself afterwards, worn out from trying to maintain a public voice for a space of time, if only on paper.

There is an entry in her commonplace book, dated September 10th 1837, which seems to begin with a neat draft of her 'Lines written' poem, but only gets two lines in before she interrupts herself. Instead, she writes out a story that was circulating in the press, about a young man who was found dead in Maryport churchyard. John Shaw, aged 38, was found dead, his throat slit, with his own epitaph written on a slate in pencil. Dorothy had often noted epitaphs in her journals and commonplace books, but in these years they seem to take on even more significance for her. The epitaph printed in newspapers differs, but the version Dorothy copies is as rich with narrative as a whole ballad:

Bury me beneath this place
Since it was my mother's case
Here for to lie
Since she did die
A broken heart has proved my end
So bury me beside my Friend
Where I may rest me safe and sure
From them who do abuse the poor

Directly beneath John Shaw's story, squeezed in at the bottom of the page, is a record of another death, this one of someone Dorothy knew well – Peggy Benson – on February 8, aged 67, 1838. Even though she seems to have escaped her own death, miraculously, death is continually on her mind.

This winter come hints that the family are divided about how to manage Dorothy in her present condition. In December, Mary writes to Dora that she and the maids have decided it would be better that Edward Quillinan does not see Dorothy that day. She 'is in her singing mood this morning', Mary explains. The problem is that William 'fancies everybody feels as he does'. (MW to Dora, December 8, 1837). It does not seem to occur to William that anyone would not want to spend time with Dorothy, who is still his beloved sister, even though she is different to how she was before her illness.

Mary, on the other hand, thinks that it is too difficult for others to be around Dorothy if she is not in one of her 'nice' moods. In October 1838 she writes of the difficulty of working out what bedrooms to put visitors in during refurbishments of the house: 'we can give *her no* neighbours but ourselves, or she would terrify strangers to death'. (MW to Dora, October 3, 1838). There are times now, Mary says, 'if you heard her talk, without seeing her, you would think nothing ailed her', but she is inconsistent and unpredictable. (MW to Dora, October 3, 1838). Mary is clearly more conscious of propriety or shame around Dorothy's condition than William is. Around the same time, William reworks a sonnet he had written for Southey, reflecting on his dementia, which he hoped to publish. William writes to Dora for her opinion, explaining that Mary 'seems to think it would be applied at once to your dear aunt'. (WW to Dora, 1838). William doesn't seem to see a problem.

There is a lot about Dorothy during this time that we do not know, that is not written down. We know she sometimes sings, and sometimes weeps, that she sometimes makes loud noises and gets agitated. In this letter Mary hints at '*manners*' that are not improved, though her memory seems to be. This echoes something she wrote to Catherine Clarkson the previous summer: 'her greatest discomforts proceed from habits that I cannot describe – and it would be painful to us both were I to attempt it'. (MW to CC, June 1837). In June 1838 Mary describes Dorothy as 'generally happy and good tempered, poor darling', adding 'she seldom uses bad expressions except in fun.' (MW to Mary Hutchinson, June 18, 1838). Dorothy's cognitive changes seem to have come with a loss of inhibitions that leave her free to swear and shout as well as sing and weep. Much speculation has been made about what Mary means when she refers to 'habits' or 'manners' with deliberate vagueness. We can make guesses at what was being alluded to – filling in what each one of us would deem most shameful, most unshareable – but like so much of Dorothy's reality in these years, we don't actually know.

SELF-LOOSENED FROM THE GRASSY SHORE

In August 1839 Dorothy sends another version of her poem to Mr. Carr, 'Five years of sickness & of pain', to Isabella Fenwick. This version splices together the original three stanzas with a poem she began in 1828, after she saw a peculiar phenomenon on Esthwaite: an unrooted island, complete with vegetation and wildlife, floating loose on the water like a ship. The 1828 poem begins with a statement about the 'Harmonious Powers' which work with Nature, and presents the mystery of the floating island 'dissevered' from the land. It is a warning of sorts. The island, she supposes, 'may survive' for many seasons, but it cannot survive forever in this state: 'Nature, though we mark her not,/Will take away – may cease to give'.

What does the floating island poem come to mean to Dorothy, during her sickness, that it did not mean before, and why does it bring completion to put these two together? In *The Fenwick Notes* – explanatory notes on his poems dictated to Isabelle Fenwick during this time – William said of the floating island poem that 'My poor Sister takes a pleasure in repeating these verses which she composed not long before the beginning of her sad illness.' There is something about the floating island, about the natural mystery of it, that seems to capture her, to connect to her present state. There seems to be something about her state that she wants to communicate through the poem.

By grafting the two poems together Dorothy makes new meaning from both of them. She has been a wanderer in the kingdom of the sick, treading a 'perilous path'. The 'tranquil shore' she has come to rest on in 'Five Years' is changed, when linked to the floating island, from a metaphor, to a real shore, an actual landscape. Thinking of this tranquil shore, and the mysterious movements of the body and soul that brought her there, she is returned to the vision of the 'slip of earth/self-loosened from the grassy shore' she saw on the lake. In the older version, she describes the slip of earth that becomes the island as having been 'by throbbing waves long undermined'. In this

1839 version it has loosened and freed itself, without violence. This impossible island, a 'peopled world', is 'passed away'; long gone, she supposes, drowned and buried in the lakebed. But this is not a loss – though the island in its past form has gone, its 'lost fragments' persist, fertilising other ground, subsumed into a large whole. It is a natural theory of entropy – nothing destroyed, only translated. But spliced together with the other poem, the body of the island becomes a version of Dorothy's own body. Once it floated loose on the water, an entire world, its trees full of birds, its wild growth blooming and fruiting. But the island was always an anomaly, and could not last. It is part of the mysterious harmony of nature that it should exist at all, but also that it should fail. This is the duteous task of nature, the work of harmonious powers. Her whole life seems like lost fragments now – scattered, confused, confusing – loosened from the shore of her life before. But like the island, it is not gone, only different. In the 1839 version she does not include the lines about Nature taking away. She had learnt this lesson. It is no longer the message of the poem. The message now is focused on continuance, in another form.

IN HER USUAL WAY

In January 1840, ten years after Dorothy's first full year of illness begins, William writes to Crabb Robinson, 'your Old friend our Sister too we think, in many respects improved'. (WW to HCR, January 23, 1840).

There are fewer and fewer accounts of Dorothy in this decade. She is no longer ill in the way she had been in the 1830s, but she is disabled, physically and cognitively. Her life is repetitive and simple. She leaves fewer and fewer accounts of herself in writing, though she does leave some. In March 1840 she writes a tribute to Reverend John Curwen – John

Wordsworth Jr's brother-in-law who died that February at the age of 40 – in perfect rhyming quatrains. Increasingly, she only appears in family letters as an aside – 'in her usual way' – nothing to remark on. Nevertheless, her life was full of small joys. The garden in summer, visits and letters from loved ones, and a thousand small amusements. She comes downstairs most evening to spend time with the family, once more part of the circle, even if she is no longer seen as an essential worker in it.

When William is given a cuckoo clock in 1840 Dorothy is delighted with it. Mary describes how she almost 'dropped from her chair, she laughed so heartily at the sudden exit of the little Mimic'. (MW to IF, April 1840). When Dora returns to Rydal in March 1841, newly married to Edward Quillinan, she notices how Dorothy finds pleasure in using Dora's married name, writing, 'it is most affecting to me to observe the childlike *fun* & pleasure she makes for herself in addressing me by my new name.' (Dora to HCR, May 19, 1841). Dorothy has been left at home whilst the rest of the family travel south for the wedding. On their return they find Dorothy 'very comfortable & delighted to see us'.

Later in the year, some friends visit Rydal Mount, and pass on to Catherine Clarkson that they saw Dorothy 'in her garden chair & could hardly perceive any decay.' (CC to HCR, November 29, 1841). One of them said 'she could not have supposed from what she saw of [Dorothy] that she ailed anything more than weakness in her limbs'. (CC to HCR, October 28, 1841).

In 1842 Edward Quillinan reports to Crabb Robinson that Dorothy 'is very well, & oftener merry than sad.' (EQ to ECR, November 28, 1842). She has, it seems, become contented with herself. By 1845, it seems to Dora, that her 'old aunty' is 'set in earthly immortality'. (Dora and WW to Isabella Fenwick, January 25, 1845).

DOROTHY AFTER WILLIAM

During a trip to London in 1847 William and Mary write a return letter to Dorothy, at home at Rydal Mount. Her own letter is lost, but from their reply we get a sense that it was typically short but carried as much news as she could manage. William begins by thanking her for her 'few lines', adding he will keep his own letter short too: 'I know you don't like long Letters and in fact I have nothing to say but that I shall be most glad to see you all again.' (WW and MW to DW, April 9, 1847). From his reply we can tell that her letter held reports on her own health and Dora's. In their absence, someone has been helping her out of doors, even in the cold of winter. 'I need not say how glad I am', William writes, 'to hear that you have a ride every day in your chair, as often as the weather permits.' (WW and MW to DW, April 9, 1847).

1847 brings losses: Jane Marshall, Dorothy's dear childhood friend, dies on January 25. In July Dora dies, after decades of ill health. There is no record of Dorothy's response to either death, but William is broken by Dora's. He describes a terrible blank in the space Dora had filled in his life. (WW to IF, December 6, 1847). Dorothy's poem for Dora's album had come true, but not in the way she expected. Dora did not need 'memorials of [her] aged Friend': it was to be Dora who went into the 'cold earth' first.

Henry Crabb Robinson passes on news of Dorothy as she approaches her 77th birthday in December 1848. Mary has told him that 'almost the only enjoyment Mr W seems to feel is in his attendance on [Dorothy] — and that her death would be to him a sad calamity.' (HCR to Isabella Fenwick, December 15, 1848). The bond between them is as strong as ever. Regardless of how other people might feel about Dorothy, to William she is the same, still the light, still the sun to his moon. Disability cannot change that.

Mary has been worried about how much Dorothy depends on William, and vice versa. In November 1848 she writes to her siblings:

> there is a difficulty about leaving Dorothy, who tho'
> I think mentally better (bodily she is well and strong)
> in some respects, is become so much the Master of her
> Brother, who humours all her waywardness as quite to
> enervate him – so that whether he will have the heart
> to deprive her of his indulgences, (which is much hap-
> pier without) by our leaving home – is doubtful. (MW to
> Thomas and Mary Hutchinson, November 1848).

She thinks they have become a bad influence on each other.
William just wants Dorothy to be happy and comfortable.
Dorothy tires William out with her demands, and he gives into
her, giving her treats to make her happy in the short term, which
in the long term make her ill. That August he had gone away for
a short trip, and Dorothy was inconsolable. Edward Quillinan
explained to Crabb Robinson, 'Miss W was in a deplorable way
for a day or two after her brother's departure: for he, you know,
spoils her, poor thing'. (EQ to HCR, August 12, 1848).

Mrs. Arnold reports to Lady Richardson in October 1849
that she found Dorothy alone at Rydal Mount, able to receive
visitors, and very conversational. Her talk seemed to be mostly
of the distant past, but centred on her early happy years with
William:

> I went to the Mount and there was poor Miss W. the sole
> representative. She was better than usual, and able to go
> back a little to old times, and said how good her brothers
> had been to her, and how William had been the especial

favourite. She talked too of his "Tintern Abbey" and said how fond Coleridge had been of it, and then she gave a tribute to him as I have heard her do before, showing how strong an impression his greatness and attaching qualities had left even on her enfeebled mind. (Mrs. Arnold to Lady Richardson, October 13, 1849).

There are other accounts from these years of visitors – both those known to the family and strangers – who saw Miss Wordsworth in her chair in the garden. She becomes part of the legend of the house for tourists; a sight to be seen. In 1846 Thomas Cooper visits and speaks with both William and Dorothy, recording in his diary that he met 'the poet's aged and infirm sister [...] being drawn about the courtyard in a wheeled chair, as we walked on the terrace'. The Duke of Argyll visits Rydal Mount in the summer of 1848 and describes realising the 'old paralytic and doited woman he saw, with a 'vacant silly stare" was the famous sister from Tintern Abbey.

In contrast, in her memoirs, Julia Wedgwood recalls meeting Dorothy Wordsworth in the summer of 1849 and finding her alert and curious. Julia was the niece of William and Dorothy's friend Tom Wedgewood, who had died in 1805. She remembers:

I was waiting at the door of Rydal Mount in the summer of 1849 when her chair drew up bearing the little shrunken figure from her daily excursion, and I looked into those "wild eyes" which kept all their life and light, though the mind had grown dim. There was no dimness in her interest when she heard my name. "From whom are you sprung?" she enquired eagerly.[106]

Dorothy clearly recognised the Wedgwood name, and thought of her old acquaintance and those long-distant times.

At the start of 1850, Dorothy seems much the same as ever. William writes to Isabella Fenwick: 'My poor Sister is as well as usual and thanks you for kind remembrance of us. She comes down-stairs to us almost every evening.' (WW to Isabella Fenwick, January 2, 1850). But in April 1850 William is taken ill. On the night of April 6 Dorothy comes to see him in his sickroom, just as he is about to fall asleep. To Mary this is yet another inconvenience. She writes to Isabella Fenwick complaining 'yet at this instant Sister is come to see him, rather inopportunely – as he is too sleepy to be kept awake, and this is not desirable just now.—' (MW to IF, April 6–7, 1850). After all these years of William coming to comfort Dorothy on her sickbed, fearing for her life, it is now time for her to do the same for him. She is there for him, even if it seems to be bad timing. Dorothy would have remembered too, I am sure, that this was the eve of his 80th birthday.

William's illness brings Dorothy into focus again. On April 23, Edward Quillinan writes to Crabb Robinson that Dorothy 'is as much herself as she ever was in her life, and has an almost absolute command of her own will!' He is amazed to find, with all her energies concentrated on her brother, that she 'does not make noises; is not all self; thinks of the feelings of others'. (EQ to HCR, April 23 1850). Later that same day, William dies. When Dorothy is told, Lee claims, she quotes 1 Corinthians: 'O Death, where is thy sting? O Grave, where is thy victory?' For all these years, it had really occurred to no one that Dorothy would outlive William and would be left to mourn him.

In September, Mary describes a bad day with Dorothy, in which she is 'unusually *stormy*, and has continued restless', partly due to thundery weather and heavy showers driving her in and out of the garden. (MW to Susan W, September 28, 1850). But in William's absence, they keep company with each other, finding a comfort in each other's presence they have missed for a long time: 'Each evening your Aunt and I passed a comfortable ½ hour together before her supper-time; last night she took it beside me – as I hope may often be the case.'

By November, Dorothy is missing the care of her brother badly. Mary writes to her sister-in-law, 'It will please Aunty if one of you will write to her – for she often tells us "nobody takes notice of her". She has been very cross lately'. Dorothy was no doubt right – nobody would take the same notice of her as her brother had continued to do, through the years. In December they are both cheered by a visit from John's little daughter Mary Louisa. As ever, Dorothy is delighted by the presence of a small child, and they are all happy to have someone else's needs and joys to focus on. They muddle on together, much the same. In April 1851, a year after William's death, Mary writes to her daughter-in-law Susan:

> Your dear Aunt Dorothy continues in her usual state –
> she gets out several times most days, for short intervals,
> for she is I think somewhat more restless [...] Otherwise
> there appears no changes in her general health. (MW to
> Susan Wordsworth, April 14, 1851).

Dorothy is still able to spend time in the garden; she takes pleasure in letters and visits from friends and loved ones. In May that year, Mary writes to a friend:

> My poor Sister was much gratified by your remembrance
> of her—She begs me to say she forgets none of her old
> friends [...] My Sister's bodily health enables her to go

out in almost all weathers—but she suffers much from nervous restlessness. (MS. Mrs. Greenwood, Swardiffe Hall, Harrogate).

The old pattern of the opening up with spring continues, even as she approaches her own eightieth birthday. That year the garden is particularly beautiful. Mary writes to her family in June: 'The garden is full to overflowing – the growth has been marvellous – Gorgeous peonies – too much blown – I never saw so many nor such fine colours'. (MW to The Hutchinsons, June 11, 1851). It is easy to imagine the pleasure Dorothy took in this. She tires easily though, and fatigue brings more pain. On a day Mrs. Arnold comes to call, specifically to check on Dorothy, she 'looked cheeringly' at Mrs. Arnold through tea, 'but afterwards she was very ill – and she complained much of her back'. It is hard for her to be alone, but also hard for her to be around people.

In the summer of 1852, Mary paints a picture of Dorothy – 'the poor thing' – oscillating between sickness and health with the weather. The same has been true all year – in January, she has what Mary calls a 'bed fit', in which it seems she does not want to get up at all, then will not sleep at night. 'It is the heavy weather that causes this', Mary thinks. (MW to the Hutchinsons, January 2, 1852). In July a 'dreadful thunderstorm' and 'intensely hot' weather disturb them all. Mary is surprised that Dorothy has managed 'often without a *fire*'. Instead, 'she comforts herself in bed, and is become comparatively *very* quiet, without any apparent increasing weakness.' (MW to IF, July 12, 1852). After all the years of singing, weeping, and shouting, this quietness in itself is worrying. The doctor is called to check up on her but pronounces her 'strong at heart'. Her bowels, for once in her life, seem unproblematic, and 'she never mentions that important <u>locality</u> of which she used for so many years to complain where her suffering lay'. Her head is kept shaved, except for three weeks when she won't let them shave it, telling Mary she 'wished her grey hair to grow it would look so <u>nice</u> hanging down her cheeks in curls ringlets.' (MW to The Hutchinsons, July 18, 1852).

In October 1853 Dorothy writes her last recorded letter, a short note to Mary, which begins, 'I have had a good night so I think I will write'. It repeats familiar themes. 'The weather was rough', she explains, so she had been in bed all day. She sends love to those who are with Mary and passes on news of the health of friends and neighbours. She wishes Mary were there, not for her own sake, but so she could share some of the good milk of the new cow they have. (DW to MW, October 22, 1853).This letter shows how even at the age of 82 Dorothy was no more or less conscious of the world around her than she had been in 1836. Whatever it is that is affecting her mind is clearly not progressive. She comes in and out of shared reality and in and out of her own particular reality.

At the close of 1854 Mary writes to her family describing Dorothy's birthday, on Christmas Day: 'her 83rd birthday was not much of a gala day with us'. Dorothy 'keeps pretty close to her bed' these days – 'the best place for her, poor thing'. She has retreated into her sickroom, her sick-bed. By January, Dorothy is quite unwell. Mary explains to her sister-in-law: 'she has been in a state (had any other Invalid been in question) I should [say] of dying – as she now seems to be'. They have expected Dorothy's death so very many times over the years, it seems implausible it will ever come. She complains 'of great pain' and loss of voice, and 'total want of appetite', but seems 'much stronger'. Dorothy, of course, was not immortal. On the afternoon of January 25, 1855 she is 'released from her gradual but *fitful* sinking'. Many of her family are gathered round her bed at the end. (MW to Mary Hutchinson, January 26, 1855).When she writes to niece Susan to give her the news, Mary reflects on the illness of twenty years earlier. Mary still cannot quite believe that Dorothy survived those five years of sickness and pain, and the terrible, mortal weeks in 1835. 'Last Wednesday', she writes, 'the Remains were laid under the Thorn in the South East corner of the Church Yard by the side of the Grave of her loved Companion my Sister.' Mary remembers how in the late spring of 1835 'it seemed to be a doubtful case which of the pair would be the first to occupy that chosen spot.' It is Sara, instead, who did not live out the year. Mary is left as the 'Solitary Lingerer', the last of the happy band, and Dorothy, the 'beloved Sufferer' with her 'restless Spirit' is at rest. Mary reflects in 1855 '20 years, all but 3 Months has your dear Aunt been the Survivor'. (MW to Susan Wordsworth, February 7, 1855).

Perhaps this is the best and most fitting way to think of Dorothy in the last quarter of her life: not as someone who had outlived herself, but as a survivor. Her life may be fragmented, but she remains. Sometimes singing, sometimes weeping, but always very much alive.

SIX

UNDIAGNOSING
DOROTHY

Posthumous diagnosis is by its very nature problematic. The ethics of diagnosing the dead are questionable, and the practicalities unfeasible. More often than not, there is no body to examine, no physical record of disease or disorder. Where there is a body, and it can be examined, it may not retain any useful evidence. Most conditions cannot be diagnosed from bones alone. Where there is no body, retrospective diagnosis relies on textual records, often letters and diaries, which may be missing key elements of the story, or worse, represent hearsay and gossip that has little to do with what the person in question actually experienced.

I know from my own experience how much diagnosis depends on asking the right questions, and how much knowing which questions to ask, and how useful the answers will be, depends on what information is available. In my case, it took a lifetime of asking the wrong questions, or the right questions with partial information, before my primary diagnoses were found, almost incidentally. It took one person to ask a simple question that hadn't been asked before, to kick off a chain reaction which led to the right tests, which lead to more questions, which lead to more answers. It was luck or chance that one of the specialists I was sent to for one genetic condition asked very thorough questions and uncovered the other genetic condition. Previous blood results that suggested it might be present had been discounted, because of partial information, a lack of understanding, a presumption that younger women did not develop this particular condition. Every step from the age of two till thirty-four that delayed my diagnoses was like this – someone looked at evidence and either misfiled it or discounted it – based on their own assumptions. This is not what I want to do with Dorothy. I want to undiagnose Dorothy, not to diagnose her. I want to ask the right questions, and to gather as much evidence as there is available. But I know two things: I have my own biases which will determine both my questions and how I interpret the answers I find, and I do not have all the information.

Lack of information and diagnostic bias has determined the diagnoses lain on Dorothy by previous biographers and commentators. Dorothy has been diagnosed with many things by many people, some of them agreeing with each other, some of them not.

The mysteriousness of Dorothy's illness has drawn attention from doctors over the years, who have attempted to diagnose her as a cold case from letters and journals entries. In the *Journal of the Royal Society of Medicine* in 1998 John Price theorises that her cognitive and mobility changes were caused by thiamin deficiency, caused by her 'vomiting and decreased food intake' during the crisis of December 1832, which developed into Wernicke-Korsakoff Syndrome.[107] Wernicke-Korsakoff Syndrome is characterised by mental confusion, vision changes, and loss of muscle coordination. It could explain some of Dorothy's symptoms, but like so many attempts to diagnose her, it does not quite seem to fit. Ironically, Price recognises the problems inherent in trying to diagnose long deceased patients from partial descriptions, comparing it to archaeology, where the 'evidence is likely to be incomplete or even fragmentary', but argues that it is possible to 'assemble the historical fragments so as to produce a recognisable whole.' In archaeology, he says, you can learn enough to tell whether shards of pottery are a cup, or a saucer.[108] Like many diagnosticians of Dorothy, Price has only looked at the published letters, alongside Gittings and Manton's biography, as his evidence base. I fear, to use his analogy, he may have confused cup and saucer after all.

In the introduction to her 1971 edition of Dorothy's journals Mary Moorman writes in passing that Dorothy was suffering from untreated gallstones which caused progressive arteriosclerosis, which in turn affected her brain.[109] Gallstone disease is known to often co-exist with coronary artery atherosclerotic disease, and studies in the last decade have sought to confirm this link.

Arteriosclerosis – known more widely now as atherosclerosis – is a condition in which plaque builds up in arteries, restricting oxygen access to organs and potentially causing blood clots, angina, heart attacks and strokes. This is a compelling idea and could explain how the acute episodes of the first half of the 1830s come to change the way Dorothy thinks and acts. A stroke or blood clots could indeed account for some of Dorothy's symptoms after her acute attacks – the swelling, discolouration and weakness of her legs, her confusion – and for her cognitive changes after the crisis of 1835. I'm not convinced Gallstone Disease fits the full range of Dorothy's bowel symptoms as collected in this chapter, but I do think the idea that something happened during those crises that affected her brain, something that could be vascular in nature, stands up. Importantly, Moorman was firm in asserting Dorothy's 'illness had purely physical causes, and if she had lived in our own age could have been treated'. She found 'the notion put about recently, that D.W.'s mind was affected by emotional distress, is not tenable'. Moorman stands out as one of the few commentators who has not identified Dorothy's illness as psychological in some or all parts. Gallstones and arteriosclerosis is the diagnosis Carl Ketchum repeats in his introduction to Dorothy's *Rydal Journals* in 1974.[110] Robert Gittings and Jo Manton's 1985 biography agrees that gall bladder disease is responsible for Dorothy's first acute illness in 1829, but suggests that her cognitive changers are unconnected.[111] They consulted an expert in age-related illnesses, who suggested 'we try too much to link all her illnesses', and that her dementia had nothing to do with her painful bilious attacks. The expert concluded she had pre-senile dementia. Dorothy managed to live an unusually long time with dementia, he theorised, because of the 'loving care' provided to her.[112] It is useful to be reminded that not every symptom is connected, but the cognitive changes occur after a physical crisis, so the idea they could be coincidental seems less likely. In her 1988 book *Dorothy Wordsworth, Writer*, Pamela Woof agrees that Dorothy was 'suffering probably from what is now known as pre-senile dementia'.[113] This diagnosis of pre-senile dementia has stuck for many, partly because of Woof's incredible expertise when it comes to Dorothy, partly because of the popular readability of Gittings and Manton's thorough *Life*.

Certainly, there are some elements of her conditions that could suggest dementia. From 1835 onwards her short-term memory seems to be impacted by her condition, yet her memory of the past seems compellingly present. In December 1837, after Elizabeth Rawson's death, William writes to Edward Ferguson that Dorothy 'talks much of Halifax and early connections there; nothing indeed seems to employ her thoughts so much.' (WW to Edward Ferguson, December 30, 1837). Evidence for dementia has also been found in Mary and William's numerous accounts of Dorothy's 'childishness' during her acute illness, and the years that follow. She becomes, Mary writes, party to 'ungovernable passions'. In other words, she wants to do what she wants to do. Visitors to Rydal Mount in her later years report on how remarkable it is that with her 'enfeebled mind' Dorothy can recite the poems of Coleridge and repeat stories of their youth.[114] It is clear how this could be read as indicating dementia, but it also only seems to me to be part of the story of Dorothy's illness, and not to explain it all. Despite apparent memory loss, and dwelling on the past, Dorothy seems to shift in and out of the present moment over her last twenty years. Although she does not write a lot during this time, she does write and recite poems and she does write some short letters. Most importantly, whatever has happened to her is not obviously progressive. Something happens in the last crisis in 1835, which changes her cognitive function for the rest of her life. But from that time on, there is no further progression, just daily fluctuations. More recently, Lucy Newlyn has combined theories to conclude that 'Dorothy's later years [...] were blighted by arteriosclerosis and dementia.'[115] It seems unlikely Dorothy could have lived with fluctuating cognitive function but have had stable health for twenty years if this were her diagnosis, no matter how much loving care she was given.

This lack of an immediate, simple explanation for Dorothy's memory and mood changes has led other scholars to discount a physical cause at all, as Moorman indicated, and assume the illness is emotional or psychogenic in some way. In this they are harking back, wittingly or unwittingly, to those Victorian commentors who believed she became ill through thinking too much, or too little, of herself. Francis Wilson diagnosed Dorothy with depressive pseudodementia, caused somehow by a *very* delayed response to no longer being the centre of William's life after his marriage. Wilson realised that Dorothy's disease progression and length does not map easily onto a diagnosis of organic dementia. It also does not map well onto pseudodementia, which is a contested diagnosis at the best of times. Even when her cognitive function is most disrupted, she has highly emotional responses to stimuli, making jokes, weeping at flowers, and becoming angry when refused something she wants, none of which fit with this functional dementia-like condition, secondary to depression, and most often recorded as a side-effect of medication. Susan Levin, despite her ground-breaking work in collecting Dorothy's poems, and careful, thoughtful, reading of her letters and journals, similarly assumes that the mysteriously fluctuating nature of Dorothy's illness means it can only be explained by 'feminine psychology'. As an invalid, Levin argues, Dorothy can do as she wants, living 'authentically' as herself, 'both the old Dorothy whom everyone knows and loves and the aggressively unacceptable crazy lady.'[116]

The idea illness offers a 'release' to Dorothy does not stand up to much scrutiny, though it repeats charges made a billion times against a billion sick women: that we are not *really* sick, just pretending, to get our own way. This psychologising always presupposes there is more to gain than there is to lose from life in the sickroom. It confuses the need all newly disabled people have to adjust to their situation and find ways to experience pleasure and joy in their changed life, and that changed life being a choice they have made towards happiness. Dorothy, it is true, finds solace in her illness, but it is clear it is not her choice. She finds solace despite her illness, not because of it. It also repeats another harm committed repeatedly against the mysteriously sick, and sick women in particular: to assume that since the cause and name of an illness it not known, the illness does not have a physical basis. It happens often in medical contexts, but it seems particularly strange to me that scholars can admire a writer or an artist from the past so much that they will spend their life dedicated to their work, but also distrust them to the point of disbelieving their own witness of their own life. Having said that, Dorothy's description of her own condition cannot always be taken entirely at face value, or as complete. There are three kinds of records we have of her illness in her own words: her poems, her letters, and her journals. The *Rydal Journals* – not written to be shared in the same way as her earlier journals were – are the most intimate of these records, and the least censored (by her own hand, at least). Her poems are made artfully, and though they reveal her own feelings about her situation, they also are formed through what she wants to feel about her situation, and what she wants to tell others. They are written to be read and shared. They are designed as communication.

In her letters, even as her condition progresses, she is very aware of her audience and their expectations. They often have a cheerful, self-deprecating tone, especially when describing the seriousness of her condition. She never wants her correspondents to worry unnecessarily. For instance, in 1830 she describes herself to her god-daughter Elizabeth Hutchinson as both old and 'infirm', but she does so to point out how entertaining her visit will be, as a 'lively companion and useful help'. (DW to Elizabeth Hutchinson, July 16, 1830). I know I self-censor my words when I tell others how I am. There are some friends I am more open with than others, but if a future archivist were to search for records of my illness, they would not find the worst of my experiences. Sometimes, they are beyond words. Sometimes I will repeat them only in person, the words floating off, ephemeral, reduced to half a sentence or an aside. Sometimes I make notes for myself, in case I need them later, but even those will not reflect the whole truth. There is so much daily body horror that goes unrecorded.

This is what I see when I am faced with the unwritten and fragmented portions of Dorothy's life: what is impossible to write down.

SEVEN

DOROTHY'S
SYMPTOMS

PAIN

One of Dorothy's most common symptoms is pain. Dorothy's pain takes many forms. She has acute pains, and chronic pains. Bone and muscle pains, pains in her limbs, pains in her stomach and bowels, pain in her teeth, pain in her head. She has intermittently experienced headaches and toothaches and stomach aches throughout her younger years, but after the illness of 1829, the pain becomes *intractable*. It lives with her, for the rest of her life. Sometimes worse, sometimes much worse than at other times, but it never really leaves.

Pain is one of the most frequently recorded symptoms in her own journals. Often, she does not elaborate on the kind of pain, or the seat of it, but only on its status. Her 1834 journal particularly becomes over-taken by pain. On August 5, 1834 she writes of being in 'too much pain to endure company', and on August 9, 'I did not venture out, being in pain'. (*RJ*, August 1834).

It is likely that the removed pages of her *Rydal Journals*, excised by Gordon Graham Wordsworth, contained more records of these pains. Although when her pain is at its worst, she does not write. In that, she is not alone.

BOWEL DISEASE

Dorothy's serious illness, as far as she and her family are concerned, begins with the digestive disorder of 1829. In November, once home at Rydal Mount and recuperating, she described this to Coleridge as a 'serious derangement of the bowels'.

In 1830, Dorothy explains her recent downturn in health to her friend Mary Lamb as stemming from 'inflammation of the bowels' the previous March or April. This varies in different letters. (DW to Mary Lamb, January 9, 1830). These months of 'serious derangement' seem to have long and lasting effect, leaving Dorothy weak and easily fatigued. Dorothy explains how her 'health had a sad shaking' and she has learnt to adjust her activities to avoid relapse:

> In June I left [Leicestershire] – and from want of care have had two or three attacks, but neither so severe, nor of the same kind; however, enough to convince me of the necessity of great care; and therefore now though perfectly well I am acting the invalid, never walk except in the garden, and am driven out whenever weather permits by my Niece in the pony chaise. (DW to Mary Lamb, January 9, 1830).

These attacks seem to be a combination of digestive pain and upset, and general malaise – fatigue, weakness, dizziness, confusion.

The gastric attacks seem to be accompanied by fluctuations in appetite, and sometimes by craving for particular foods, which cause problems when certain foods are identified as exacerbating her symptoms rather than helping them.

In *What She Ate*, Laura Shapiro puts the bowel inflammation of 1829 down to eating black pudding: richer, denser, and less digestible than her normal plain fare. I'm not sure the severity of her symptoms can be blamed on black pudding, but diet does seem to affect her. In her journals, when she can write, she tries to keep track of her appetite, her diet, and her symptoms, to see if they correlate. The last year of her journal in particular pays attention to her sickness and her food intake. When her stomach is at its worst, she cannot eat solid food or keep any food down. When it is slightly better, she is able to eat plain biscuits and arrowroot bread, and avoids food considered heavy and hard to digest at the time, like meat.

Dorothy has what we might consider a 'flare' of her digestive symptoms in spring 1831, and another bad one in December 1831 into January 1832, which was accompanied by symptoms that suggest her circulatory system has been affected (blackened ankles and swollen legs).

In a letter to Christopher Wordsworth in May 1832, William notes that Dorothy's 'pain is only occasional, proceeding from extreme flatulence', suggesting a lot of her pain at this time is abdominal discomfort caused by her bowel condition. (WW to CW, May 5, 1832).

These digestive symptoms flare up again in the autumn of 1832. Writing to Jane Marshall she describes suffering 'flatulence and pains in the Bowels', but also describes 'horrid cravings' and a 'gnawing appetite' which have eased by the time of writing. (DW to JM, November 20 1832).

Dora writes to Jane Marshall that Dorothy 'fancies her appetite bad – but we know she eats quite enough for one who only moves out of bed to have it made.' (Dora to JM, Fragment, 1832).

In December, her bowel symptoms worsen further and in late January William writes to John Keyon that Dorothy 'has been five weeks confined to her room by a return of the inflammatory complaint which shattered her constitution three years ago.' (WW to John Kenyon, January 26 1832). In February 1833 William explains this to Henry Crabb Robinson as a relapse of the 1829 illness – the 'inflammation in the Bowels, caught by imprudent exposure' in Whitwick. At this point William traces her current downturn to the relapse a year prior, in the winter of 1831/2, since which she 'never has been well or strong.' (WW to HCR, February 5, 1833).

In January 1834 Dorothy is enjoying food again. She writes to Julia Myers to thank her for sending her oysters – 'indeed I thought I had never eaten any that were so good'. (DW to Julia Myers, January 3, 1834).

However, by the time of her birthday that year, the following Christmas, Dorothy is worse again. Mary writes to Jane Marshall to thank her for Dorothy's birthday presents, because Dorothy is too ill to do so herself – she has had a 'rather severe bilious attack' – a description used most often to describe a combination of digestive disorder and a sick headache, including abdominal pain, nausea, dizziness, sleep disturbance, fatigue, vomiting, and diarrhoea. The word bilious refers to bile – a bilious attack was seen to stem from an excess of bile. What were known as bilious attacks are often now explained as stemming from gallbladder or liver disorders, although bilious attacks were also seen to be part of cholera symptoms in the nineteenth century. It could also be used to describe cyclical vomiting syndrome, which is characterized by chronic nausea, vomiting, fatigue, abdominal pain, dizziness, and vertigo that may last for hours to days.

It might or might not be of consequence that Dora and William both also had digestive disorders at this time - although Dora's lack of appetite is seen to be tied to a wider illness ('she suffers less pain, - but as yet we cannot look for an increase of strength as very little improvement has taken place in her appetite'), whilst William's to be quite unconnected in Mary's mind, though she describes him as having 'been inconvenienced by irregularity of digestion' for two weeks. Meanwhile, Mary and William's son John's family in Workington have all been affected by a 'bilious diarrhoea' which is described as 'general' in the town – perhaps what we know now as Norovirus, or Winter Vomiting. Mary recounts these as distinct from Dorothy's attack, either because of differing symptoms or lack of contact or because it seems more obvious to view Dorothy's acute illness that Christmas as a recurrence of her relapsing and remitting illness, and not as something separate. Before Mary manages to send the letter, Dorothy has recovered enough to get dressed and to be sitting in her chair waiting for them when they return from chapel.

In spring 1835 William reports that Dorothy has again lost weight and is 'troubled with squeamish sickness'.

By the close of 1835 her appetite has returned so much that it becomes remarkable to the family. In November she requests Crabb Robinson send her some Norfolk Beefins – large, rosy winter apples she ate during her happy teenage years in Norfolk. She is craving fruit, but, as William writes, 'none are left now', out of season. (WW to HCR, November 25, 1835). By Christmas, her appetite is unquashable. 'Our poor Sister smiled at the passage in your kind letter where you speak of your wish to bring her aught to "*stimulate* her appetite"—that alas! is keen enough, for she told me poor Creature this morn^g that "'she is never happy but when she is eating"'. (WW dictating to MW to HCR, December 16, 1835). In March 1836, Crabb Robinson sends Dorothy a crate of oranges. (HCR to MW, March 8, 1836).

Food remains a problem for her, and her digestion remains fragile, though she does not seem to have the serious 'attacks' of the early 1830s later. Her diet is managed, as William records in his 1838 Christmas letter to Jane Marshall:

> Her bodily health has been remarkably good—except that within the last two days—owing to her having eaten some trifle, in which she is not generally allowed to indulge—her stomach has been a little disordered—so that we find it is quite necessary to be careful to confine her to such food as we know to be suitable to her. (WW to JM, December 26, 1838).

The Wordsworth family clearly viewed this bowel disorder as Dorothy's primary condition, and the other symptoms or linked conditions to be co-morbid or causal. There could be so many explanations for the centrality of this bowel complaint to Dorothy's ongoing illness. The relapsing remitting nature of it could suggest an inflammatory bowel disease, such as Crohn's Disease or ulcerative colitis. Untreated, Inflammatory Bowel Disease (IBS) can cause complications including arthritis, osteoporosis, skin disorders, and eye problems. What is most important, perhaps, in tracing the importance of this bowel disorder to Dorothy's illness, is that it did not start in 1829 from nothing. Dorothy does write that she suffered no 'serious illness' before 1829, but looking back at the previous thirty years it is obvious that she has had many smaller attacks of illness, often centred in her stomach. In 1801 William writes to their brother Richard that they have both been well, except 'Dorothy being subject to bilious sickness from time to time', which suggests her regular stomach upsets were simply a part of her life even then. (WW to RW, November 21, 1801). She often experienced headaches and digestive disorders at the same time, which has lead to the presumption that the digestive symptoms were secondary to migraine. Iris Gibson diagnoses Dorothy with Migraine in an article in the *British Medical Journal* in 1982, counting '63 probable references to migraine in the journals', though also pointing out 'there were erasures in the manuscript by an unknown person and some of these referred to illness', acknowledging the incomplete patient history the journals present.[117] It has since become standard to understand her headaches as migraines, to the point that Dorothy is used as an example case by Mark Wetherall in a review of a book about the history of neurological patients as an example of a historical patient who was an 'active agent' in her own health. He is certain 'there can be little doubt that her problem was migraine'.[118] In an essay about reading the journals as a migraneur, published in the *LA Review of Books* in 2020, Alicia Wright notes that 'The *Grasmere Journal* contains seventeen mentions of "head-ache", beginning on the very first page.'[119] However, she also directs herself away from the confirmation bias that may have driven Iris Gibson's reading of Dorothy's symptoms, skirting away from the temptation to 'retroactively diagnose Wordsworth's headaches as being representative of any particular condition'. Her journals, the same as her letters, are full of references to bad bowels and bad heads, though not always together.

In her journal on May 19, 1802 she notes 'Coleridge's Bowels bad, mine also', and mentions being tired, but no headache. The next day she writes that she lay in bed late, and was 'somewhat tired', but the following week is a litany of having to go to bed early, unwell, or very poorly. On Sunday 23 she writes, 'I was ill in the afternoon, took laudanum', and the painkiller allows her to walk half a mile or so to Banerigg wood in the evening. On Thursday 27 she can't get up at all but is 'in bed all day – very ill'. No more details are given. On May 30 she notes, 'I had been obliged to go to bed before tea & was unwell all day.' A headache is never specifically mentioned, but the combination of bad bowels and fatigue is already a familiar pattern.

In early 1804, Dorothy had such a 'sad attack' that she wrote to Catherine Clarkson asking her to pass on details of her symptoms to the famous doctor Thomas Beddoes and ask for his expert medical advice on 'what is proper to be done' to alleviate an attack. She starts off describing how it 'began, as usual with sickness, followed by a complaint in my Bowels with a violent looseness that lasted four days.' Later in the letter, she adds: 'I began with sickness, violent head-ache, yellow and pale looks, afterwards came on the [?]ness with pains in the Bowels, thirst, and want of appetite—I had then no sickness, but what seemed to come from weakness and pain.' Frustratingly, one word is obscured by the letter's seal. As she writes, she thinks of more she needs to add to her patient history for Dr. Beddoes, about situations which seem to precipitate these attacks:

> By the bye if it seems to be worth while, you may tell Dr Beddoes that at all times when I am not in uncommon strength (as I was before the last attack) after writing for any length of time or doing any thing that exercises my thoughts or feelings, I have a very uneasy sense of want and weakness at my stomach, a mixture of emptiness, gnawing, and a sort of preparation for sickness—eating always removes it for a time.

This seems to show a direct relationship between fatigue, appetite changes, and the subsequent attacks.

This letter also shows the importance of corroboration of witnesses in recording symptoms, as she adds:

> William after reading over my letter is not half satisfied with what I have said of myself—he bids me add that I always begin with sickness and that any agitation of mind either of joy or sorrow will bring it on—if any thing puts me past my sleep—for instance—also being in much company and hot rooms. Ever since I can remember going into company always made me have violent headaches.' (DW to CC, February 26/27, 1804).

This last sentence particularly sounds familiarly migrainous, but the other details are interesting. Lack of sleep, anxiety or excitement can occasion flare ups of all sorts of conditions. They are triggers I recognise myself as agitators of all my chronic symptoms. Dorothy herself comes to recognise that emotional upset can trigger her symptoms (for example, John Wordsworth's death in 1805 brings sickness). This has encouraged later readers to assume that they are psychosomatic episodes, but that side-steps the effect distress or excitement has on any background condition. Just because emotion makes it worse, does not mean emotion causes it.

Dr. Beddoes recommends Dorothy take some medicine, and a change in diet, though the details are lost. He also asks her for more details about her digestion and food reactions. She replies:

> In answer to Dr Beddoes's enquiry respecting flatulence I must tell you that formerly I was very much troubled with it both in stomach and bowels, and am so now frequently though in a far less degree. I cannot say that I have observed that any particular sort of food that comes in the common course of our plain diet disagrees with me regularly though several things seem to do so when I am not quite well. When I am well my appetite is often much larger than that of any of my female friends but it is very irregular. (DW to CC, March 25, 1804)

Meanwhile she has described the episode further to Coleridge, her fellow sufferer in all complaints of the bowels, sparing no details: 'I began with sickness but this soon went off and was followed by a violent looseness that lasted 4 days and weakened me much'. (DW & WW to STC, March 6, 1804). William adds his description to the second half of the letter: 'it came on all at once; the first day sickness [...] and afterwards violent looseness, coming on the moment she took any refreshment, and pains in the Bowels, leaving her at last very thin and weak, though she recovered as if by magic.' He and Mary have been 'rather alarmed' by this 'shock' of ill health, not least because Dorothy had seemed 'uncommonly well before' it came on. Although Dorothy can't see any pattern in her eating that might relate to the symptoms, William remembers that before she was taken ill her appetite had been unusually good, and 'she had been eating heartily of sausages unusually heartily'.

These symptoms – sudden onset of sickness and/or diarrhoea, changes in appetite, and weakness – seem to be exactly what comes to trouble her so much more acutely in the 1830s. Dr. Beddoes treatment does not act as a cure, whatever it was. By 1805, she has started to think of her condition as chronic, a part of her life she simply has to accept. She writes to Lady Beaumont, 'I have fits of illness occasionally, and probably shall have all my life – sickness with head-aches'. (DW to LB, October 27, 1805).

In April 1808 Dorothy writes to Catherine Clarkson that she has 'had a violent inflammation in [her] Bowels', in parallel with 'severe weather' that has been making them all ill. This bowel attack seems to make her particularly weak and confused. She writes a long letter, but adds 'my head is muddy, or I would have taken a larger sheet of paper.' (DW to CC, April 22, 1808). That summer, her bowels flare up again, on a weekend visit to John Wilson's new house at Orrest Head. A long walk on a hot day brings on a bad headache, which turns into a 'violent sickness' at tea-time. Dorothy writes to Catherine Clarkson, 'I continued vomiting and retching till 12 o'clock at night, and a thousand times I wished myself at home'. The following day, she reports feeling 'quite well, but very languid'. She is fine the whole next day, but on the Sunday, during a trip on horseback, she is suddenly ill again. Her illness perplexes her. 'I know not how it was', she writes, 'but my Bowels grew bad.' They have to make a stop at a house in Ambleside, where she is 'very poorly'. William and John Wilson are so alarmed by how ill she looks, John Wilson arranges for a chaise to carry her onwards. They stop again at their friends', the Luffs, in Patterdale, where she is again 'poorly'. 'Poorly' here seems to be standing in for diarrhoea. She blames herself for going out at all, at her illest writing that she was 'thoroughly vexed with myself for having left home'. By the evening she feels better again. The accompanying headache with the sickness and stomach upset could seem to agree with the migraine theory, but Dorothy's bowel problems are not always accompanied by a headache. As she gets older, the bowel symptoms with no other sign of a migraine become more dominant. It is tempting to see a headache and sickness together and think it must be migraine, but the irregular occurrence and progression of her bowel symptoms suggest that even if her headaches are migraine, there is something else happening with her digestive system which gets worse over time, building up to the crises of the 1830s. Migraine, like any chronic condition, can be co-morbid with others.

It is hard to unravel enough detail from the clues left to be certain of any particular cause and effect. Her bowel problems always seem to be accompanied by pain and urgency, and leave her exhausted and weak afterwards. There are hints that she looks different when she is ill too. In one of William's letters to Mary in 1810, famed as love letters, he compares a sickness Sara Hutchinson experiences whilst travelling to one of Dorothy's episodes. He reassures Mary that the problem was not serious or lingering, and only caused by not being able 'to have attended leisurely to a call of Nature', but adds that when she was unwell, she was 'as to complexion etc as bad as Dorothy in one of her worst fits'. (WW to MW, August 19, 1810).

In June 1815 Dorothy is left in charge of the household and the children whilst William and Mary are away, and they are all ill with 'violent coughs – fever, hoaresness &c &c –.' Dorothy remarks on her own illness separately, and that it has left her 'quite unable to use much exercise', though she expects to regain strength. (DW to CC, June 28, 1815). During the summer she complains of 'want of strength and appetite', typical of her bowel flare-ups, but assures Catherine Clarkson that she is 'eating like a ploughman' again by August. (DW to CC, August 15, 1815).

During her trip through Europe with Mary and William in 1820, Dorothy's digestive disorder flares up, she believes, brought on by 'excessive heat' and by walking too far. (MW and DW to Sara Hutchinson and Dora, July 21, 1820). Her 'bowels were much affected' she writes in a letter to Catherine Clarkson, which in turn 'brought on weakness'. She reports not being well enough to 'go out as much as the others', and when she does walk out to see a view, finds the exertion 'too much' for her, and that she is left 'overpowered and exhausted'. Her sleep is disturbed – she wakes early but has to go back to bed because of pain in her legs caused by the bowel disorder. She admits 'my legs ached so much from the state of my Bowels that I was forced upon the bed again.' This combination of digestive disorder, leg pain, and weakness can be seen repeated more dramatically in the acute episodes she experiences between 1829 and 1835. This flare up affects the rest of the trip. Several times she has to return to bed and rest, or rest in the carriage instead of sightseeing. Even when she feels better, she limits her walks in case exercise brings on another flare. At this stage in her illness, she is already learning what will become central to her disease management later – to pace herself. She is 'resolved now to do always less than I *can* do', she claims, and hopes this will limit her 'suffering', though it is clear she sees not being able to walk as much as she wants to as a 'privation'. In Cologne she was a 'prisoner' in her room, only able to watch the busy world through the window, presaging her later illness. She is forced to face her aging, admitting, 'I certainly am not so strong as I was twenty years ago. This I am now obliged to confess and I must manage myself accordingly.' (DW to CC, July 23, 1820).

By the time they reach Interlaken in August 1820, she has had two bad episodes. Though both made her weak at the time, with 'hardly [...] strength for the walking up and down the stairs', she believes she has recovered her strength completely. She hopes if she avoids 'the sort of hurry which upsets' her and takes 'the proper diet' she can put off a relapse. She has been ill enough to noticeably have lost weight, writing to Mary Hutchinson, 'I am now quite well; but you never saw me so thin in your life.' (DW to Mary Hutchinson, August 8, 1820). To Dorothy, thinness was always a sign of illness. She was a small woman, under 5 feet tall, and her weight fluctuated with her health. After all but one of her teeth are pulled in April 1820 she tells Sara Hutchinson she is looking quite healthy, despite dramatic weight loss: 'I have lost 8 lbs since I was last weighed, being now only 6 stone 12 lb'. Fatness was a sign of robustness to Dorothy. She associates fatness with strength and good health. Crossing the Alps, and recovered temporarily, she writes to Sara, 'I am growing fatter and am, I think, the strongest of the Party', adding, 'climbing the Passes of the Alps is not near so fatiguing as our mountains.'

By the time they reach Paris in October, her health has largely settled again, though she still has the odd flash of unexpected fatigue. She writes to Catherine Clarkson that she feels 'strong' and has 'never but once been tired' during their time in

Paris. (DW to CC, October 14, 1820). Little did Dorothy know this would be her last trip abroad.

FATIGUE

Whenever Dorothy is ill, from her earliest writings, fatigue is one of her most frequently recorded symptoms, perhaps because she finds it particularly frustrating.

During the crisis years she has to learn to pace herself to avoid bringing on worse fatigue. It is a hard lesson for her to learn. Early on in autumn 1829 she learns the dangers of pushing herself too quickly. In November she writes to Mary Anne Marshall, Jane's daughter, that she has learnt the hard way as 'no conviction is so strong as that which is produced by experienced'. She has realised that she has to keep 'acting the Invalid, however strong and well I feel myself to be: for I find that exercise amounting to the slightest degree of fatigue invariably disorders me'. (DW to Mary Anne Marshall, November 19, 1829). In 1832 she writes to Jane Marshall, 'I am grown so careful of myself that I endeavour always to prevent fatigue by leaving off writing while I have yet a hundred things to say.' (DW to Jane Marshall, November 20, 1832). Earlier in the year, she found even a change of air 'exhausted her a good deal.' (Dora to EQ, April 12, 1832).

In 1833, after the third crisis, William reports to Crabb Robinson that 'she can walk about 20 or 30 steps, but always with exhaustion'. (WW to HCR, June 5, 1833).

By 1834, fatigue has begun to drastically affect her capacity to communicate. She writes to Julia Myers, 'I must hasten to tell you the little news I have—good and bad—for I have already written one short letter and am tired even when I begin with you. You will forgive my brevity—knowing that the will is good, though the power tottering and crazy—' (DW to Julia

Myers, January 2, 1834). Here Dorothy could be referring not only to fatigue, but to cognitive problems, perhaps what people now refer to as 'brain fog'. She wants to write – 'the will is good', but the power to do so is 'tottering and crazy' – uncontrollable and uncontrolled.

Like her bowel flare-ups and her headaches, episodes of fatigue have been with her since her teenage years, if not before. In 1793 she confesses to Jane Pollard that she has been suffering from 'lassitude and weariness which hung upon me and absolutely deprived me of the Power of exerting myself'. She describes how if she does something as little as walking upstairs too quickly, she has palpitations and sudden exhaustion which would make her have to lie down, and her 'limbs to ache to a most distressing degree'. She realises she can walk on the flat, if she walks slowly, for as far as six miles 'without *very great* Fatigue', but walking upstairs makes her feel she 'could scarcely support [her] body'. Interestingly, she has had no headaches during this period of fatigue. At the times she thinks it was brought on by an episode of worms, and helped by an unspecified medicine, though the reference to worms may indicate an early manifestation of her bowel disorder.In the summer of 1805, when she is 34, her eldest brother buys her a pony because he worries she is wearing herself out by walking too much. He could see she was 'at that time not very strong'. This allows Dorothy to travel further without worrying so much about fatigue, though it also reminds her that when she was younger, she 'could never ride half a dozen miles without great fatigue'. (DW to LB, October 27, 1805). It seems fatigue has been a part of her life since girlhood.

As early as 1815, Dorothy realises that she has to rest after illness or her fatigue will last longer. She writes to Catherine Clarkson that she has 'contented [her]self with strolls – and creeps', only able to take slow, shortish walks, concluding: 'I am now well convinced by experience that fatigue from walking is the worst thing possible for people who have any sort of weakness at the chest or elsewhere internally.' (DW to CC, June 28 1815). Later in the same summer she admits that though she is, 'in general as well able to walk as ever' she has found 'a little illness tells [more] than formerly', and she 'could not take a long walk … with so little fatigue as 15 years ago.' (DW to CC, August 15, 1815).

POST EXERTIONAL MALAISE

Dorothy's fatigue can be seen to extend into what may now be termed Post Exertional Malaise, particularly during the crisis years: the worsening of symptoms following even minor physical or mental exertion.

She frequently notes that she fails to 'gain strength' between episodes. By November 1829 she is 'convinced by experience, that exercise of any kind that amounts even to a slight degree of fatigue is injurious' to her health, however strong she feels to begins with. (DW to John & CW Jr, November 18, 1829). More importantly, she begins to find that resting does not help. She writes to her nephews John and Chris: 'Even letter writing has fatigued me, and I have shrunk from any work that was not absolutely necessary, till within the last ten days.'

In July 1832 William writes to Crabb Robinson that Dorothy 'never quits her room but for a few minutes, and we think is always weakened by the exertion.' (WW to HCR, July 21, 1832). Exercise not only tires her, but makes her obviously more ill, and hinders her recovery further.

The same becomes true of any activity that requires concentration, so that between Christmas and New Year 1834, Mary relates to Jane Marshall that 'letter-writing always exhausts her'. (MW to JM, December 27, 1834).

Throughout 1834 her journals show her trying to balance activity with fatigue, as pushing at her exhaustion will leave her ill and in more pain for days. On August 19, 1834 she has a busy day, with visitors reading poetry to her, demanding concentration, and Mary helping on one of the rugs she was making for friends. Afterwards, despite the weather being fine, she knows she 'durst not go out with so much in door labours'. (*RJ* August 19, 1834). She cannot do both. Like Dorothy's bowel problems, this sense of unremitting fatigue, which gets worse with activity, is a feature of her periods of bad health throughout her life. A few weeks before her twentieth birthday, she writes to Jane Pollard that she has been ailing all year 'without being absolutely ill' but 'less able to support any Fatigue'. In other words, when she gets tired, she cannot recover from the tiredness. She reports having had 'an extreme Weariness in my limbs after the most trifling Exertions such as going up stairs' and being 'more troubled with Headache'. She is ill enough to have resorted to 'taking medicine', which she calls 'a thing so rare with me that I can hardly reconcile myself to its Necessity while I cannot, in fact, say that I am ill.' (DW to Jane Pollard, December 7, 1791).

In 1806 she writes to Catherine Clarkson that during a stay with Lord and Lady Beaumont in Coleorton she has found herself uncommonly well: 'I eat most heartily, am never fatigued with exercise and they all tell me I never looked so well in my life.' (DW to CC, November 24, 1806). That this is remarkable shows how usual it is, even in the years she considers herself generally well and strong. But from 1829 onwards she has to learn to accept that any kind of exertion, even the smallest kind, takes a great toll on her health, and can set her back for days or weeks.

TOOTH LOSS

Dorothy's toothlessness has attained mythological status.

On the tour of Dove Cottage, which we all learnt by following other tours until we 'had our own', we used to say that Dorothy Wordsworth had lost all of her teeth by the time she was forty. It was an inaccurate statement in several ways, making it sound like Dorothy's teeth just wandered off like stray sheep. We would say this in the ground floor bedroom, whilst talking about William and Mary's double-washstand, and the slightly stretched truth that when the Wordsworths lived in Dove Cottage people brushed their teeth with twigs and ash.

This story, passed on and on, has found its way into the popular consciousness, as into poetry. Carol Ann Duffy's poem 'Dorothy Wordsworth is Dead' opens with 'who came to lose every tooth in her head' and turns on 'whose tongue travelled her empty gums'.[120] In reality, Dorothy had problems with her teeth for many years, and did indeed lose many of them without intervention. As Margaret Drabble pointed out in her review of Francis Wilson's *Ballad of Dorothy Wordsworth* one of the most revealing and poignant entries in Dorothy's *Grasmere Journal* is that for May 31, 1802: 'My tooth broke today. They will soon be gone. Let that pass, I shall be beloved—I want no more'. She is only 31. Her journals note various toothaches, and it's possible that some of her headaches were tooth-related, since her dental problems were so severe. Even as early as May 1791, when she is only nineteen, she writes to Jane Pollard about going to have two teeth drawn in Norwich.

In August 1819 Dorothy admits in a letter to Catherine Clarkson that her toothlessness is aging her. She feels as strong as ever and has 'as much enjoyment in walking' as when she moved to Cumbria twenty years earlier, but she is now 'in face a perfect old woman.' She explains that by this time she has 'only eight teeth remaining – two in the upper jaw, the rest below and of those two or three are on the point of coming out.' (DW to CC, August 1, 1819).

Dorothy's tooth story culminates in a costly trip to a London dentist in April 1820. The dentist wanted 50 guineas to remove her remaining teeth. She was 49 years old.

She writes to Mary Hutchinson after the work is done:

> He drew all my remaining teeth (8 in number including stumps) on Monday—all but one sound one, which is left to steady the new set for the time it will last; and when it goes I can have a false one in its place. The tooth-drawing was not half so bad as I expected, though bad enough. He is certainly a delightful operator; and I hope my gums will be sufficiently healed by next Thursday to be measured for the new set. If they should not answer—but every body encourages me to expect they will—I shall only have the 50gs to regret, for I rejoice in having got rid of my old teeth. My mouth has not been so comfortable for many months, and I wish that poor Sara, whose mouth is for ever growling, were in exactly my state.—I confined myself to the house two days in which I was fully employed in writing. (DW to Mary Hutchinson, May 5, 1820).

Dorothy has to wait for her gums to heal from the extractions before moulds can be made by the dentists, and her false set of teeth made to measure. She explains to Mary how she was able in London to meet up with Catherine Clarkson, who tries to assure her that her appearance is 'not so much changed by the want of teeth as she expected', but Dorothy sees herself quite altered by the absence: 'for now my mouth is drawn up to nothing, and my chin projects as far as my nose'. She looks 'healthy enough' though, she concludes, though she has lost weight again, presumably because she has struggled to eat.

Dorothy's early tooth decay and loss could be indicative of an underlying health condition. Even in a time before regular dental care, it seems unusual for an otherwise healthy woman of Dorothy's abstemious eating habits to lose her teeth so dramatically, so early. Many chronic conditions can affect tooth health, from diabetes to connective tissue disorders. It could also potentially be linked to Dorothy's bowel disorder, if it led to malnutrition, or acid damage.

COLD INTOLERANCE

After her bowel illness in 1829, Dorothy develops a marked intolerance for the cold. The following Christmas she writes to William Pearson of how the cold limits her ability to be out-of-doors in a way it did not used to: 'This weather is charming for the young and strong – Moonlight and at Christmas used to be delightful, thirty years ago. I now enjoy a short, sharp walk in the garden, and a peep out of doors, on the Evergreens and sunshine, from a warm fire-side.' (DW to William Pearson, December 29, 1830).

Two years before her illness she had written to Crabb Robinson of how 'the present moon has brought that kind of fine weather [with snow] which is delightful to the Strong for exercise; but very trying to invalids'. (DW to HCR, February 18, 1827). At the beginning of 1834 she writes to her nephew 'I begin this year m[uch] better than the last—I only fear ... the cold—' (DW to WW Jr, January 2, 1834).

Her *Rydal Journals* and her letters are full of similar references to the cold, and it seems obvious to everyone around her that the weather and her condition are linked.She has by this time entirely linked cold and damp weather with a worsening of symptoms, and particularly of pain. William echoes this later that spring when he writes to Crabb Robinson that 'the mild air has proved singularly beneficial' to Dorothy, and that 'she has suffered much less pain than heretofore'. (WW to HCR, April 3, 1834).

In the autumn she experiences another relapse, shortly after writing to Catherine Clarkson 'cold is my horror'. (DW to CC, October 18, 1834).

This link between the external weather and the internal weather of the body seems so obvious to Dorothy and to her family that her reports of stormy weather begin to stand in for both. Whether this link is an observation, or an assumption based on medical advice is harder to be sure of. William's assertion to Henry Crabb Robinson that the bowel disorder was caused by an 'imprudent exposure, during a long walk, when she lived with her Nephew in Leicestershire' makes the weather the culprit. (WW to HCR, February 5, 1833). It was widely believed at the time that 'imprudent exposure' of the body to cold and damp could cause bowel complaints. Imprudent exposure appears in nineteenth century medical textbooks as causation in digestive disorders. It might seem like a leap to believe cold could cause stomach disorders, but without other theories, they had to look to cause and effect to explain symptoms and try and avoid them. In the midst of one of his famous love letters to Mary in 1810, for instance, William writes that his 'stomach failed about a fortnight since from too much talking, or rather from not being sufficiently alone'. (WW to MW, August 11, 1810). Is Dorothy listening to her body when she avoids the cold, or listening to medical advice? Dorothy is clearly frustrated by having to limit her exercise, whether because she is already too fatigued, or in the hope of avoiding fatigue and other symptoms. She does tell Crabb Robinson many times over the years that she is following the advice of those who know better when she keeps indoors. She complains about being kept inside, but never about avoiding the cold itself. Being warm, on the other hand, does seem to make her feel better, and just as she increasingly avoids the cold as her illness progresses, she increasingly seeks heat.

In October 1833 Sara Coleridge writes to a friend that Dorothy's gains in health seem entirely dependent on a mixture of stimulants (brandy and laudanum) and the use of hot water bottles, suggesting 'if her stimulants & hot bottles were withdrawn it is feared that debility would ensue & she will require the utmost care during the winter.' (Sara Coleridge to Elizabeth Wardell, October 30, 1833). In May 1835 a heat wave aggravates all the sick women in the household. William notes 'the thermometer for these last three days has never been under 68 [°F – i.e. 20°C] in my sister's room in any of the 24 hours, and often at 78 [°F – i.e. 25.5°C]'. (WW to HCR, May 1835). In June he writes that 'the weather of last month was by the sharpness of its changes of temperatures very hurtful to our Invalids', and though he calls the heat 'oppressive', Dorothy is suddenly much better. (WW to Mrs. Williamson, June 7, 1835).

Dorothy's relapses also coincide with cold or wet weather. This is true when she feels unwell even long before her serious illness. In June 1820, when she is staying in London for a protracted visit to see a dentist, she writes to Dora that it is the first day that has been warm enough for her not to have a fire, but even so, in the morning she was 'obliged to put on [her] Bonnet to walk half of an hour to warm [her]self'. (DW to Dora, June 23, 1820).

Similarly, one of her bad episodes in 1801 seems to be brought on by putting her head under a spring of cold water. This cold intolerance did not begin suddenly in 1829, but whatever happened that year catalysed the exaggeration of something pre-existing, as it may be with many of these symptoms.

In her reports on Dorothy's illness, Mary often complains about Dorothy demanding a fire in her room at times Mary deems inappropriate – in the middle of the summer, for instance – when other members of the family are easily warm enough. This is conspicuously worse after the 1835 crisis and has been interpreted by later readers as proof of dementia.In July 1837 Mary writes to William:

> You asked about Sister's fire. We cannot conquer in her the love of it. During this fine summer she is never contented without she has a perfect winter's fire – she says "it is the only things that does her good". "Stir the fire" is her first salutation when her room is like an oven – and that must either be done, or a hubbub ensues. (MW to WW, July 29–31, 1837)

Mary is sure these fires must be contributing to Dorothy's discomfort, complaining to Dora in August that 'the heat of the weather and her large fires must affect her – but to tell her so, or attempt to reduce the fire, makes her *outrageous*.' (MW to Dora, August 14, 1837). Dorothy is adamant that the reverse is true – they are the only thing that makes her comfortable. Each one thinks the other outrageous. I have more sympathies with Dorothy, having spent many summer days shivering in jumpers and a coat in my brother's house whilst he sits steaming in shorts and sandals. It doesn't seem to occur to anyone around her that Dorothy really does feel cold and need her fires, rather than it being a sign of delusion. She seems genuinely cold, in a way that baffles even her. In June 1834 she notes in her journal 'the thermom^r never below 58 or 60—yet my limbs like marble—' (*RJ*,

June 21, 1834). She cannot help what her body feels, even if it seems to make no sense. When the thermometer reaches 72°F (22°C) in early July, she does not find it oppressive. Conversely, when she gives in during a damp spell and lights a fire, she 'feel[s] the good effects'. (*RJ*, July 12, 1834). She realises during storms that summer that a fire can stave off the pain the damp gives her, writing in August, 'I think the fire agrees with me'. (*RJ*, August 24, 1834). That September she is tormented by hot damp, when she cannot light a fire, and so 'could do nothing but loll on my chair–& suffer twisting pains'. (*RJ*, September 25, 1834). It is no wonder a fire becomes a requirement for her as her discomfort increases. Mary also worries about the cost of Dorothy's require-ment for heat: 'This is an *intolerable* expense, and coals are now to us 17 1/2 d a cwt.' (MW to Dora, August 14, 1837).

Cold intolerance can come along with many conditions, from Thyroid disorders, to hormonal changes, to problems with circulation, blood pressure, and the nervous system. Perhaps it is simply the inactivity necessitated by her weakness and pain that makes cold unbearable. It could also suggest damage to the hypothalamus – the part of the brain that produces the hormones that regulate body temperature – which could also tally with some of her other symptoms (changes to appetite and weight, emotions, behaviour and memory, and to body clock). The hypothalamus in turn controls the pituitary gland, which controls the adrenal glands, thyroid, and ovaries. A problem with her hypothalamus – whether from a growth, blood vessel damage, or an underlying disorder or auto-immune disease – could explain many Dorothy's 'mysterious' systemic symptoms.

PHYSICAL WEAKNESS AND MOBILITY PROBLEMS
In 1833 William reports that Dorothy is 'deplorable weak; and cannot we fear remain long with us.' At this point she 'has not

left her room for five week & scarcely her bed.' (WW to HCR, February 5, 1833).

In June Dora reports to her cousin Chris that Dorothy 'has neither gained nor lost strength the last six weeks. She can walk a little by aid of two sticks, ride round the garden several times in her little carriage, work a little, talk a little, read a great deal, eat well, and sleep tolerably'. (Dora and WW to CW Jr, June 17 1833). Her mobility and her activity are greatly limited, though the fact she can walk a little is a sign of some recovery. Hartley Coleridge reports to his mother in the autumn that Dorothy 'looks well in the face but is very decrepit & aged in figure & motion'. (Sara Coleridge to Elizabeth Wardell, October 30, 1833).

Her legs are increasingly affected by her acute episodes – each one seems to leave her less able to stand by herself, and to walk – both through pain and weakness. In July 1834 she writes to Crabb Robinson: 'my legs are but of little use except in helping me to steer an enfeebled Body from one part of the room to the other. The longest walk I have attempted has been once round the Gravel Front of the House.' (Dora and DW to HCR, July 24, 1834).

Isabella describes her aunt as 'dreadfully weak and languid' in May 1835, reflecting language Dorothy uses about herself in both poems and journal entries. (Isabella Wordsworth to Charles Wordsworth Jr, May 18 1835). In the summer of 1836, Mary relates that she seems in a continual state of 'surprise & disappointment at finding herself unable to walk'. In her inability to remember the facts of her illness 'she is constantly raising herself, fully expecting each time that she can walk as usual'. (MW to JM, 1836?)

By 1837, once she has stabilised as much as she ever will, she can walk a little unsupported on good days, but not far, and never beyond the garden, which she mostly visits in her chair.

SWOLLEN ANKLES

In the crisis of January 1833 Dorothy's lower legs swell up and develop discoloured areas, which William describes as 'blackened spots'. (WW to CW, January 29, 1833).

A fragment of a letter by Dora to Jane Marshall provides an important record of these swollen, blackened ankles. Dorothy at the time is in recovery: 'the blackness about the ancles which alarmed us so much is rapidly dispersing & the swelling nearly abated'. (Dora to Jane Marshall, n.d. 1833?).

William Knight includes this letter of Dora's in his 1907 collected *Letters of the Wordsworth Family*, but dates it at 1835. Most importantly, he edits the letter, omitting mention of the swollen, blackened ankles. The Wordsworth Trust has it dated as possibly 1832, but placing it alongside other records suggests it was written between March and May 1833.

Many conditions can cause lower leg swelling. They could perhaps support a diagnosis of atherosclerosis, although the most likely causes of swelling and discoloration in both ankles are chronic venous insufficiency, causing blood-pooling in the lower limbs, or lymphedema, both of which would be eased by elevation of the limbs.

Around the same time, Mary describes raised and swollen areas like flea bites on Dorothy's legs, accompanied by heat. This, and William's description of 'blackened spots' could be plausibly suggestive of Erythema Nodosum, an inflammatory skin condition which can be secondary to Inflammatory Bowel Disease, and can also cause fever, malaise, weight loss, and painful, swollen and stiff joints. The lesions can haemorrhage under the skin, causing blackened areas. Could this explain the relationship between Dorothy's bowel flare-ups and her leg pain, and particularly why her legs became so discoloured and swollen during this crisis?

Her legs continue to swell during bad episodes. In her journal in September 1834 as she recovers from a bowel flare-up she writes, 'I think my limbs grow stronger, and the swelling at bed-time is less'. (*RJ*, September 7, 1834).

SPASMS OR SEIZURES

In February 1833 Dorothy calls 'spasms in the legs' one of the worst features of her latest episode. (WW & DW to EQ, February 22, 1833).

Dora's letter fragment to Jane Marshall also notes 'sad spasms wh[ich] were so distressing'. (Dora to JM, undated, 1833?). It is not clear whether these were muscle spasms or something else, but they seem to be aggravated by exercise. In her journal in July, Dorothy says her 'legs, though the change has of late been most rapid, are still very weak—and spasms after much exercise'. (*RJ*, July 18, 1833). Both the spasms and the swelling in her legs are eased by massage, which is usually William's job, twice a day. Crabb Robinson offered to help, as he did with support and conversation. Dorothy records how he '<u>would</u> have rubbed my feet and ankles; but this I <u>could</u> not consent to'.

Again in 1833 William mentions a seizure of spasms that occurs during a bad episode, and she notes 'night spasms' in her journal in October 1834. (*RJ*, October 16, 1834).

ORTHOSTATIC INTOLERANCE

In September 1834 Dorothy writes to Elizabeth Hutchinson, 'I rise late and go to bed before sunset, because it tires, and in other respects disagrees with me to sit up more than from 4 to 6 hours in the day'. (DW to Elizabeth Hutchinson, September 14, 1834).

It seems not being in bed is a problem for Dorothy, and she has established this clearly enough by 1834 to have altered her routine to account for it. By the spring of that year, she has become 'afraid of the fatigue of down stairs'. (*RJ*, March 14, 1834). Dorothy's shortened days might suggest not only chronic fatigue, but another problem common to many chronic illnesses – one suggested by the phrase 'other respects disagrees with me' – an intolerance to being upright. Being upright, even sat in a chair downstairs, for more than a few hours, makes Dorothy ill. I know many people reading this will feel as I did when I first read this letter – a jolt of recognition in the need to be as horizontal as possible – to have feet up, head down.

Medically, this is known as Orthostatic Intolerance; literally, an intolerance to being upright. Orthostatic is a word applied mostly to falling people and to standing stones.

In the Christmas letter to Jane Marshall in 1835 Mary shows Dorothy writing in bed, unable to lift herself up from her pillow: 'From the specimen on the other page you are not to suppose that our dear Sister is not capable at times to guide a pen better—but she was "too *lazy* to rise from her pillow" Dora says'. (MW and DW to JM, December 1835). Before my diagnoses, I too, may have thought of this need to be horizontal as only weariness, or worse, laziness. This is what we are told, and tell ourselves. That having to lean, sit down, lie down is only tiredness.

Now I know it is more than and different to fatigue, and must be treated differently. It is not a problem with being awake, it is a problem with being vertical.

It makes me think of the Sylvia Plath poem 'I am vertical', with its first line, 'But I would rather be horizontal.' So many times I have found myself thinking this, that it is, as she writes, more natural to be lying down, in parallel to the sky. Then I think of Dorothy, lying in a ditch in John's Grove, staring at the sky of 1802, aged 31. And Dorothy only able to be vertical for a few hours a day, at a great cost, thirty years on. In May 1835, she reports in a letter to her nephew Charles, 'though I write lying on my back it wearies me'. (DW to Charles Wordsworth Jr, May 18, 1835). Even being horizontal does not offer complete relief.

I am lucky that my orthostatic intolerance is less severe now than before my diagnosis, and responds well to basic treatment: drinking a lot of water, eating a lot of salt, and avoiding the vertical. It means that I can write in a chair, unlike Dorothy, so long as I remember to respect gravity. I keep my feet up as much as possible. Even now, in the twenty-first century, the best advice to manage orthostatic intolerance is to keep horizontal: feet up, head down, take the day slow, rise late, rest early. All the things Dorothy was doing for herself.

DYSAUTONOMIA

Orthostatic Intolerance is one of many manifestations of dysautonomia. Dysautonomia is the partial or total failure of the autonomic nervous system – the involuntary system which usually controls blood pressure, body temperature, breathing, heart rate, and much more – without us knowing or noticing. When the autonomic nervous system fails, however, we cannot help but notice.

We are cold when we should be hot, hot when we should be cold. When we get cold, we can't get warm. When we get too hot, we can't cool down. When we stand, or exert ourselves, our heart races and our head spins. Our blood pressure falls or rises erratically. We cannot correct it against gravity. We stand up, and our blood sinks down, and we cannot get it back up again. We get dizzy. We feel sick. Sometimes we faint. Sometimes we lose control of our words, our limbs.

To me, Dorothy's accounts of her needing to have her feet up clearly suggests she is experiencing orthostatic intolerance, but her other accounts suggest she might have been experiencing a broader dysautonomia.

Dysautonomia can take many forms and have many causes. Symptoms can include all or some of the following: an inability to stay upright; dizziness; fainting; nausea; chest pain; gastrointestinal problems; visual disturbance; weakness; fatigue; breathing difficulties; mood swings; anxiety; fatigue; exercise intolerance; migraines; tremors; disrupted sleep; inability to regulate body temperature and blood pressure; appetite changes and concentration and memory problems.

It can be exacerbated by anything that makes the heartbeat rise suddenly, such as walking up hill or stairs quickly, or excitement or stress. This could explain the symptoms which come on when she exerts herself or gets upset or excited from her teens onwards, such as the months in 1793 when she gets suddenly exhausted walking upstairs.

COGNITIVE IMPAIRMENT

When Dorothy writes to Julia Myers in January 1834 that she has to finish her letter it is not only because she knows she is growing too tired; she could be referring not only to fatigue, but to cognitive problems, perhaps what people now refer to as 'brain fog'. She wants to write – 'the will is good' – but the power to do is 'tottering and crazy' – uncontrollable and uncontrolled. During the second winter of her illness, she described her mind as 'perfectly fallow' and herself entirely 'without the power to think'. (Dora to JM, nd, 1832?).

Anyone who has been very ill, or suffered great pain, might be familiar with the memory loss and confusion that can come along with it, and how disconcerting it can be. There are also many conditions which affect memory, and a person's ability to access memory, more directly. Dorothy's problems with *the power to think* seem to grow worse with each crisis she experiences between 1829 and 1835, and are accompanied by other changes suggestive of cognitive impairment: mood changes, memory loss, loss of inhibitions.

Although she has little memory of the acute episode of December 1831, between serious flares, she is able to read and sew. In April 1832 William tells Christopher that, though confined to her room and physically very weak, 'she reads much, both religious and miscellaneous works'. (WW to CW, April 1, 1832). In 1832 when she is recovering from another acute episode Dora writes that 'she cannot yet read at all to herself nor can she bear to listen to reading for more than 5. minutes together unless it is something she is perfectly familiar with as certain Chap:s in the Bible Psalms Hymns – &c &'. Her concentration levels have suffered, and she has little memory of the period of the peak of illness itself.

In the summer of 1833 she requests reading from Henry Crabb Robinson and passes on tips for his trip to the Isle of Man. (WW to HCR, June 4, 1833; WW to HCR June 5, 1833).

When he visits Rydal Mount he is pleased to find Dorothy 'could partake of conversation' for short periods of time, but noted that she was 'too nervous to bear disputation' – in other words, she couldn't face a good debate. (HCR to TR, July 4, 1833).

In the autumn of 1833 Dorothy writes to Kate Southey, the poet's daughter, with news and love, adding a request for more books: 'if you can send me any Books that you think will interest and amuse an invalid I know you will set them aside to be brought by Jane at her return. My taste lies in the *Biography, Missionary* and *Travels* line'. (DW to Kate Southey, October/November 1833). As usual, her letter is short – she writes in bed – but apart from length it shows no change in intellectual capacity. She describes her output in 1834 as 'short, dull letters' to her nephew William, though she still gives him a page of domestic and political news. (DW to WW Jr, January 2, 1834). But later, her ability to concentrate much at all seems to have wavered.

The crisis of May–June 1835 seems to irrevocably damage Dorothy's short-term memory. William notes immediately that 'her recollection is greatly impaired since the event', clarifying 'I mean her recollection of recent events.' (WW to HCR, July 6, 1835). He relates that Dorothy herself has said Sara's death has effected a 'sad shattering' of her faculties: 'she complains of foolishness of mind', showing that she herself has noticed a change. As she recovers some physical strength, her memory seems to come and go, or is very partial. She cannot remember much of the illness, but she can recite poetry: 'Her memory is excellent this morning', William tells Henry Crabb Robinson, 'I chanced to mutter a line from Dyer's *Grongar Hill*, she immediately finished the passage, reciting the previous line, and the two following.' (WW to HCR, July 6, 1835).

By the autumn of 1835 Mary is reporting her mind as 'in a state of childishness', and her 'thoughts and manners ... quite childlike'. (MW to HCR, November, 1835). She seems to simultaneously take 'wild pleasure in her sallies' and 'bemoan her sufferings', which the family find confusing – how can she be suffering and also enjoying herself? – and take as further proof of damage to her mind. That Mary hopes 'her intellect ... may be recovered' shows that they consider it to be damaged.

Mary recalls how at one point in her illness, Dorothy's memory for 'passing events [...] was quite gone' – she couldn't keep a grasp on the present moment – though she could still concentrate on things that mattered to her. Her 'retrospective' memory was 'perfect, & her mind if it could be fixed on books or serious matters as vigorous as ever.'

Withdrawing opium in November 1835 – which they hope will help her memory – brings 'no comfort with respect to the *mind*'. (WW to HCR, December 16, 1835). On New Year's Day 1836 William writes of Dorothy's continued cognitive problems as 'inflammatory affection in her head' (WW to Miss Murray, January 1, 1836), a theory he repeats to his nephew in February: 'her mind, owing *we think* to some inflammatory action in the brain, is sadly weakened and disturbed.' (WW to CW Jr, February 8, 1836).

On January 18 William reports to Isabella Fenwick that 'My poor Sister's health especially as affecting her mind is to us a constant source of anxiety'. (WW and MW to IF, January 18, 1836).

She has a 'confused recollection' of the crises in her health. (WW and MW to HCR, March 17 1836). By March she is able to write positively about her health, convinced she is better, although unable to walk unsupported. William sees a calming in her mental state – her mind no longer 'disturbed by fits of violence as it used to be'. (DW, MW, and WW to CW Jr, Late March 1836).

Dorothy is clearly changed in her personality and her thinking, although the changes are neither consistent nor progressive.

At some point in the late spring of 1836 Mary writes to Jane Marshall giving a full picture of Dorothy's state. On the one hand, 'she is perfectly rational – indeed more than that – she is acute, & correct in her judgements – & takes interest in matters independent of herself & read a little'. On the other hand, she has a complete absence of memory 'regarding herself' and her illness. 'She has no consciousness of what she has passed through' to the extent that she keeps forgetting that she can't walk, and can't remember the illness leading up to it at all. Every time she tries to walk and finds she can't, 'the disappointment seems ever new to her.' She seems to think she will be able to walk to Grasmere. Mary describes her awareness of her body's baffling changes as 'personal wonders' – absolutely inexplicable and almost unbelievable to her. She has so far forgotten her illness that she is planning trips abroad, and seems 'as happy & as amiable as possible' doing so. (MW to JM, 1836?)

In May, Mary describes Dorothy as 'like a very <u>clever</u>, <u>tyrannous spoilt</u> Child', qualifying 'for she is acute & discriminating to a marvellous degree'. She switches between 'impatient discomfort' and 'intervals of mildness', during which she is 'overcome by her old affections'. In yet other moods, 'she is very languid & weeps'. She is hyper-emotional, quick to anger, and quick to joy. (MW to Mary Anne Marshall, May 4, 1836).

In June, Mary writes again to Jane Marshall that though her old friend is 'often acute, & as much her own dear self as ever' Dorothy has started to take pleasure in making strange noises, and enjoying the attention:

> in consequence of the noises she makes (the strength of her voice would astonish you) we have been induced to change her <u>sitting-room</u> to the back part of the house – to prevent the sounds reaching the ears of the Tourists & others, who we have lately observed, stand & look up – & it is remarkable in her, that her delight is to attract attention, & whenever she knows (& she finds out every thing) strangers are in the house – or grounds – she is determined to make herself heard. (MW to JM, June 28, 1836).

This determination to make herself heard, and delight in attracting attention, seems alien to the version of Dorothy in her youth – awkward, restless, quiet – which so often dominates.

In July Mary reports to Crabb Robinson that Dorothy is 'at times, & for a *short space* her own acute self, retains the power over her fine judgement & discrimination – then, & at once, relapses into child-like feebleness –& gives vent to some discomfort by merry sallies or with the impatience of a *petted child* contrives one *want* after another, as if merely to provoke contradiction.' She comes and goes from lucidity, from her old familiar self, to what seems to the family a completely different character. They don't think she has 'delusions', but Mary considers her state as 'premature Dotage' – what we might now call dementia.

In September Mary reports again on the 'most strange' nature of Dorothy's 'partially' good memory. She both recites and improvises poetry: 'sometimes she amuses herself by pouring out verses – as by inspiration – in a moment & seemingly without thought she will write down (& in as good a hand as ever she wrote) 6 or 8 very respectable lines'. Though, Mary notes, the lines of poetry, 'generally addressed to her attendants' are not on 'very elevated' subjects. It does not seem to be as simple as her remembering things past and forgetting the present. Her memory for both near and far events seems to waver in and out of focus. She reads the newspapers – though Mary points out 'an old one – read a doz[en] times – pleases equally with a new one.' (MW to HCR, September 28, 1836). In October Crabb Robsinson includes a witty epigram of Coleridge's in a letter, and in return, Mary writes that though they of course all knew it, 'yet is was new to poor [Dorothy's] mind – as many *gone-by* things are–& it made her laugh heartily.' (MW to HCR, November 1, 1836). She understands completely why the rhyme is funny but does not remember that she had found it funny before. Throughout this time, though she is not keeping a journal, she still writes and reads. That September, though, William writes to Catherine Clarkson that Dorothy is a 'wreck [...] both in mind and body' – strong words indeed – though 'she still remembers and thinks of her dear old Friends'. Dorothy has been aware enough to write a note to Catherine, whose only son has just died. It's hard to know exactly what William means when he calls Dorothy a wreck in body and mind, and to measure how much we might infer from our own experiences when we read those words.In December 1838, the task falls back to Mary to write to Jane Marshall to thank her for her gifts to Dorothy, because even though Dorothy talks about writing herself, 'her *intentions* are not to be depended upon'. (WW to JM, December 26, 1838). Mary records how Dorothy jokes in a 'waggish way' about the present, adding, 'this habit of bantering, which now is not unfrequent with her—so different to her character in former days—shews a great change, yet a wonderful acuteness and quickness of mind.' Dorothy's memory is improved, Mary repeats, her 'mind less feeble', but 'for a much longer space we can keep her interested by conversation, tho' her uncomfortable *habits* are still as bad as ever.'

Henry Crabb Robinson visits the family again over Christmas 1840 into January 1841. He writes to his brother that he finds 'Poor Miss W: in an unexpectedly improved state'. He calls her 'mind feeble' but adds that now 'she talks nothing absolutely insane or irrational, but she has so little command of herself that she cannot restrain the most unseemly noises, blowing loudly & making a nondescript sound more shrill than the cry of a partridge & a turkey'. She still finds pleasure in reciting poetry, and remembers it by heart. Crabb Robinson suggests the only way to re-focus her is 'a request to repeat Verses which she does with affecting sweetness', including her own poetry. (HCR to TR, January 12, 1841).

In 1843, when the family receive a copy of Harriet Martineau's memoir of her illness, *Life In The Sick Room*, and read it aloud to each other, Dorothy is left out, ironically, as Edward Quillinan writes, not because she cannot understand, but because she cannot concentrate for long periods of time: she 'could not bear sustained attention to any book, but [...] would be quite capable of appreciating a little at a time.' (EQ to HCR, December 9, 1843).

In some ways, Dorothy's memory and cognitive ability seem to improve over time, rather than degenerate. William's death in 1850 is seen to jolt her out of apathy in some way.

A late letter from Mary to the Hutchinson family in July 1852, when Dorothy is 70, shows her drifting in and out of lucidity within hours. This is, like 'every thing about her most strange':

> she sometimes <u>looks</u> as if she were dying, & then starts
> up looking blither & begins to joke or sing. But last night
> before & at her bedtime, she was as it were quite <u>lost</u> –
> Hannah had to carry her up & down in & out & when
> in bed, she prayed that we might let her <u>go to bed</u>, it was
> all she wanted & when told she <u>was</u> there still pleaded to
> go – & then was as earnest, until after 11 oC to go out of
> doors. (MW to the Hutchinsons, July 18, 1852).

Dorothy continues to be 'a strange case' all this time, as Mary put it in 1838. (MW to Dora, October 3, 1838).

OPIUM USE AND WITHDRAWAL

It has been speculated – as it often is with nineteenth century invalids – that the entirety of Dorothy's illness may have been caused by the side-effects of opium use and by withdrawal.

Opium, as laudanum, was the only painkiller of any effect available to people at this time. Dorothy would have used a locally available 'tincture of opium': a preparation of opium simmered into a syrup with fortified wine, spices, and fruit juice. In her *Grasmere Journals* she notes when she takes it for toothache, headaches or unspecified pain, but it only appears three times over the three years. Laudanum's addictiveness and side-effects were beginning to be understood. As friends of both Samuel Taylor Coleridge, who was addicted to laudanum for much of his adult life, and of Thomas De Quincey, who wrote the first addiction memoir about his experiences with laudanum – *Confessions of an English Opium Eater*, published in 1821 – they well knew the potential pitfalls of the drug. Back in 1808 Dorothy had written to Catherine Clarkson that she was worried news from Coleridge would never be anything but 'one distressing detail of illness after another' if he 'continues the practice of taking Opiates as much as ever.' (DW to CC, February 5, 1808).

The moral panic over opioids is not a twenty-first century invention. Mary calls laudanum Dorothy's 'treacherous support'. By the close of 1835 the family have decided that Dorothy's cognitive problems, and other of her symptoms, may be being exaggerated or even caused by the use of opium.It had 'been thought necessary for her' during her illness, and prescribed regularly since 1833, but in the autumn of 1835 they withdraw the medication based on their doctor's recommendation, as Dorothy's physical health is so much better. (WW to HCR, November 25, 1835).

They call it an 'experiment', and hypothesise that with her improved health, since she does not need the pain relief so much, the laudanum is doing nothing but making her mental health worse. In early November Mary writes to Crabb Robinson that 'this has nearly been effected without bad consequences', and it gives them hope of recovery from her current 'state of childishness'. (MW to HCR, November 1835). But a few weeks later William warns Crabb Robinson that if he comes to stay, as intended, he might find them in a bad way. Her 'present sufferings appear to be, from withdrawing this medicine so severe, that we would rather you were not conscious of them to the extent that would be unavoidable, if you were with us.'

Nevertheless, they 'expect in the course of a fortnight to get rid of it altogether'. They will only stop the experiment if a diarrhoea comes on, as William phrases it. (WW to HCR, November 25, 1835).

What has been hoped is that withdrawing the laudanum will bring Dorothy back to a lucidity of thought that has been missing during her crises. In mid-December William can conclude, now the effects have settled, that the experiment has not had the effect they hoped for on her mental state and memory, though she is able to focus more in the moment: 'The recollection of passing objects is indeed greatly restored – but is more than counterbalanced by increasing irritability, which when her wishes are necessarily opposed amounts to rage & fury.' (WW to HCR, December 16, 1835).

This could suggest the laudanum was masking other cognitive changes; it could be that increased pain inevitably results in increased irritability. At the end of December, Mary once again writes to Dorothy's friend Jane Marshall to thank her for a gift to Dorothy, and to update her on Dorothy's condition. Dorothy has been suffering again from 'a good deal of pain in her bowels'. Whether this is from Dorothy's usual digestive disorder, or from the withdrawal, is hard to say – it could be either, or both.

By this time, Mary admits to not having 'much hope respecting any improvement in her mind'. 'Her memory', she writes, 'is less confused and I think gradually strengthens—but the same childishness governs her—and lately her passions have been *more* ungovernable.' (MW and DW to JM, December 1835).'She fancied herself ill-used', Mary reports, describing how, when Jane's gift was given to Dorothy, 'her countenance glistened' with joy, and she admonished Mary, 'You see, I *have* good friends who care for me, tho' you do not.'

The gift is two chickens and a turkey, and these too, and Dorothy's response to them, are held against her as signs of cognitive change. Dorothy, once so abstemious, is seen here as greedy and selfish. She is utterly delighted by the gift of the meat to eat, and according to Mart declares aloud 'she should eat them every bit herself.' (MW and DW to JM, December 1835).

The cognitive changes Mary describes in this letter – failures of memory, childishness, paranoia, ungovernable passions – are often used as evidence of dementia. But put in the context of 'the experiment', they might shift meaning. It is impossible to know at this distance how many of the symptoms Dorothy was experiencing at this time were side-effects from laudanum, how many were masked by the laudanum, and how many are entirely independent of laudanum and only coincidental. But two things are obvious from the letters. Dorothy is already physically much better before withdrawal – it is the 'wonderful change [...] in her constitution' whilst still taking laudanum that encourages the doctor to try withdrawing it. (MW to HCR, November 1835). This suggests it is not laudanum causing her physical symptoms. As William notes 'the *bodily* improvement had taken place before – or what has been done *could not* have been effected'. (WW to HCR, December 16, 1835). Secondly, withdrawing laudanum has little effect on either Dorothy's physical, emotional or cognitive state.

By the end of the year, Mary can admit this. She starts to hypothesise that Dorothy's changes in temperament were due to withdrawal, but then checks herself, remembering 'before we began to reduce the Opium, she was (except that her memory was then gone) much as she is at present.' (MW and DW to JM, December 1835).

*

To assume the record we have of Dorothy's symptoms is complete and uncensored would be a mistake.

The letters of the Wordsworth family and their friends have been an invaluable resource in piecing together the timeline and the details of Dorothy's illness, though I am very aware when turning to them of two things: when they are not Dorothy's own letters, the reports of her condition are necessarily second hand. They are not her own accounts of her feelings or experiences, although in some key places, they do include notes to the recipient dictated directly by her. William Knight published a selection of the letters of the Wordsworth family to Henry Crabb Robinson in the transactions of the Wordsworth Society. In 1907, he then published a three-volume edition of the family letters. In his introduction he explains that many of the original letters have 'disappeared' since transcriptions were made – they are either irrecoverable or unseen to him – in private collections or entirely lost. In some cases he is working with second-hand transcriptions by the letter's owners. 'It is impossible', he admits, 'to give a full list of those which have been recently seen, read, and transcribed by me; or to state where they are now.' Knight took the same attitude to editing the Wordsworth family letters as he did to Dorothy's journals. He omitted repetitions and things he considered unnewsworthy or 'too minutely domestic'. He regularised punctuation and spelling – lamenting the family's 'arbitrary and casual' attitude to both. What he does not make clear though is that when the content became too personal in his mind, he skipped words, phrases, sentences, and even whole paragraphs. Much of what is skipped in the later letters refers to Dorothy's illness.

In 1927, Edith Morley publishes a collection of letters between the Wordsworth family and Henry Crabb Robinson that seeks to replace what Knight has edited out.

Edith Morley is at pains to point out where her editing style has differed from Knight's. 'There is nothing', she believes, 'in the correspondence that can in any way injure the reputation of the writers, and after so long an internal of time I prefer to give the letters exactly as I find them.' Knight's policy of omitting 'purely personal or family matter, and trivial details' to her mind removed also too many of the original and characteristic elements Knight championed.[121] Like Knight, she finds parts of the letter undecipherable, due to bad handwriting, but unlike Knight, she has retained spelling and punctuation differences, and not truncated openings and closings of letters.

It is in these unredacted letters so carefully transcribed by Edith Morley that I have found many of the telling symptoms that have since disappeared from the record. Importantly, she recognised that whilst some details in the letters might seem of 'no literary bearing', they could have 'interest to specialist investigators in other directions.'[122] It is because of her conscientious work a hundred years ago, and her anticipation of interests beyond her field, that I am able to present the evidence I do.

Different publications of the letters of the Wordsworth family and their friends were censored in different ways. Vital details of Dorothy's symptoms were left out by various people at various times, as either irrelevant, or too awful to share in public. So often, in searching letters for reports of Dorothy's health, I found that authoritative sources will only contain a partial record of the correspondence. I have searched the collected letters, unpublished letters in manuscripts, letters published in the Wordsworth Society Transactions by William Victorian admirers, who removed bodily functions seen as too embarrassing, letters collected and published in the 1920s, and letters collected and transcribed or re-transcribed by contemporary academic projects. All individually give only a fragmentary glimpse into Dorothy's condition at various points. Between edits, and the omission of whole letters, the details of Dorothy's illness became increasingly hazy, and increasingly partial through the twentieth century. It is inevitable that the understanding of the nature of her illness became increasingly hazy and partial too. I'm sure I have missed more vital clues, but I hope I have gathered together some important details that have not been put in sequence before, and could not be understood as a whole disease narrative.

As with any person's symptoms, it is hard to unravel the precise cause of some of Dorothy's problems. It is clear, for example, that she finds it increasingly hard to be up and out of her bedroom as the years pass, but is this because of fatigue, discomfort, pain, cognitive problems which make it difficult to be in company, something else entirely, or a combination of the above? This, I can only guess at, but I can at least lay out the evidence. In these early years of the twenty-first century, it is impossible for us to know what exactly did ail Dorothy in the middle years of the nineteenth century. But we can at least, I hope, learn to take her own words for what she experienced, to believe her testimony, and not to deny the reality of her illness because we do not understand the precise nature or mechanics of it.

CODA

FINDING DOROTHY

August 1842 sketch by John Harden (1772–1842) of
Brathay Hall, depicting Dorothy Wordsworth being
wheeled around the garden at Rydal Mount.

Sinead Morrissey began the final reading of the 2014 *Dorothy Wordsworth Festival of Women's Poetry* with her poem '1801', the opening poem in her 2014 TS Eliot Prize-winning collection *Parallax*. As Morrissey explained, standing at the front of St. Oswald's, Grasmere, that April evening – the church the Wordsworths are buried by and attended and wrote of – the poem is written in the voice of Dorothy Wordsworth as recorded in her famous *Grasmere Journals*. On her recording of the poem on the Poetry Archive website Morrissey describes it as 'inspired by Dorothy Wordsworth's Journals'.[123] At the festival reading, Morrissey was keen to point out that '1801' is not a found poem, calling it instead 'all my own language pretending to be Dorothy Wordsworth's language', adding, of the final image of 'moonlight … like herrings', 'but I have stolen one of her best lines'. Morrissey recounted being 'so blown away by her [Dorothy's] writing that I wanted to *capture her voice*.' What she describes is in effect a poetic ventriloquism of Dorothy: absorbing the voice of her journals, taking it on, or putting it on, to make a new arrangement of words in an old pattern. Morrissey's reading was followed that night by Northumbrian poet Gillian Allnutt, who read her small, beautiful poems, with no Dorothy content within them, before Carol Ann Duffy gave the festival's final reading. Duffy – then UK Poet Laureate and patron of the *Dorothy Wordsworth Festival* – opened her closing set with *her* Dorothy Wordsworth poem: 'Dorothy Wordsworth is dead'. Both Morrisey and Duffy wrote their Dorothy poems after visits to the Wordsworth Trust – a creative campus centred around Dove Cottage – the house where Dorothy wrote her journals, and lived with her brother, and then his growing family, from 1799-1808. Many writers who visit the cottage, officially or unofficially, write about the Wordsworth siblings. A strange kind of elegy, Duffy's Dorothy poem falls into a wider category of Dorothy poems, in which the details seem drawn from a mixture of the tour of the cottage and museum and from received wisdom trickled down through memoirs and biographies, perpetuating those preconceptions about Dorothy Wordsworth's life and character: Dorothy as muse, as toothless aunt, as keen eye, as tireless walker and worker, as undervalued sister to the more-famous poet.

Dorothy's words have found their way into many poet's works. Arthur Quiller-Couch was perhaps right when he predicted that all future poets owe her dues.[124] Dorothy's published journals are collaged amongst other words or rearranged into new forms in poetry collections as varied as Catherine Simmonds' *We Have Heard Ravens* (2008), Dan Beachy-Quick's *This Nest Swift Passerine* (2009), and Sarah Corbett's *A Perfect Mirror* (2018). In the centre of Sina Queyras' 2009 collection *Expressway* is 'Lines Written Many Miles from Grasmere': a fourteen-part poem that occupies ten pages, section V of IX: 'Some Moments from a Land Before the Expressway'. In the notes, Queyras calls this poem 'crafted from the text of Dorothy Wordsworth's *Grasmere Journals*'.[125] The text is entirely found, lineated, but also reordered, re-shaped, and made to mean new things in new arrangements, as well as still encompassing a careful précis of the matter of the journals. Dorothy's abbreviations are kept, so William appears as Wm., and a sense of her own fragmented syntax and juxtaposed images remain in the fragmentary style. The first person to turn Dorothy's journals into poems and publish them was an American poet, Hyman Eigerman. His book *The Poetry of Dorothy Wordsworth: edited from the journals* was published in 1940. The introduction, by Professor Hoxie Neale Fairchild, compares these free verse renderings to the imagist poets of the early twentieth century. Eigerman drew on Knight's editions, so follows his edits, but the spare, free verse poems he made would seem familiar to many readers of later similar projects. Directly and indirectly, Dorothy's words continue to inspire new work, from Sarah Doyle's 2021 poetry pamphlet *Something so wild and new in this feeling*, which collages words from the *Grasmere Journal*, to appearances in Alison Bechdel's 2021 graphic memoir *The Secret to Superhuman Strength*. Bechdel even has a panel in which William is seen pushing Dorothy in a bath chair around the garden at Rydal Mount. Doyle has spoken of her process in making her collage poems from Dorothy's journal:

> Throughout the writing process I remained committed to treating the source text with sympathy, sensitivity, and respect; to treat the journals ethically, and to always bear in mind that these were originally the private journals of another woman.[126]

The poems become a 'hybrid of Dorothy's voice' and her own 'sensibilities'.

Before it occurred to me that I could write this book, I realised I could bring the *Rydal Journals* to new readers by making them into poems, taking her words, and rearranging them to make new meanings. In 2017 I was asked to contribute to a collaboration responding to Dorothy's *Grasmere Journals*, by artist Zoe Benbow, and poet Sarah Corbett. Their exhibition, 'Dorothy's Colour', included landscape painting by Benbow and a sequence of poems in conversation with the *Grasmere Journals*, which became the title sequence of Corbett's *A Perfect Mirror*. For years, I had been talking with my friend and co-conspirator Dr. Emily Stanback – an expert in Romantic Disability Studies – about the possibility of publishing a collaborative transcription of Dorothy's *Rydal Journals*. We believed that access to the full journals would change the narrative around Dorothy's later years, by allowing everyone to see her own words, and not their partial summary. But permissions were complicated. Meanwhile, the *Rydal Journals* still rested in this obscure zone: referred to but not citable, barely accessible even for the few scholars who could travel to Grasmere to see the manuscripts, presupposed to have no merit in themselves.

Creatively I could do what I could not do as an academic. My aim was not to re-make Dorothy's narrative in free verse, as Eigerman had, but to use her words to reveal something about a shared experience of chronic pain and illness. Without knowing it, I was making my own version of her sick-bed consolations. Returning to the *Rydal Journals* I saw again how they reveal the connection between the landscapes within and without. I found repeated parallels between the external weather of the Lake District, and the internal weather of the body in pain. This connection between external and internal weather gave me the basis for the long poem 'Dorothy's Rain', first written for the launch of Benbow and Corbett's exhibition, which gathers every reference to rain made in her Lakes-based journaling from 1824 to 1833. The accumulation and persistence of rain reflects the accumulation and persistence of pain: the repetition and the length encapsulate the repetitive nature of chronic illness.

I was attracted by the same things every poet has been who has used Dorothy's words – the sparse beauty of her phrasing; her particular way of seeing things. My findings in Dorothy's late journals became a way to connect experiences, to link parallel bodily experience in the same place, in different times. To find a language for pain and articulation of the body through the repurposing of the words of another. Petra Kuppers has written of how 'in multiple ways, pain disrupts the clear boundaries of self and language, truth and embodiment, as the history of poetic practices by people in pain shows.'[127] By combining Dorothy's language with my structure, I wanted to embody in the text something of this disruption. I also hoped I could begin to start a different conversation about Dorothy and disability: one focused more on Dorothy's findings than her loss.

The *Rydal Journals* show a different side to Dorothy as an individual, beyond her role as a co-partner in the Wordsworthian Life. They show Dorothy in pain, Dorothy in doubt, a Dorothy who is often frustrated, confined, explicit about the failings of the body. They also show the same keen eye that has been lauded in her early journals, turned not just on the world around her, but on the world inside. I hope this book can be the beginning of many more conversations, and many more findings.

DOROTHY WORDSWORTH:
A LIFE IN A TIMELINE

1771 Dorothy Born, December 25, Cockermouth, Cumbria, third child of Ann Cookson and John Wordsworth.

1778   Ann (Dorothy's Mother) dies March 8, at the age of thirty. Dorothy, aged only six, is taken to live with Ann's cousin Elizabeth Threlkeld in Halifax, Yorkshire. Dorothy befriends Jane Pollard.

1781 Dorothy sent to a boarding school at Hipperholme, near Halifax.

1783 John Wordsworth, Dorothy's Father, dies December 30. Dorothy is twelve.

1784 Dorothy is transferred to a day-school in Halifax, with her dear friend Jane Pollard.

1787 In May, Dorothy is sent to live in Penrith with her Mother's parents, above their draper's shop. Here she befriends Mary and Peggy Hutchinson. Reunited with her brothers in the school holidays. In December, Grandfather Cookson dies.

1788 In October Dorothy's uncle William Cookson marries Dorothy Cowper. Dorothy moves with them to their rectory in Forncett, Norfolk.

1789 Dorothy runs a Sunday school teaching nine younger girls, and plans a School of Industry for girls. William Wilberforce visits Forncett. Revolution in France.

1790 William goes on a walking tour of France, Switzerland, and Germany with his friend Robert Jones and writes long letters to Dorothy.

1791 William returns to France; meets Annette Vallon.

1792 William's daughter with Annette Vallon, Caroline, is born. Dorothy spends three months (August-November) living in Windsor where her Uncle Cookson has become the Canon.

1793 France declares war against Britain, and William is unable to return to Annette and Caroline. He does not see his daughter until she is nine years old.

1794 Dorothy visits Aunt Threlkeld – now married and Aunt Rawson – in Halifax in February. Reunited with William and together they visit the Lake District, walking through Grasmere, to stay at William's friends Raisley and William Calvert's house, Windy Brow, in Keswick. They live cheaply, and get a sense that they could live in this way permanently. Dorothy tours around family members and friends in Cumbria, then visits Newcastle in April.

1795 Raisley Calvert dies in January, leaving £900 to William, with a stipulation that some must be set aside for Dorothy. Dorothy visits Mary and Peggy Hutchinson, now living at their brother Tom's farm at Sockburn, and goes on to visit Aunt Rawnson (Threlkeld) in Halifax, attending Jane Pollard's wedding to John Marshall. In September, Dorothy and William move to Racedown Lodge in Dorset, where they take on the care of Basil Montagu, aged three.

1796 Peggy Hutchinson dies and Mary travels down to stay with Dorothy and William at Racedown Lodge from November until June 1797.

1797 Dorothy and William meet Coleridge and his wife, Charles Lamb, and other people who will be important to them throughout their lives. They move to Alfoxden House in Somerset, close to Coleridge's cottage in Nether Stowey.

1798 In January Dorothy begins her journal, only keeping records until May before breaking off until 1800. In July Dorothy and William walk through the Wye valley, visiting Tintern, inspiring William's poem. In the autumn the first editions of *Lyrical Ballads* are published. Dorothy, William and Coleridge travel to Germany. The Wordsworths' budget is very limited.

1799 In February Dorothy and William leave Goslar after a freezing winter to stay with the Hutchinsons in Sockburn. In December, she and William walk to their new home in Grasmere.

1800 Dorothy and William's younger brother John joins them in Grasmere from January. In May, Dorothy restarts her journal. The Coleridges visit in Grasmere then move to Greta Hall in Keswick in July. Dorothy becomes close with Catherine and Thomas Clarkson whilst they are living nearby.

1802 Peace of Amiens. In August, Dorothy and William travel to Calais to see Annette Vallon and Caroline (now 9). They bathe in the sea. William writes sonnets. In September they visit Basil Montagu and Charles and Mary Lamb, who becomes a firm friend to Dorothy. October 4, William is married to Mary Hutchinson in Gallow Hill, Yorkshire. Dorothy is too ill to attend the ceremony. Sara Coleridge born in December at Greta Hall.

1803 January 16 is the last entry in Dorothy's *Grasmere Journal*. William and Mary's first child, John Wordsworth, is born

June 18. Dorothy, William and Coleridge go on tour of Scotland. England and France at war again. Robert Southey and his family join the Coleridges at Greta Hall, taking over the tenancy in 1804.

1804 William and Mary's second child Dora (Dorothy) Wordsworth born August 16. Dorothy and William take a short tour around the Duddon Valley in the autumn.

1805 John Wordsworth dies as sea, February 5. In July, Aunt Rawson visits Grasmere.

Richard Wordsworth buys Dorothy a pony 'for her health', and Dorothy and William have a week's pony-tour in Ullswater in November. Dorothy's journal of this is revised into part of William's 1822 *Guide to the Lakes*.

1806 The Wordsworth family stay at Coleorton for eight months at Lord and Lady Beaumont's invitation. William and Mary's third child Thomas Wordsworth born June 15. Catherine and Thomas Clarkson move to Bury St. Edmund's for the sake of Catherine's health. She becomes one of Dorothy's most treasured correspondents.

1807 In March, the Act for the Abolition of the Slave Trade is passed in parliament. April-May Dorothy stays at Coleorton, looking after the children whilst William and Mary travel. They return to Grasmere. Thomas De Quincey calls at Dove Cottage – his third attempt after backing out twice – and finally meets the Wordsworths.

1808 Green children of Grasmere orphaned in March after their parents are lost in a blizzard. Dorothy writes their story to raise funds for the children. In May, the Wordsworth family move to Allan Bank, a much larger newbuild at the other end of Grasmere. William and Mary's fourth child Catherine Wordsworth born September 6. De

Quincey stays at Allan Bank from November – February 1809.

1809 Dorothy prepares Dove Cottage for De Quincey to move in, which he does in October.

1810 William and Mary's fifth child Willy (William) Wordsworth born May 12. The Wordsworths' friendship with Coleridge under strain. In July, Dorothy and William stay with Lord and Lady Beaumont at the new Coleorton Hall. Dorothy visits Catherine Clarkson in Bury St. Edmunds, via Cambridge; Charles and Mary Lamb in London, accompanied by Henry Crabb Robinson, and her Uncle William Cookson. In October, the Dorothy and the children move temporarily to John Wilson's house in Windermere to avoid an outbreak of Scarlet Fever in Grasmere.

1811 The Wordsworth family move from Allan Bank to the Old Rectory in Grasmere.

1812 Catherine Wordsworth dies June 4. William and Mary are both away, and Dorothy has to arrange the funeral. Dorothy visits Aunt Rawson and Jane Marshall in July. Thomas Wordsworth dies December 1.

1813 William appointed to Distributor of Stamps for Westmorland. In May, the Wordsworth family move to Rydal Mount, a few miles South of Grasmere, so that Mary does not have to see the graves of her children daily.

1814 Dorothy stays with Mary Barker in Keswick for three months, helping to nurse Basil Montagu. In the autumn, Dorothy accompanies Sara Hutchinson to Radnorshire to stay with her brother Tom. In France, Caroline's wedding is postponed in the hope Aunt Dorothy will be able to travel to France to attend, but war makes it impossible.

1815 William's poems include three 'By My Sister'.

1816 Caroline marries Jean Baptiste Baudouin, February 28. None of the Wordsworth family are able to be there. Her daughter, born December, is named Louise Dorothée. Dorothy visits Aunt Rawnson in Halifax. Richard Wordsworth, Dorothy and William's brother, dies.

1818 Climbs Scafell Pike with Mary Barker. Keats calls at Rydal Mount, finds no one at home.

1820 Visits dentist in London whilst staying with her brother Christopher – remainder of her teeth removed, and false teeth fitted. Otherwise well enough to tour the Continent from July-November with William and Mary, Mary's cousin Thomas Monkhouse and his new wife, and joined by Crabb Robinson en route. In September they stay in Paris to see Annette, Caroline and Caroline's two children. Before sailing home, they stay with Mary Barker at her new home in Boulogne. Back in England, they visit their brother Christopher in Cambridge in November, and Dorothy spends December with the Clarksons at their home near Ipswich.

1821 Edward Quillinan and his wife Jemima move to Rydal. Dorothy and Mary nurse Jemima Quillinan after the birth of her second daughter, Rotha. William is made her Godfather. De Quincey publishes his *Confessions of An English Opium Eater*, with evocative descriptions of Dove Cottage, and his response to Catherine Wordsworth's death.

1822 Jemima Quillinan is badly burnt after her dressing gown catches fire. Dorothy, left alone at Rydal Mount, nurses her, and arranges her funeral. William writes an epigraph. Jemima is buried in St. Oswald's, Grasmere. Her pet canary goldfinch, which dies shortly after her, is buried with her. In the autumn, Dorothy and Joanna Hutchinson make a tour of Scotland.

1823 Dorothy visits Edinburgh.

1824 Dorothy visits friends and family in London, Oxford and Cambridge, followed by a stay with the Clarksons. She begins to keep a journal again, which she continues, on and off, until 1835.

1826 From February-September Dorothy and Joanna Hutchinson stay with Tom Hutchinson and his family at their farm in Herefordshire. From this base, she visits Gwerndovennant, Manchester, Leamington, the Wye Valley and Worcester. Before returning home, Dorothy spends October in Coleorton.

1827 From June-September Dorothy stays with Aunt Rawson in Halifax.

1828 In the summer Dorothy visits the Isle of Man with Joanna Hutchinson and her brother Henry. Visits Maria Jane Jewsbury in Manchester. In November, she travels to Leicestershire to prepare John Wordsworth's new home in Whitwick.

1829 Dorothy becomes serious unwell during her extended visit to Whitwick. Mary Wordsworth travels there to nurse her. Dorothy returns home in September via Aunt Rawson in Halifax and is taken ill again.

1830 Dorothy continues to recuperate at home. Felicia Hemans visits Rydal Mount. In October John Wordsworth, now living in Moresby, near Whitehaven, marries Isabella Curwen.

1831 In September Dorothy stays briefly with the Curwen family at their house on Belle Isle, in Windermere. Illness worsens in December, and Mr. Carr tells the family she is likely to die.

1832 Dorothy begins her collection of poems as 'sick-bed consolations'. Dorothy begins to take laudanum daily in an attempt to manage her pain.

1833 In January Dorothy has another acute episode, and it seems certain she will not survive. By September she has recovered enough to sit for a portrait by Samuel Crossthwaite.

1834 Coleridge dies in July, and Charles Lamb in December.

1835 Acute crisis in May-June, which leaves Dorothy with cognitive changes. Sara Hutchinson dies. Withdrawal from laudanum use in November. Last entry in journal in November.

1836 Dorothy's health stabilises, and remains much the same for the rest of her life.

1841 Dora and Edward Quillinan are married in Bath. Dorothy cannot travel to attend the wedding.

1847 Dora dies in July.

1850 William dies in April.

1853 Dorothy writes her last recorded letter, to her sister-in-law, Mary.

1855 Dorothy dies, aged 84, on January 25.

NOTES

1   Ernest De Sélincourt, *Dorothy Wordsworth* (Oxford: Clarendom, 1933), pp.393–94.

2   Helen Darbishire, 'Introduction' in *The Journals of Dorothy Wordsworth* (London: Oxford University Press, 1958), p.xvii.

3   Francis Wilson, *The Ballad of Dorothy Wordsworth* (London: Faber and Faber, 2021), p.14.

4   Wilson, p.231.

5   Wilson, p.232.

6   Carl Ketcham, 'Dorothy Wordsworth's Journals, 1824-1835', Notes and Partial Transcript, The Wordsworth Trust, Grasmere (1978?), p.49.

7   Millicent Fawcett, *Some Eminent Woman of Our Time* (London: MacMillan and Co., 1889), p.184.

8   Ketcham, p.50.

9   Catherine MacDonald Maclean, *Dorothy and William Wordsworth* (Cambridge: CUP, 1927) p.25.

10 Iris Gibson, 'Illness of Dorothy Wordsworth', *British Medical Journal* 285, 18-25 (December 1982), p.1813.

11 Thomas De Quincey, 'William Wordsworth', *Tait's*, 1839. These early parts of De Quincey's series of Lake Reminiscences now appear in vol. 11 of *The Works of Thomas De Quincey.*

12 Pamela Woof, *Dorothy Wordsworth: Wonders of the Everyday* (Grasmere: Wordsworth Trust, 2013), p.xvi.

13 Wilson, p.7.

14 Michael Blastland, George Davey Smith and Marcus Munafò, 'Covid-19's known unknowns', *BMJ* (2020); 371.

15 Stephen Gill, *Wordsworth and the Victorians* (Oxford: Clarendon Press, 1998), p.3.

16 Edmund Lee, *Dorothy Wordsworth: The Story of a Sister's Love* (London: James Clarke & Co, 1886), p.ix.

17 Lee, *Dorothy Wordsworth*, p.227.

18 Lee, *Dorothy Wordsworth*, p.ix.

19 Lee, *Dorothy Wordsworth*, p.16.

20 Lee, *Dorothy Wordsworth*, p.17.

21 Lee, *Dorothy Wordsworth*, p.19.

22 Lee, *Dorothy Wordsworth*, p.17.

23 Lee, *Dorothy Wordsworth*, pp.67–68.

24 Lee, *Dorothy Wordsworth*, p.77.

25 Lee, *Dorothy Wordsworth*, p.20.

26 Lee, *Dorothy Wordsworth*, p.26.

27 Lee, *Dorothy Wordsworth*, p.61.

28 Lee, *Dorothy Wordsworth*, p.61.

29 Lee, *Dorothy Wordsworth*, pp.70–71.

30 Lee, *Dorothy Wordsworth*, p.71.

31 Lee, *Dorothy Wordsworth*, p.231.

32 Lee, *Dorothy Wordsworth*, p.213.

33 Lee, *Dorothy Wordsworth*, p.217.

34 Lee, *Dorothy Wordsworth*, p.192.

35 Lee, *Dorothy Wordsworth*, p.193.

36 Stopford A. Brooke, *Dove Cottage: Wordsworth's Home from 1800-1808* (London: Macmillan and Co., 1890), p.19.

37 Brooke, p.19.

38 Brooke, *Dove Cottage: Wordsworth's Home from 1800-1808* (London: Macmillan and Co., 1890), p.15.

39 *Edmund Lee, Some Noble Sisters* (London: James Clarke & Co., 1892), p.167.

40 Lee, *Dorothy Wordsworth*, frontispiece.

41 Lee, *Some Noble Sisters*, p.xi.

42 Brooke, p.9.

43 Brooke, p.5–6.

44 Brooke, pp.47–48.

45 Brooke, pp.28–29.

46 Brooke, p.52.

47 Christopher Wordsworth, *Memoirs of William Wordsworth, 2 vols* (London: Edward Moxon, 1851), p.90.

48 Edith Coleridge, *Memoir and Letters of Sara Coleridge* (London: Henry S. King & Co., 1875), p.50.

49 Harriet Martineau, 'Lights of the English Lake District', *Atlantic*

Monthly, 7 (1861), pp.541-58, p.545.

50 Martineau, p.545.

51 Martineau, p.557.

52 Martineau, p.557.

53 Edith J. Morley (ed), *The Correspondence of Henry Crabb Robinson with the Wordsworth Circle, 1808-1866* (Oxford: The Clarendon Press, 1927), p.3.

54 Mary E. Burton, *The Letters of Mary Wordsworth, 1800-1855* (Oxford: The Clarendon Press, 1958), p.xxix.

55 Burton, p.xxix.

56 Margaret Oliphant, 'William Wordsworth', *Blackwood's Magazine*, (1871), p.307.

57 Oliphant, p.308.

58 Oliphant, p.308.

59 Oliphant, p.308.

60 John Campbell Shairp (ed), *Recollections of a Tour Made in Scotland* (New York: G.P. Putnam's, 1874), p.xxx.

61 Shairp, p.xxx.

62 Millicent Fawcett, *Some Eminent Woman of Our Time* (London: MacMillan and Co., 1889), p.176.

63 Fawcett, p.179.

64 Fawcett, p.184.

65 Maurice Hewlett, 'The Other Dorothy', *Last Essays of Maurice Hewlett* (London: William Heinemann, 1924), p.228.

66 Arthur Quiller-Couch, 'Dorothy Wordsworth. II', *Studies in Literature, Third Series* (Cambridge: Cambridge University Press, 1933), p.91.

67 Virginia Woolf, *The Common Reader Second Series*, (London: The Hogarth Press, 1935), pp.164–65.

68 William Knight, *Journals of Dorothy Wordsworth,* 2 vols (London: Macmillan and Co, 1904), I, p.viii.

69 Knight, *Dorothy Wordsworth*, I, p.viii.

70 William Knight, *Letters of the Wordsworth Family, 1787–1855,* 3 vols (Boston and London: Ginn and Co.,1907), I, p.x.

71 Gordon Graham Wordsworth, Extracts from *The Journals of*

Dorothy Wordsworth 1831–1833, Dove Cottage Manuscripts DCMS 118.

72 Knight, *Dorothy Wordsworth*, I, p.xii.

73 Lee, *Dorothy Wordsworth*, pp.21-22.

74 Catherine MacDonald Maclean, *Dorothy and William Wordsworth* (Cambridge: CUP, 1927), p.22.

75 Martineau, 'Lights of the English Lake District', *Atlantic Monthly* 7 (1861), pp.541-58.

76 Tilar J. Mazzeo, *Plagiarism and Literary Property in the Romantic Period* (Philadelphia: University of Pennsylvania Press, 2007), p.69.

77 Kathryn Aalto in *Women on Nature* ed. by Katharine Norbury (London: Unbound, 2021), p.14.

78 Nicola Healey, *Dorothy Wordsworth and Hartley Coleridge: The Poetics of Relationship* (London: Palgrave Macmillan, 2012), p.172.

79 Elizabeth A. Fay, *Becoming Wordsworthian: A Performative Aesthetic* (Amherst: University of Massachusetts Press, 1995), p.7.

80 Healey, p.170.

81 Fay, p.2.

82 Fay, p.16.

83 Fay, p.26.

84 Anne Wallace, "Inhabited Solitudes': Dorothy Wordsworth's Domesticating Walkers', *Nordlit*, 1 (University of Tromso, 1997), pp.99–126.

85 Healey, p.176.

86 Healey, p.177.

87 Jack Stillinger, *Multiple Authorship and the Myth of Solitary Genius* (Oxford: Oxford University Press, 1991) p.71; Healey, p.176.

88 Healey, p.176.

89 Healey, p.167.

90 Lucy Newlyn, *All in Each Other* (Oxford: Oxford University Press, 2013) p.11.

91 Newlyn, p.62.

92 Newlyn, p.44.

93 Oliphant, p.315.

94 William Wordsworth, 'Home at Grasmere', *Home at Grasmere, Part First, Book First, of The Recluse, by William Wordsworth,* ed. by Beth Darlington, MSB, l.874, l.866.

95 Alethea Hayter, *The Wreck of the Abergavenny: The Wordsworths and Catastrophe* (London: Pan Macmillan, 2003).

96 William Wordsworth, 'When first I Journey'd Hither', in *Poems, in Two Volumes, and Other Poems, 1800-1807, by William Wordsworth,* ed. by Jared Curtis, (Ithaca: Cornell University Press, 1983), l.36-8.

97 'When first I Journey'd Hither', l.82.

98 'When first I Journey'd Hither', l.88.

99 'When first I Journey'd Hither', l.9-10.

100 Samuel Taylor Coleridge, 8 April 1805, *The Notebooks of Samuel Taylor Coleridge,* ed. by Kathleen Coburn, 4 vols (London: Routledge, 1957-1990), II (1962), p.2529.

101 Anne D. Wallace, 'Home at Grasmere again: Revising the family in Dove Cottage', in *Literary Couplings: Writing Couples, Collaborators, and the Construction of Authorship*, ed. by Marjorie Stone and Judith Thompson (Madison: University of Wisconsin Press, 2006), pp.103-123, p.106.

102 William Wordsworth, *The Fenwick Notes of William Wordsworth,* ed. by Jared Curtis (London: Bristol Classical Press, 1993), p.32.

103 Morley, p.5.

104 Sylvia Plath, *The Journals of Sylvia Plath*, ed. by Frances McCullough (New York: Anchor, 1998) p.23.

105 Ellen Samuels, 'Six Ways of Looking at Crip Time', *Disability Studies Quarterly,* Vol. 37, no. 3 (2017), n.p.

106 Julia Wedgwood, *The Personal Life of Josiah Wedgwood The Potter By His Great-Granddaughter, The Late Julia Wedgwood*, (London: Macmillan & co., 1915), p.332.

107 John Price, 'Dorothy Wordsworth's Mental Illness', *Journal of the Royal Society of Medicine*, Vol. 91 (1998), pp.390-393, p.390.

108 Price, p.390.

109 Mary Moorman, 'Introduction', *Journals of Dorothy Wordsworth* (Oxford: Oxford University Press, 1971), p.xix.

110 Ketcham, pp.26-27.

111 Robert Gittings and Jo Manton, *Dorothy Wordsworth* (Oxford: Oxford University Press, 1985), p.258.

112 Gittings and Manton, pp.282-3.

113 Pamela Woof, *Dorothy Wordsworth, Writer* (Grasmere: The Wordsworth Trust, 1988), p.14.

114 See note to *Wordsworth's Letters* no. 2126 (WW to Isabella Fenwick, January 2, 1850) detailing Mrs. Arnold's 1849 visit to Rydal Mount as recounted to Lady Richardson.

115 Lucy Newlyn, 'Heaney, the Wordsworths, and wonders of the everyday', *OUPBlog* (September 16, 2013), https://blog.oup.com/2013/09/heaney-dorothy-william-wordsworth/

116 Susan M Levin, *Dorothy Wordsworth and Romanticism*, (New Brunswick and London: Rutgers, State University, 1987), p.64.

117 Gibson, p.1813.

118 Mark Weatherall, 'Writing Patients' Histories', *Brain*, Volume 136, Issue 9 (September 2013), pp.2918–2921, p.2918.

119 Alicia Wright, 'On Writing About Dorothy Wordsworth's The Grasmere Journal', *Avidly* (May 8 2020), http://avidly.lareviewofbooks.org/2020/05/08/on-writing-about-dorothy-wordsworths-the-grasmere-journal/

120 Carol Ann Duffy, *The Bees* (London: Picador, 2011), p.14–15.

121 Morley, p.vii.

122 Morley, p.ix.

123 Sinead Morrissey, '1801', *Parallax* (Manchester: Carcanet, 2013), http://www.poetryarchive.org/poem/1801/

124 Arthur Quiller-Couch, 'Dorothy Wordsworth. II', *Studies in Literature, Third Series* (Cambridge, Cambridge University Press, 1933) p.91.

125 Sina Queyras, *Expressway* (Toronto: Coach House Books, 2009), p.101.

126 Sarah Doyle, 'Introduction to poems read out during online launch', *Something so wild and new in this feeling* (Droitwich: V. Press, 2021).

127 Petra Kuppers, 'Poetry-ing: Feminist Disability Aesthetics and Poetry Communities', *English Language Notes* 49.2 (2011), pp.73-82, p.75.

BIBLIOGRAPHY

Aalto, Kathryn, *Writing Wild: Women Poets, Ramblers, and Mavericks Who Shape How We See the Natural World* (Portland: Timber Press, 2020)

Beachy-Quick, Dan, *This Nest, Swift Passerine* (North Adams, MA: Tupelo, 2009)

Bechdel, Alison, *The Secret To Superhuman Strength* (Boston: Houghton Mifflin Harcourt, 2021)

Bertucci, Paula, 'Shocking Subjects: Human Experiments and the Material Culture of Medical Electricity in Eighteenth-Century England' in *The Uses of Humans in Experiment: Perspectives from the 17th to the 20th Century*, ed. by Erika Dyck and Larry Stewart (Leiden: Brill Rodopi, 2016)

Bradshaw, Michael (ed), *Disabling Romanticism* (London: Palgrave, 2016)

Brooke, Stopford A., *Dove Cottage: Wordsworth's Home from 1800-1808* (London: Macmillan and Co., 1890)

Burton, Mary E. (ed), *The Letters of Mary Wordsworth, 1800-1855* (Oxford: The Clarendon Press, 1958)

Coburn, Kathleen (ed), *The Letters of Sara Hutchinson, 1800-1835* (London: Routledge and Kegan Paul, 1954)

— *The Notebooks of Samuel Taylor Coleridge,* 4 vols (London: Routledge, 1957-1990), II (1962)

Coleridge, Edith, *Memoir and Letters of Sara Coleridge* (London: Henry S. King & Co., 1875)

Coleridge, Samuel Taylor, *Collected Letters of Samuel Taylor Coleridge, Volume I, 1785-1800*, ed. by Earl Leslie Griggs (Oxford: Oxford University Press, 1956)

— *Collected Letters of Samuel Taylor Coleridge, Volume VI*, 1826-1834, ed. by Earl Leslie Griggs (Oxford: Oxford University Press, 1971)

Corbett, Sarah, *A Perfect Mirror* (Liverpool: Pavillion Poetry, 2018)

Curtis, Jared (ed), *The Fenwick Notes of William Wordsworth* (London: Bristol Classical Press, 1993)

Darbishire, Helen (ed), *The Journals of Dorothy Wordsworth* (London: Oxford University Press, 1958)

De Sélincourt, Ernest, *Dorothy Wordsworth* (Oxford: Clarendom, 1933)

— *The Letters of William and Dorothy Wordsworth: Volume I. The Early Years 1787-1805*, 2nd edn, rev. by Chester L. Shaver (Oxford: Clarendon Press, 1967)

— *The Letters of William and Dorothy Wordsworth: Volume II. The Middle Years: Part 1. 1806-1811,* 2nd edn. rev. by Mary Moorman (Oxford: Clarendon Press, 1969)

— *The Letters of William and Dorothy Wordsworth: Volume III. The Middle Years: Part 2. 1812-1820,* 2nd edn, rev. by Mary Moorman and Alan G. Hill (Oxford: Clarendon Press, 1969)

— *The Letters of William and Dorothy Wordsworth: Volume IV. The Later Years: Part 1. 1821-1828,* 2nd edn, rev. by Alan G. Hill (Oxford: Oxford University Press, 2000)

— *The Letters of William and Dorothy Wordsworth: Volume V. The Later Years: Part 2. 1829-1834,* 2nd edn, rev. by Alan G. Hill (Oxford: Oxford University Press, 2000)

— *The Letters of William and Dorothy Wordsworth: Volume VI. The Later Years: Part 3. 1835-1839,* 2nd edn, rev. by Alan G. Hill (Oxford: Oxford University Press, 2000)

— *The Letters of William and Dorothy Wordsworth: Volume VII. The Later Years: Part 4. 1840-1853,* 2nd edn, rev. by Alan G. Hill (Oxford: Oxford University Press, 2000)

De Quincey, Thomas, *The Works of Thomas De Quincey*, ed. by Grevel Lindop and others, 21 vols (London: Pickering & Chatto, 2000–3)

Doyle, Sarah, *Something so wild and new in this feeling* (Droitwich: V. Press, 2021)

Duffy, Carol Ann, *The Bees* (London: Picador, 2011)

Fay, Elizabeth A., *Becoming Wordsworthian: A Performative Aesthetic* (Amherst: University of Massachusetts Press, 1995)

Eigerman, Hyman, *The Poetry of Dorothy Wordsworth* (New York: Columbia University Press, 1940)

Fawcett, Millicent, *Some Eminent Woman of Our Time* (London: MacMillan and Co., 1889)

Gill, Stephen, *Wordsworth and the Victorians* (Oxford: Clarendon Press, 1998)

Gittings, Robert and Jo Manton, *Dorothy Wordsworth* (Oxford: Oxford University Press, 1988)

Gibson, Iris I.J.M., 'Illness of Dorothy Wordsworth, *British Medical Journal*, 285, 18-25 December 1982

Hayter, Alethea, *The Wreck of the Abergavenny: The Wordsworths and Catastrophe* (London: Pan Macmillan, 2003)

Healey, Nicola, *Dorothy Wordsworth and Hartley Coleridge: The Poetics of Relationship* (London: Palgrave Macmillan, 2012)

Hewlett, Maurice, 'The Other Dorothy', *Last Essays of Maurice Hewlett* (London: William Heinemann, 1924)

Hill, Alan G. (ed), *The Letters of William and Dorothy Wordsworth: Volume VIII: A Supplement of New Letters* (Oxford: Oxford University Press, 2000)

Jones, Kathleen, *A Passionate Sisterhood: Women of the Wordsworth Circle* (London: Constable, 2000)

Ketcham, Carl H., 'Dorothy Wordsworth's Journals, 1824-1835', *The Wordsworth Circle*, Winter 1978

— 'Dorothy Wordsworth's Journals, 1824-1835', Notes and Partial Transcript, The Wordsworth Trust, Grasmere (1978)

Knight, William (ed), *Journals of Dorothy Wordsworth*, 2 vols (London: Macmillan and Co, 1904)

— *Wordsworthiana: A Selection of Papers read to the Wordsworth Society* (London: Macmillan, 1889)

— *Letters of the Wordsworth Family, 1787–1855*, 3 vols, (Boston and London: Ginn and Co., 1907)

Kuppers, Petra, 'Poetry-ing: Feminist Disability Aesthetics and Poetry Communities', *English Language Notes 49.2* (2011)

Lee, Edmund, *Dorothy Wordsworth: The Story of a Sister's Love* (London: James Clarke & Co., 1886, 2nd edtn. 1894)

— *Some Noble Sisters* (London: James Clarke & Co., 1892)

Levin, Susan M., *Dorothy Wordsworth and Romanticism* (New Brunswick and London: Rutgers, State University, 1987)

— (ed), *Dorothy Wordsworth: A Longman Cultural Edition* (New York, San Francisco, Boston, London: Pearson Longman, 2009)

Levy, Michelle, 'Bookmaking and Archiving in Dorothy Wordsworth's Notebooks', in *After Print: Eighteenth-Century Manuscript Cultures*, ed. by Rachael Scarborough King (Charlottesville: University of Virginia Press, 2020)

Maclean, Catherine MacDonald, *Dorothy and William Wordsworth* (Cambridge: CUP, 1927)

Martineau, Harriet, 'Lights of the English Lake District', *Atlantic Monthly*, 7 (1861), 541-58

Mazzeo, Tilar J., *Plagiarism and Literary Property in the Romantic Period* (Philadelphia: University of Pennsylvania Press, 2007)

Moorman, Mary (ed), *Journals of Dorothy Wordsworth* (Oxford: Oxford University Press, 1971)

Morley, Edith J. (ed), *The Correspondence of Henry Crabb Robinson with the Wordsworth Circle, 1808-1866* (Oxford: The Clarendon Press, 1927)

Morrissey, Sinead, *Parallax* (Manchester: Carcanet, 2013)

Newlyn, Lucy, *All in Each Other* (Oxford: Oxford University Press, 2013)

Norbury, Katharine (ed), *Women on Nature* (London: Unbound, 2021)

Oliphant, Margaret, 'William Wordsworth', *Blackwood's Magazine*, 1871.

Plath, Sylvia, *The Journals of Sylvia Plath*, ed. by Frances McCullough (New York: Anchor, 1998)

Price, John, 'Dorothy Wordsworth's Mental Illness', *Journal of the Royal Society of Medicine*, Vol. 91 (July 1998), 390-393.

Queyras, Sina, *Expressway* (Toronto: Coach House Books, 2009)

Quiller-Couch, Arthur, 'Dorothy Wordsworth. II', *Studies in Literature, Third Series* (Cambridge: Cambridge University Press, 1933).

Samuels, Ellen, 'Six Ways of Looking at Crip Time', *Disability Studies*

Quarterly, Vol. 37, no. 3 (2017)

Shairp, John Campbell, 'Wordsworth: The Man and Poet', *The North British Review*, 41 (Edinburgh: Edmonston and Douglas, 1864), 1-54.

Shapiro, Laura, *What She Ate: Six Remarkable Women and the Food That Tells Their Stories* (London: 4th Estate, 2018)

Simmonds, Catherine, *We Have Heard Ravens* (Milbourne: Flagon, 2008).

Stanback, Emily B., *The Wordsworth-Coleridge Circle and the Aesthetics of Disability* (London: Palgrave, 2016)

Stillinger, Jack, *Multiple Authorship and the Myth of Solitary Genius* (Oxford: Oxford University Press, 1991)

Utell, Janine, 'View from the Sickroom: Virginia Woolf, Dorothy Wordsworth, and Writing Women's Lives of Illness', *Life Writing*, vol. 13 (2016), 27–45.

Wallace, Anne D.,"Inhabited Solitudes': Dorothy Wordsworth's Domesticating Walkers', *Nordlit*, 1 (University of Tromso, 1997), <http://www.hum.uit.no/nordlit/1/wallace.html>

— 'Home at Grasmere again: revising the family in Dove Cottage', in *Literary Couplings: Writing Couples, Collaborators, and the Construction of Authorship*, ed by Marjorie Stone and Judith Thompson (Madison: University of Wisconsin Press, 2006), pp.103-123.

Weatherall, Mark, 'Writing Patients' Histories', *Brain*, Volume 136, Issue 9 (2013)

Wedgwood, Julia, *The Personal Life of Josiah Wedgwood The Potter By His Great-Granddaughter, The Late Julia Wedgwood*, (London: Macmillan & co., 1915)

Wilson, Frances, *The Ballad of Dorothy Wordsworth* (London: Faber and Faber, 2008, 2021)

Whelan, Timothy (ed), *The Letters of Henry Crabb Robinson*, (2013) <https://www.qmul.ac.uk/sed/religionandliterature/online-publications/crabb-robinson-letters/>

Woof, Pamela, *Dorothy Wordsworth, Writer* (Grasmere: The Wordsworth Trust, 1988)

— (ed) *The Grasmere and Alfoxden Journals* (Oxford: Oxford University Press, 2002)

— *Dorothy Wordsworth: Wonders of the Everyday* (Grasmere: Wordsworth Trust, 2013)

— 'Dorothy Wordsworth, Writer: The Middle Years', *The Wordsworth Circle,* Vol. 45, No. 1, Winter 2014

— 'Dorothy Wordsworth and Old Age', *The Wordsworth Circle*, Vol. 46, No. 3, June 2015

Woolf, Virginia, *The Common Reader Second Series*, (London: The Hogarth Press, 1935)

Wordsworth, Christopher, *Memoirs of William Wordsworth*, 2 vols., (London: Edward Moxon, 1851)

Wordsworth, Dorothy, *DCMS 104, DCMS 118, DCMS 120,* Grasmere, The Wordsworth Trust Collections

— *Recollections of a Tour Made in Scotland* ed. by John Campbell Shairp (New York: G.P. Putnam's, 1874)

— *The Continental Journals, 1798-1820*, ed. by Helen Boden (Bristol: Thoemmes, 1995)

Wordsworth, William, *Home at Grasmere, Part First, Book First, of The Recluse, by William Wordsworth*, ed. by Beth Darlington, (New York: Cornell University Press, 1977)

— *Poems, in Two Volumes, and Other Poems, 1800-1807, by William Wordsworth*, ed. by Jared Curtis (Ithaca: Cornell University Press, 1983)

— *Lyrical Ballads and Other Poems, 1797–1800 by William Wordsworth*, ed. by James Butler and Karen Green (Ithaca: Cornell University Press, 1992)

— *Sonnet Series and Itinerary Poems, 1820-1845, by William Wordsworth*, ed. by Geoffrey Jackson (Ithaca: Cornell University Press, 2004)

— *The Thirteen-Book Prelude by William Wordsworth, Volume I*, ed. by Mark L. Reed (Ithaca: Cornell University Press, 1991)

Wright, Alicia, 'On Writing About Dorothy Wordsworth's The Grasmere Journal', *Avidly*, May 8 2020

ACKNOWLEDGEMENTS

There are many people without whom it would not have been possible for me to write this book, not least my partner Will Smith, who has been a patient aid all the way through the thinking, researching and writing processes. Without his support and his exceptional ability to chase a research lead through the interstices of the internet, this book would not exist. Without Dr. Emily Stanback, I might never have thought to turn to the *Rydal Journals* to search for overlooked evidence of Dorothy's condition, and her partial transcripts of the journals, along with those made by Dr. Anastasia Stelse and those made by Kathleen Winter have been foundational in my own readings of the journals. Her friendship and fellowship through the years has been even more invaluable. I am also grateful for the input at the eleventh hour of Susanne Sutton and Professor Nick Mason, who generously shared their transcripts from their forthcoming edition of the *Rydal Journals* with me.

Thanks are due to The Wordsworth Trust for allowing me access to the manuscripts, and permission to quote from the journals, and particularly to Jeff Cowton, for his continual support and enthusiasm. I'd also like to thank Yennah Smart for her diligent proofreading.

This book is underpinned by the work of countless scholars, many of whom have not gained the full recognition they deserve for their work on Dorothy, most notably Pamela Woof, Susan Levin, Beth Darlington and Nicola Healey, and indeed, Edmund Lee. Without you, I would have nothing to build on.

Grasmere, September 2021

INDEX